Fundamentals of Entrepreneurship Principles, Policies and Programmes

Fundamentals of Entrepreneurship Principles, Policies and Programmes

Dr. K. K. Patra

Professor of Finance,
Rourkela Institute of Management Studies,
Chhend, Rourkela - 769015,
Odisha.

Himalaya Publishing House

• MUMBAI • NEW DELHI • NAGPUR • BENGALURU • HYDERABAD • CHENNAI • PUNE
• LUCKNOW • AHMEDABAD • ERNAKULAM • BHUBANESWAR • INDORE • KOLKATA

First Edition : 2011

Published by : Mrs. Meena Pandey for **Himalaya Publishing House Pvt. Ltd.,**
"Ramdoot", Dr. Bhalerao Marg, Girgaon, **Mumbai - 400 004.**
Phone: .022-2386 01 70/2386 38 63, Fax: 022-2387 71 78
Email: himpub@vsnl.com Website: www.himpub.com

Branch Offices:

New Delhi : "Pooja Apartments", 4-B, Murari Lal Street, Ansari Road, Darya Ganj, New Delhi - 110 002. Phone: 011-23270392/23278631, Fax: 011-23256286

Nagpur : Kundanlal Chandak Industrial Estate, Ghat Road, Nagpur - 440 018. Phone: 0712-2738731/3296733, Telefax: 0712-2721215

Bengaluru : No. 16/1 (Old 12/1), 1st Floor, Next to Hotel Highlands, Madhava Nagar, Race Course Road, Bengaluru - 560 001. Phone: 080-22281541/22385461, Telefax: 080-22286611

Hyderabad : No. 3-4-184, Lingampally, Besides Raghavendra Swamy Matham, Kachiguda, Hyderabad - 500 027. Phone: 040-27560041/27550139, Mobile: 09848130433

Chennai : No. 85/50, Bazullah Road, T. Nagar, Chennai - 600 017. Phone: 044-28344020/32463737/42124860

Pune : First Floor, "Laksha" Apartment, No. 527, Mehunpura, Shaniwarpeth (Near Prabhat Theatre), Pune - 411 030. Phone: 020-24496323/24496333

Lucknow : Jai Baba Bhavan, Church Road, Near Manas Complex and Dr. Awasthi Clinic, Aliganj, Lucknow - 226 024. Phone: 0522-2339329, Mobile: 09305302158/09415349385/09389593752

Ahmedabad : 114, "SHAIL", 1st Floor, Opp. Madhu Sudan House, C.G.Road, Navrang Pura, Ahmedabad - 380 009. Phone: 079-26560126, Mobile: 09327324149/09314679413

Ernakulam : 39/104 A, Lakshmi Apartment, Karikkamuri Cross Rd., Ernakulam, Cochin- 622011, Kerala. Phone: 0484-2378012/2378016, Mobile: 09344199799

Bhubaneswar : 5 Station Square, Bhubaneswar (Odisha) - 751 001. Phone: 0674-2532129, Mobile: 09861046007.

Indore : Kesardeep Avenue Extension, 73, Narayan Bagh, Flat No. 302, IIIrd Floor, Near Humpty Dumpty School, Narayan Bagh, Indore- 452 007(M.P.), Mobile: 09301386468

Kolkata : 108/4, Beliaghata Main Road, Near ID Hospital, Opp. SBI Bank, Kolkata - 700 010, Mobile: 09910440956

DTP by : HPH Editorial Office, Bhandup (Asmita Pankar)

Printed by : Shri Krishna offset Press Delhi-93

Dedicated To

The Sacred Memory of
My Father

PREFACE

This book **'Fundamentals of Entrepreneurship Principles, Policies and Programmes'** has given me an impetus to treatise on the subjects in Bachelor of Commerce, Bachelor of Business Administration and Master of Business Administration who would be holding key posts in corporate sector either in India or abroad and can possess superior knowledge and skills in entrepreneurial developments. This book is designed for students in colleges and universities, as well as others in industry and public service, who seek to learn the essentials of entrepreneurship.

Entrepreneurship and small business has been recognized as the engine of economic development and industrialisation. The prosperity of a nation and society is measured by the entrepreneurial spirit of its people. Entrepreneurs are expected to play a vital role in the process of development by introducing innovations and demonstrating leadership qualities in the dynamic situation. Entrepreneurship has been found as a low cost and long-term strategy for ensuring supply of right kind of entrepreneurs in the economy to sustain the development tempo.

Considerable effort has been made in this book to explore the fundamentals of entrepreneurship which will provide an insight into the processes that drive and sustain entrepreneurship. This book will no doubt make the task of a teacher easy in teaching their students even the students would become self-illuminated by easy assimilation of knowledge treasured in this book. This textbook has ten chapters and each chapter vividly describes in an easy-to-understand method. This book may essentially be termed as '*Entrepreneurship Made Easy*!'

I am thankful to all the members of RIMS family for their assistance in enabling me to obtain the requisite literature on the subject. I thankfully acknowledge the moral support and guidance offered by them during the manuscript preparation. I am grateful to Mr. C. Panigrahi, Management Consultant, SSI, and Accreditated Entrepreneurial Motivation Trainer, NIESBUD, New Delhi, who was associated with the study initially and who made valuable contribution to the thinking on the formulation of the study and the organisation of data collection.

I shall be failing in my duties, if I do not express my appreciation and manifold help from my family members. They not only encouraged me to proceed with my work, but rendered their invaluable help at the hours of my need. I am particularly indebted to my spouse, whose patience, support, encouragement and sacrifice made me completely free to translate my dreams into reality. I am very much thankful to her. Without her active co-operation, this work would not have been completed in right time.

I am also thankful to Mr. Bijoy Kumar Ojha and the editorial board members of M/s Himalaya Publishing House, Mumbai for their constructive suggestions which has added value to this book. Last, but not the least my sincere gratitude to my daughter, who has edited the whole text despite her busy schedule. My son has patiently bore with my negligience and long absence from home during the time of data collection. I sincerely welcome any comments or suggestions from the teachers and students for further improvement of this book.

Dr. K. K. Patra

CONTENTS

CHAPTER

ENTREPRENEURSHIP: AN INTRODUCTION

> *"...We pass through three major stages in our lives: a time to learn, up until the age of twenty; a time to expand, between twenty and forty; and a time to grow wise, from forty onwards..."*
>
> ***— Bernard Lievegoed, 1979***

Chapter Overview:

At the end of this chapter, you will be able to understand:

1. The importance of entrepreneurship.
2. Factors influencing entrepreneurship.
3. Exploring the concept of vision for entrepreneurial venture.
4. Exploring the concept of mission for entrepreneurial venture.
5. Qualities and skills of an entrepreneur.
6. Entrepreneurs who have changed the face of India.

INTRODUCTION

An entrepreneur represents the starting point of an entrepreneurial venture. He is business' first and most valuable human resource. An entrepreneur is a person who organizes, operates and assumes the risk for a business venture. Every successful business person is someone who can identify a problem and come up with a solution before somebody else does. An entrepreneur is the first and foremost mindset of any business who is finding profitable solutions to problems. An entrepreneur invests, hence he has to face risks; an entrepreneur is ambitious, so he has to be careful and an entrepreneur wants to stay in the business, hence he should have knowledge, skill and foresight.

Entrepreneur basically means 'Capitalist' and 'Industrialist' i.e., producer, maker, manufacturer. Here in the broader sense, the macro vision, entrepreneur does mean the producer of new things, new ideas, languages and all those innovations in the world. Thus an entrepreneur is the crown of all the present day academic, spiritual, cultural, scientific and technological innovations and developments in the world. Had not there been an entrepreneur we all would have been still in the primitive age moving in the jungles without proper food, clothing and shelter. It is by the zeal and perseverance of the entrepreneurs of the past that it has become possible for us to live in this modern age quite cozily with all the comforts in life. Many developing countries owe their success to those entrepreneurs who despite their comfort of working in a company jumped out to build an enterprise to give jobs to other people and to help the nation. What makes a good entrepreneur? What attributes do successful entrepreneurs possess? What are the qualities that make an entrepreneur effective? The answer to these questions must arise from an understanding of either what entrepreneurs actually do or what they are expected to do; it would require, in other words, an analysis of the entrepreneurial skills. Entrepreneurship is likely the biggest career decision one will make. There are a hundred reasons to stay working as an employee, and there are a hundred more reasons to give self-employment a proper go. Everyone is different, but which one is the better option for an individual. Whether working from 9 AM to 5 PM or going self-employed?

Entrepreneurship is becoming an increasingly popular career choice in today's market place. Understanding the difference between **self-employment** and **employee** status is extremely important. There are two ways of living in the society i.e., (i) Service, or (ii) Self-employment. The difference between an employer-employee relationship and self-employment lies in one small wording 'change'.

Entrepreneurship is a dynamic process of creating incremental wealth by individuals who take risk of equity, time and career to infuse resources with value of society. Entrepreneurs have an important effect on world economies and are playing an important role in maintaining and developing new values. Entrepreneurship is the process of creating, identifying, developing, and bringing a vision to life. The vision may be an innovative idea, an opportunity or simply a better way to do something. The end result of this process is the creation of new venture, formed under conditions, risk and considerable uncertainty.

Entrepreneurship is the process of looking at things in such a way that possible solution to problems and perceived needs may evolve in venturing. It is the dynamic process of creating incremental wealth. It is also the process of creating something new with value by devoting the necessary time, effort, assuming the accompanying financial, physical and social risks and receiving the resulting rewards of monetary, personal satisfaction and independence. Following are the few differences between an employee and an entrepreneur:

Service vs. Self-employment

Sr. No.	Basis	SERVICE (Employee)	SELF-EMPLOYMENT (Entrepreneur)
1.	Status	Employee	Employer
2.	Nature	Dependent	Independent
3.	Growth	Limited	Unlimited
4.	Performance	Mechanical	Independent
5.	Earning	Hand to mouth	Recurring
6.	Satisfaction	Slavery	Self satisfaction
7.	Routine	Same overall routine every day.	Chosen as per one's own working hours.
8.	Survive	If you can't work, you can't survive.	If you can't sell your product or service, you can't survive.
9.	Contract	Contract of service with an employer-employee relationship.	Contract for services sets up self-employment.
10	Source	It's a fairly reliable source of income.	Income depends on finding work.

Meaning and Definitions of Entrepreneurship

Entrepreneurship is the marriage between profitability and growth. It is the recognition of opportunities (needs, wants, problems, and challenges) and the use of resources to implement innovative ideas for new, thoughtfully planned ventures. Following are the few definitions of entrepreneurship:

Entrepreneurship involves bringing about change to achieve some benefit. This benefit may be financial but it also involves the satisfaction of knowing you have changed something for the better.

— **Lily Kretchman *et. al.*, Toronto**

Entrepreneurship is essentially the act of creation requiring the ability to recognize an opportunity, shape a goal, and take advantage of a situation. Entrepreneurs plan, persuade, raise resources, and give birth to new ventures.

Richard Bodell *et. al.*, Toronto

Real opportunities lie within a person, not outside, what lies behind you and what lies before you are tiny matters compared to what lies within you.

Ralph Waldo Emerson

The role of entrepreneurship is to assemble and deploy resources in new combinations that disrupt the otherwise static nature of the market.

Schumpeter, 1934

Entrepreneurs innovate. Innovation is the specific instrument of entrepreneurship. It is the act that endows resources with a new capacity to create wealth. Innovation, indeed, creates a resource.

Drucker, 1985

Entrepreneurship is the process of acquiring, assembling, and deploying resources in the pursuit of perceived opportunities for long-term gain.

Bowman and Upton, 1991.

Entrepreneurship is the discovery of new combinations of resources under uncertain situations that generate entrepreneurial rent as reward for risk taking.

Rumelt, 1987

A firm-creating entrepreneur creates and perhaps operates a new business firm, while an innovating entrepreneur transforms inventions and ideas into economically viable entities.

Baumol, 1991

Characteristics of Entrepreneurship

An entrepreneur attacks life head on, takes charge of his own life, and has a persistent determination to create his own path in life. According to **Napoleon Hill**, "An educated person is not necessarily a person with any specialized knowledge, but an educated person is one who has so developed the higher faculties of his mind that he can acquire anything he wants without violating the rights of others." The typical characteristics that make up an entrepreneur in today's world are:

1. The entrepreneurs have an enthusiastic vision and passion to drive the force of an enterprise.
2. The entrepreneurs express a great amount of enthusiasm in the work supported by interlocked collection of specific ideas.
3. The entrepreneur expresses a great amount of enthusiasm and promotes the vision with enthusiastic passion.

4. The entrepreneurs are goal-oriented in their quest to reach their desired outcomes.
5. The entrepreneurs have creative imagination and with their persistence and determination, develop strategies to change the vision into reality.
6. Entrepreneurs have a positive attitude when it comes to building their business and business relationships.
7. Entrepreneurs are very quick decision makers in their business endeavours and ideas.
8. An entrepreneur must have positive attitude, passionate about achieving their goals, innovative, creative, versatile, persistent, self confident, self reliant, have a strong sense of commitment etc.

Factors Influencing Entrepreneurial Performance

Entrepreneurship development has made significant contribution in providing employment to millions of people, generating foreign exchange for the growing economy, contributing to value addition and utilizing the vast human and natural resources of the country. Entrepreneur is a person who habitually creates and innovates to build something of recognized value around perceived opportunities. In view of the above contributions, entrepreneurship development through small enterprises has come to occupy crucial role in the economic progress of the nation. Businesses are made by people. A business can only be successful if the people who make it up are properly directed and are committed to make an effort on its behalf. An entrepreneurial venture also needs the support of people from outside the organization such as customers, suppliers and investors. To be an effective, an entrepreneur needs to demonstrate a wide variety of skills in the way he or she deals with other people. The successful entrepreneur must not only use these skills but learn to use them and to learn from using them. Entrepreneurs should constantly audit their abilities in these areas, recognize their strengths and shortcomings, and plan how to develop these skills in the future. Following are four factors influencing entrepreneurial performance:

(a) Industry knowledge

(b) General management skills

(c) Personal motivation

(d) Human relationship skills

Entrepreneurial performance results from a combination of industry knowledge, general management skills, personal motivation and human relationship skills. The success of an entrepreneurial venture depends on the entrepreneur. The entrepreneur is the leader and driver of the venture who requires supports to make the venture a grand success. The major factors that influence entrepreneurship include natural, technological, political, cultural, economical, psychological and external environmental and the skill set of the entrepreneur.

1.	**Natural Environment**	✓ Anti-pollution pressures ✓ Changing role of governments ✓ Increased energy costs ✓ Shortage of raw materials
2	**Technological Environment**	✓ Accelerating pace of technological change ✓ Increased regulation of technological change ✓ Unlimited opportunities for innovation ✓ Varying research and development budgets
3.	**Political Environment**	✓ Government support to economic development ✓ High rate of taxation ✓ Non-availability of infrastructure ✓ Unstable political conditions
4.	**Cultural Environment**	✓ Customary practices and beliefs ✓ Perceptions, preferences, and behaviours of people ✓ Significant impact on basic values
5.	**Economical Environment**	✓ Economic slowdown or recession ✓ General purchasing power of the people ✓ Gross National Products and per capita income ✓ Reluctant to invest during recession ✓ Trade cycle and balance of payment
6.	**Psychological Environment**	✓ Ability to draw up a comprehensive business plan ✓ Ability to manage and minimize risk ✓ Hard work and persistence ✓ Inclination having a contingency plan
7.	**External Environment**	✓ Competitors ✓ Customer ✓ Employees ✓ Shareholders ✓ Suppliers

Evolution of Entrepreneurship in India

The evolution of entrepreneurship in India can be discussed under following headings:

1. Promotion of business
2. Preparation of blueprints
3. Procuring necessary finance
4. Setting necessary organization
5. Forecasting and decision making
6. Conducting the affairs of the business
7. Distributive functions
8. Risk taking.

1. Promotion of business: An entrepreneur is the sole person who promotes a business. He is the person who takes all the necessary decision to start a business. He takes decisions after researches have been done for the concerned business and selects the best alternatives out of all ideas.

2. Preparation of blueprints: An entrepreneur is the person who thinks to take all the decisions about the concerned business from the existing till the end of the business.

3. Procuring necessary finance: An entrepreneur is the person who takes necessary actions to arrange funds for the business to start and if the business has started then for its expansion. He decides the way in which he can collect sufficient finance for the business.

4. Setting necessary organization: An entrepreneur is the person who sets the necessary organization and takes all efforts to start and expand the business.

5. Forecasting and decision making: An entrepreneur needs to forecast the market of the product of the concerned business and take necessary decision to increase the sale and make it more popular between the customers so that its demand increases.

6. Conducting the affairs of the business: An entrepreneur is the person who is in-charge of preparing the affairs of the business and then taking necessary actions to increase the sale and maximize the profit scale of the business.

7. Distributive function: An entrepreneur plans out the functions of the business and give the work to different person which is known as distribution function of work of the business.

8. Risk-taking: An entrepreneur is the person who takes all the necessary risk for the development of the business. He does all the necessary work and research in taking the necessary decision which involves risk.

The Entrepreneurial Process

An entrepreneur is the key figure in the process of economic growth. He is an economic man who tries to maximize his profits by innovations. Entrepreneur is the individual who lies at the heart of entrepreneurial process that is the manager who drives the whole process forward. The entrepreneurial process consists of opportunity, resources and organizations. Opportunities are the potential to serve customers better than they are being served at present. Resources include the money invested in the venture, the people who contribute their efforts, knowledge and skills to it etc. Organization consists of number of factors such as their size, their rate of growth, the industry they operate in and the types of product they deliver, etc.

Entrepreneurship and the entrepreneur, is at the core of what makes an enterprise succeed, whether we call it an entrepreneurial firm, a small business, a family business, a home-based business, or a new business. He is the kingpin of the business who conceptualizes, builds and manages a business enterprise. It is only the diligent effort of the entrepreneur, which will make our society aspire for a happy and prosperous tomorrow. A successful entrepreneur always stands out with innovative, groundbreaking ideas. Entrepreneurship cycle consists of 3'S, i.e., stimulatory, support and sustaining. Stimulation indicates that entrepreneurs are born and they cannot be made or trained. But in the ever-changing business, it has now changed that entrepreneurs can be made and not born. Stimulation includes proper training and guidance, which helps an entrepreneur to excel in his performance. Supports are the assistance from the registration of a unit up to the marketing, which includes proper infrastructure with adequate quantity, quality and reliability. Sustaining includes the promotion, expansion, modernization, diversification, consultancy, policy measures, reservation of items etc. For entrepreneurship development it requires to balance the above elements of the entrepreneurial cycle.

1. Entrepreneurial Education
2. Planned publicity for entrepreneurial opportunities
3. Identification of potential entrepreneurs through scientific method
4. Motivational training to new entrepreneurs
5. Help and guidance in selecting products and preparing project reports
6. Making available techno-economic information and project reports
7. Evolving locally suitable new products and processes
8. Availability of local agencies with trained personnel for entrepreneurial counselling and promotions
9. Creating entrepreneurial forum
10. Recognition of entrepreneurs

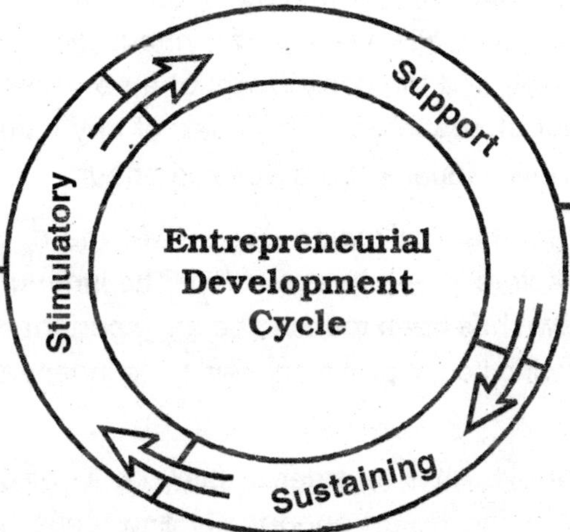

1. Registration of unit
2. Arranging finance
3. Providing land, shed, power, water etc.
4. Guidance for selecting and obtaining machinery
5. Supply of scarce raw materials
6. Getting licence/import licences
7. Providing common facilities
8. Granting tax relief or other subsidies
9. Offering management consultancy
10. Help marketing product
11. Providing information

1. Help modernisation
2. Help diversification/expansion/substitute production
3. Additional financing for full capacity utilisation
4. Deferring repayment/interest
5. Diagnostic industrial extension/consultancy source
6. Production units legislation/policy change
7. Product reservation/creating new avenues for marketing
8. Quality testing and improvident services
9. Need-based common facilities centre

*Akhouri, M.M.P. Dr., 1977 Balancing the imbalances caused by the known factors of Enterepreneurial Development, Paper presented in the Workship on Technology and Entrepreneur, Kuala Lumpur, 25-30 May 1977.

Fig. 1.1: Entrepreneurial Development Cycle

WHO IS AN ENTREPRENEUR?

An entrepreneur is a person who organizes, operates and assumes the risk for a business venture. Simply entrepreneur is the agent who unites all means of production and who finds in the value of the products, the re-establishment of the entire capital he employs, and the value of the wages, the interest and rent which he pays, as well as profits belonging to him. An entrepreneur is a person who initiates and establishes an enterprise. Entrepreneurship refers to the decisions he takes in setting up and running a new enterprise. The individual constitutes the most important element in entrepreneurship. It is an individual who takes a decision to start or not to start an enterprise. And it is 'HE' or 'SHE' who strives to make it a success.

According to **Schumpeter**, "The entrepreneur is the innovator who implements change within markets through carrying out new combinations. The carrying out of new combinations takes several forms like introduction of new goods or quality thereof, the introduction of new method of production, the opening of a new market, and the consequent of a new source of supply of new materials or parts, the carrying out of new organisation part of any industry." There are four parameters which encourages an individual to be an entrepreneur:

(i) Decision to become an entrepreneur: The first major step is that the decision must be his own. This is one of the most crucial factors to entrepreneurship. The inner urge of the individual to do something new, to be on his own has been found to be an important factor. This may be reinforced by one or more of the following i.e., to prove oneself, to be independent, to do something unique, to excel etc.

(ii) Identification and selection of an opportunity: In order to fulfil the inner desire to be an entrepreneur, the individual starts searching for an opportunity and focus on his entrepreneurial desires. He looks around for different possibilities of business, reads about them, and meets people who could give ideas and inspiration, and collects information on several possibilities.

(iii) Business plan formulation and its implementation: An entrepreneur makes the movements in the direction of project detailing. His efforts are directed towards visualising the establishment of the enterprise. He studies the feasibility and profitability of the project, which combines various factors of production.

(iv) Entrepreneurial continuum: Once an entrepreneur establishes the enterprise, he will have to manage it well by translating the problems into opportunities. Entrepreneurial continuum can be achieved through a series of entrepreneurial decisions and actions directed towards new product development, product diversification or expansion, research and developments etc.

TYPES OF ENTREPRENEURSHIP

Entrepreneurship is the practice of starting new organizations, mature organizations, particularly new business generally in response to identified opportunities. There are basically two types of entrepreneurship which are (1) Opportunity-based entrepreneurship, and (2) Necessity-based entrepreneurship.

(1) Opportunity-based entrepreneurship: It is entirely prompted, encouraged and nurtured by positive opportunities thrown up by events, circumstances. When an entrepreneur perceives a business opportunity and chooses to pursue this as an active career choice is known as opportunity-based entrepreneurship.

(2) Necessity-based entrepreneurship: It is based on *'Necessity is the mother of invention'*. As the necessity is the greatest force to be reckoned with, in all kinds of human endeavour, an entrepreneur is left with no other viable option to earn a living. It is not the choice but compulsion, which makes him/her, choose entrepreneurship as a career.

TYPES OF ENTREPRENEURS AND THEIR FUNCTIONS

(A) On the basis of Types of Business:

1. **Business entrepreneur:** Entrepreneurs who deal in manufacturing and trading aspect of any business are called business entrepreneurs. They convert ideas into reality. For example, small trading houses, manufacturing business are few of them.

2. **Trading entrepreneur:** Entrepreneurs who undertake trading activities and are very much concerned with marketing activities at domestic and international levels are trading entrepreneurs. For example, export and import houses.

3. **Industrial entrepreneur:** Entrepreneurs who undertake only manufacturing activities such as new product development like textile, electronics etc., are known as industrial entrepreneur.

4. **Corporate entrepreneur:** Entrepreneurs who are interested in management part of the organisation and coordinate skills to manage a corporate undertaking like Ambanis, Tatas etc., are corporate entrepreneurs.

5. **Agricultural entrepreneur:** Entrepreneurs who are interested in the production and marketing of agricultural inputs and outputs like dairy, horticulture, forestry etc., are known as agricultural entrepreneurs.

(B) On the basis of Technology

1. Technical entrepreneur: Entrepreneurs who are interested in the production process and possess innovative skills in manufacturing, quality control, product design etc., are known as technical entrepreneurs.

2. Non technical entrepreneur: Entrepreneurs who are interested in the marketing, distribution and development of cheaper products are known as non-technical entrepreneurs.

3. Professional entrepreneur: Entrepreneurs who are interested in creating new ideas or technology and selling them are known as professional entrepreneurs.

(C) On the basis of Motivation

1. Pure entrepreneur: Entrepreneurs who are motivated by psychological and economical rewards are known as pure entrepreneurs.

2. Induced entrepreneur: Entrepreneurs who are motivated by incentives, concessions, benefits offered by government are known as induced entrepreneurs.

3. Motivated entrepreneur: Entrepreneurs who are motivated by sense of achievement and fulfillment are known as motivated entrepreneur.

4. Spontaneous entrepreneur: Entrepreneurs with inborn traits of confidence, vision and initiative are known as spontaneous entrepreneur.

(D) On the basis of Growth

1. Growth entrepreneur: Entrepreneurs who enter a sector with a high growth rate and are positive thinkers are known as growth entrepreneurs.

2. Super growth entrepreneur: Entrepreneurs who enter a business and show a quick, steep and upward growth curve are known as super growth entrepreneur.

3. Classical entrepreneur: Entrepreneurs who give more importance to consistent returns than to growth and are concerned about customer and market needs are known as classical entrepreneurs.

(E) On the basis of Stages in Development

1. First generation entrepreneur: Entrepreneurs who are innovators, risk takers and are among the firsts in family to enter into business are first generation entrepreneurs.

2. Modern entrepreneur: Entrepreneurs who consider feasibility of business and can adapt to changes and dynamic market are known as modern entrepreneurs.

(F) On the basis of Areas

1. Rural entrepreneur: Entrepreneurs who establish their business unit in rural areas to enhance the improvement of the living condition of the rural people is known as rural entrepreneur.

2. Urban entrepreneur: Entrepreneurs who are establishing their business unit in urban and developed areas are known as urban entrepreneur.

(G) Other categories of Entrepreneurs

Besides the above classification, there are some other categories of entrepreneurs. They are:

1. Male entrepreneur: Any enterprise owned, managed and controlled by a male member is known as male entrepreneur.

2. Female entrepreneur: Any enterprise owned, managed and controlled by a female member is known as female entrepreneur.

3. Small-scale entrepreneur: An undertaking having an investment in plant and machinery of not more than Rs. 1 crore is known as small-scale entrepreneur.

4. Medium-scale entrepreneur: An undertaking where people are working on the optimum size to derive maximum efficiency in production.

5. Large-scale entrepreneur: Undertakings where large number of workers are working with power driven machines are known as large scale entrepreneurs.

Entrepreneur vs. Intrapreneur

Entrepreneurship is the practice of embarking on a new business or reviving an existing business by pooling together a bunch of resources, in order to exploit new found opportunities. Intrapreneurship is the practice of entrepreneurship by employees within an organization. Intrapreneur is a person who focuses on innovation and creativity and who transforms a dream or an idea into a profitable venture, by operating within the organizational environment. The main points of distinction between an entrepreneur and an intrapreneur are summarized below:

	ENTREPRENEUR	INTRAPRENEUR
1.	An entrepreneur is the owner of the business.	An intrapreneur works for the business.
2.	An entrepreneur is his own boss and enjoys an independent status as the owner of the business.	An intrapreneur is a salaried employee of an entrepreneurial business and is not enjoying independent status.
3.	Every small business does not need an entrepreneur	Every small business needs an Intrapreneur.
4.	Entrepreneurial ideas are always converted into reality.	Intrapreneur ideas always create a new idea.
5.	An entrepreneur operates from outside the organization.	An intrapreneur operates from within the organization.
6.	Entrepreneurship involves in innovations and creativity.	An intrapreneur thinks iike an entrepreneur and looking out for opportunities, which gives profit to the organization.

Effective Qualities of an Entrepreneur

Entrepreneur provides a bridge between the small business manager and the chief executive of large firms. In growing venture, the entrepreneur transforms the role of acquiring resources into that of creating and Intaining structures of management. It involves development and change within the organisation and changes in the way in which the organisation grows. Essential qualities of an entrepreneur are as follows:

A	Ability to take risk	N	Nurture entrepreneurial spirit
B	Balancing family and business	O	Out of box thinking
C	Creativity and innovations	P	Proper business plan
D	Determination and commitment	Q	Quest for continuous learning
E	Enjoyment of responsibilities	R	Resource utilization
F	Financial risk taker	S	Seek professional advice
G	Goal oriented leadership	T	Team building
H	Honest and trustworthy	U	Upright and honest
I	Interpersonal skill	V	Vision (smart)
J	Jealous of none	W	Work pattern
K	Know your industry	X	Xtraordinary human being
L	Learn from failure	Y	Youthful spirit
M	More work, less talk	Z	Zest for fairness and justice

1. Ability to take risk: An entrepreneur is a pivot around which the entire business rotates. To be an effective entrepreneur, one has to bear all the risks and uncertainties associated with the setting up, running and the ultimate outcome of the enterprise. Risk and failure are integral parts of any successful entrepreneur's life. One cannot expect success straightaway.

2. Balancing family and business: Work-life balance identifies the key need or reason for introducing work-life balance policies. An entrepreneur must build the commitment to work-life balance in order to fulfil his vision or values. One should be very much effective in the day-to-day work life and personal life. There is no perfect, one-size fits all, balance one should be striving for. Work-life balance will vary over time.

3. Creativity and innovations: Creativity is the ability of an entrepreneur to use insights and come up with new solutions to old problems. An entrepreneur is doing things in a different way or follows a different approach for conventional things to work together. An entrepreneur is the head of a business who always thinks of new ideas, new product and new marketing methods - all these are fertile ground for creative thinking.

4. Determination and commitment: Business success never comes easy. To overcome the obstacles that will be thrown in entrepreneur's path, it requires an incredible amount of hard work and resilience. Successful entrepreneurs learn from their mistakes. They are not easily discouraged and never give up. This involves being self-reliant and personally disciplined. Endeavour without goal would be like groping in darkness.

5. Enjoyment of responsibilities: Every work and the consequent result is a self-portrait of the person who does it, regardless of what job he does. The feeling of a job well done is a reward in itself. It is better to do small things well, than do big things poorly. We all take pride in our performance. Pride gives a winning edge. It enthuses one to put in required effort and hard work.

6. Financial risk taker: A good entrepreneur realizes that loss and failure are inherent in any business endeavor. Thus, an entrepreneur must always be ready to make calculated risks and face whatever consequences those risks might have. Entrepreneurs must have the courage to face failure and start again despite those setbacks. As in all fields of endeavor, the characteristic of a successful entrepreneur is in never giving up and in picking up the pieces and continuing the journey even if failure momentarily obstructs the way.

7. Goal-oriented leadership: Successful people tend to write down their goals, check them daily, and regularly review them until they achieve success. Entrepreneurs take a lot of satisfaction in setting and reaching achievable business-related goals. This helps them find satisfaction in their accomplishments. As a leader of the enterprise, he has to set examples of dedication, devotion and self discipline to inspire the various persons working with him.

8. Honest and trustworthy: Entrepreneurship is concerned with the development of a range of skills and capabilities including planning, coordinating and organizing, using initiatives, working independently, effective time management, risk management skills, good communication skills, adaptability, flexibility, taking responsibility, decision making and the ability to innovate and exercise vision. Honesty and integrity means to firmly adhere to a code of moral and ethical principles.

9. Interpersonal skill: An entrepreneur is a natural leader with the vision and the drive to do things right and steer his company towards success with ease. Effective leaders have the ability to relate and communicate well with people from all walks of life. Their sociability and enthusiasm inspires those around them and enables them to lead others to achieve their business vision. This quality is not present in everybody, it is a very scarce characteristic, hard to find among individuals.

10. Jealous of none: It is sometimes said that, '*Jealousy is the tribute mediocrity pays to genius.*' Entrepreneurs are zealous. They are so bound by their passions that they often forget about the risks and simply go after what they desire. Sometimes this leads to greatness while other times it leads to utter failure. The common thread in either case is an unyielding desire to pursue what is important to them, regardless of the cost.

11. Know your industry: Entrepreneurs perceive new opportunities and create and grow ventures around such opportunities. Entrepreneurs are specific people who engage in the creative process. We can talk about entrepreneurs in abstract terms, but that will never have an impact on our communities. All persons in business have some entrepreneurial traits, but all business owners/operators are not entrepreneurs.

12. Learn from failure: Failure to an entrepreneur is nothing more than an opportunity waiting to be discovered and the entrepreneurs learn from their failures and those of others. This is an untrue notion that entrepreneurship is often difficult and tricky. Entrepreneur is often synonymous with "founder". Most commonly, the term entrepreneur applies to someone who creates value by offering a product or service.

13. More work, less talk: The key to quality is doing something, not just talking about it. This provides an introduction to the key areas of quality analysis. The basic quality techniques are applied to the individuals and this approach concentrates on identifying customers, analyzing their needs and finding ways of servicing these needs. Successful entrepreneurs do not start with all the knowledge, skills and insights necessary to create thriving ventures.

14. Nurture entrepreneurial spirit: Entrepreneurship is the complex process by which entrepreneurs envision, create and grow ventures. To understand entrepreneurship, we need to understand the necessary components of the process i.e., Creativity, Innovation, Motivation and Capacity.

15. Out of box thinking: A successful entrepreneur believes in his abilities. He is not scared to explore un-chartered territories, take risk and take difficult decisions. A person can have high self-confidence in one situation and totally lack in another. This is one of those skills that can be developed by training. Self-confidence is a key entrepreneurial skill for success.

16. Proper business plan: Success is the offspring of a plan well executed. An entrepreneur should have good perception of an idea, credible business plan, clarity of what he wants to do and above all belief in him/her to become successful. The ambition and aspiration will be fruitful when one work with a sense of direction, i.e., a good plan of action strictly adhered to.

17. Quest for continuous learning: Learning is generally considered to be any change in an individual's response or behavior resulting from practice to experience. Learning is the process by which individual acquires various habits, knowledge, skill and attitude that are necessary for meeting certain objectives. Continuous learning changes the behaviour of entrepreneur. There are three focal areas in psychology of learning. They are (i) learner (ii) the learning process and (iii) the learning situation.

18. Resource utilization: Entrepreneurs are not wild risk takers in the gambling sense. They are very good at assessing and managing risk. Second, most grown businesses are not rooted in some high tech invention. Third, most entrepreneurs are not experts. Rather they are very good at assembling a team to ensure key competencies. Fourth, most entrepreneurs do not have a fully sorted out vision of their enterprise. Successful entrepreneurs whether online or offline tend to be willing to take carefully calculated risks after careful thought and planning.

19. Seek professional advice: 'Compassion for people' or 'humanity' is another value that should be cherished and discussed on equal terms with professionalism, integrity, ethics and other values. Business entrepreneurs who adhere to creative values are defined as intrapreneur as their principal objectives includes personal development and social change. Every entrepreneur expect to do everything i.e., high-level work, ground work, business developments, brand developments, human resources, operations, finance etc.

20. Team building: A key element to motivate staff is enabling them to take ownership of any problems arising and to give them a framework, either individually or in groups, to solve these problems. It is empowering to staff members to take action. The most effective approach is usually within groups which can take the form of quality improvement teams or quality circles. If an entrepreneur expects to have a successful team at any level, one must have strong leadership. Most people are not born with leadership qualities and need good training to learn these skills. Team work enables a wide variety of skills to be brought together to solve the problem.

21. Upright and honest: An important mark of a good entrepreneur is to be honest and honourable in all the business dealings and interpersonal relationships – whether it is between business partners, employees, peers and investors. Entrepreneurs are not super humans. What is different is their approach towards things, their vision, their inclination towards treating challenges in a more creative and positive way, and their determination to achieve their vision against all odds. The positives of an entrepreneur include control of one's own future, have the satisfaction of making one's own money and not for someone else, and to put one's talent to use.

22. Vision (smart): A vision is the ability to see what others cannot see. The visionary entrepreneur is able to see exactly what his or her business is going to look like in every detail when it is finished. The visionary entrepreneur uses leverage to his or her full advantage. Leverage is simply the ability to do more with less. An entrepreneur must be a visionary for further growth and development, commitment to constructive change and energy to achieve results.

23. Work pattern: One who assumes risk in order to combine knowledge, capital, and resources to create a venture that will hopefully return a profit. Entrepreneurs are generally highly independent, which can cause problems when their ventures succeed. In a small company the entrepreneur is able to personally manage most aspects of the business, but this is not possible once the company has grown beyond a certain size. Management conflicts often arise when the entrepreneur does not recognize that running a large stable company is different from running a small growing company.

24. Xtraordinary human being: Passion, resourcefulness, willingness to improvise and listen to others and strong determination to succeed is what makes an entrepreneur successful. Entrepreneurs don't need to be told to be entrepreneurs. Risking everything and becoming an entrepreneur is not a vocation that is typically encouraged or even suggested. The successful entrepreneur is also described as having strong drives for independence and success, with high levels of vigor, persistence, and self-esteem.

25. Youthful spirit: Self improvement is about knowing who we really are. It's a journey of self discovery; leaving our comfort zone and exploring uncharted territory. It has nothing to do with getting a better paid job, having lots of friends or taking better care of our families. It is about honesty, compassion and integrity to one's self. Because everyone is different, there is no one path in the journey toward self improvement. Each person must find their own way and in their own time.

26. Zest for fairness and justice: It's the innovative entrepreneur whose ideas, passion and dedication, create new companies in new industries, requiring new skills, that foster the economic growth and new jobs that turn the situation around. The biggest winners in life have also been the biggest failures at one point or another. Entrepreneurship is a dynamic process that involves a blend of vision, change, and creation. Entrepreneurship is a practice involving traits and behaviours that can be cultivated and developed to better manage an entrepreneurial venture.

ENTREPRENEURIAL SKILLS

The skills of an entrepreneur make him or her ideally suited to spot opportunities. As an entrepreneur, one has to strive for excellence. However, few entrepreneurs have the wisdom of excellence versus perfectionism, that is, the ability to judge when striving for excellence. It is based on the principles of "If you want something done right, you have to do it yourself." Following are the variety of skills required by an entrepreneur.

E	**Enthusiastic:** Entrepreneurs should be enthusiastic and interested in various activities, thereby being able to gather knowledge and experience from various walks of life. The builty-in and learned passion is the main thing that helps him to stand ahead of the crowd.
N	**Nurturing:** No entrepreneur becomes successful overnight. Their success stories are the product of hope and believe that they carry with themseleves. When paired with sustainable growth, developmental steps taken by them over the years towards creativity, it leaves behind a beautiful creation that is looked up to in the years to come.
T	**Tactful:**The work of an enterpreneur is no less than a business tycoon. They have to be skillful and master the art of sensitively dealing with each stakeholder who are associated either directly or indirectly with their business by taking into consideration the long time perspective of their organizations survival.
R	**Righteous:** Entrepreneures are expected to be ethical, morally right and justifiable towards their work and their associates. By being righteous the entrepreneur will be able to keep the motivation of all associates high and at the same time boost them to engage in the well being of his business.
E	**Exceptional:** Entrepreneures are the ones who have an exceptional approach towards business. Their thoughts are often quite distinct from the ones existing, likewise is their way of working as well. It is because of this exceptional quality that they are able to attract a large number of people and engage them either directly or indirectly in their endeavour.
P	**Productive:** The productivity of the entrepreneurs should be visible in their actions and not just merely be restricted to their thoughts. Without achieving the targets it would be very difficult for the entrepreneur to sustain himself and be able to win the trust of the people, because at the end all people are merely interested in the results.
R	**Revolutionary:** Entrepreneurs should be able to bring about complete changes. Changes initiated towards the welfare of all is the key to all success as this would be able to bring about differences. Men today looks for changes, craves for betterment and seeks well being.

E	**Efficient:** Hardwork is the key to all success. The entrepreneurs should be able to work productively with no wastage of money, efforts and resources. This efficiency should be limited to not just to self but lined up and demanded from all stakeholders for healthy growth.
N	**Novelty :** The quality of being new and unusual is what makes an entrepreneur different from common man. There are plenty of areas that are to be rebuilt and this requires the efforts of a person who is novel in their approach to make the situations better for a lot more people.
E	**Exemplary :** Entrepreneures are the best of their kind. They give others a reason to live, a reason to be happy and tension free. Their innovative steps are truly commendable as they in their own way are able to erradicate, if not all but a few problems of mankind.
U	**Utilitarianistic:** It requires immense dare to do something different in the world. The entrepreneurs are able to fulfil their dreams only because they believe that the greatest happiness of the majority is the guiding principle that guides their behaviour.
R	**Rejuvenating:** The realistic dreams that are set out by the entrepreneurs makes life more lively and youthful. The fact that the entrepreneurs are successful is because their dreams, beliefs and hopes find place in the world of a lot many who are not as daring as them to take the bold steps but, are happy to be a part of it.
S	**Self-reliant:** Successful entrepreneurs are proactive people, who set goals and always try to take full responsibility for their actions. They know the difference between what they are today and what they are going to be tomorrow. Everything depends upon their own choices and decisions.
H	**Humanitarian:** All entrepreneurs concentrate a lot in the human welfare. They are highly socialable people and the steps that they take engages a large number of people. Their sociable approach is greately appreciated as they are allowed to operate in the society and not in isolation.
I	**Irrepressible:** It is very difficult to restrain any entrepreneur from taking different steps. The way in which entrepreneurs analyses and intreprets a situation is very different. It is this characteristic of the entrepreneurs that help them to compete and survive in the competitive and ever changing world.
P	**Practical:** Entrepreneurs believe more in actually doing something rather than just being restricted to theory. The entrepreneurs are more successful because they stress more on getting the things done rather than sticking to how to get the things done?

Entrepreneurial Leadership

Leadership is one of the essential ingredients for entrepreneurial success yet it is conceptually elusive. We recognize leadership when we see it but it is very hard to say what we are recognizing. The challenge is not just to understand leadership but also to provide recommendations on how leadership skills can be developed and used to enhance organizational performance. Entrepreneurial leadership can be classified into following eight categories.

1. **Personal vision:** The entrepreneur's vision is the driving force behind leadership. It is the vision which transforms a disparate group of stakeholders into the people who will act to move the venture forward.

2. **Communication with stakeholders:** An entrepreneur must relate their vision to stakeholder through a variety of communication channels and forums. Such communications is not simply a passion of information; it is a call to action.

3. **Organisational culture:** It is the web of rules which define how it goes about its tasks. The relationship between leadership and culture is reciprocal. Leadership creates the organisation's culture and in return, the organisation's culture creates a space to be filled by a leader.

4. **Knowledge and expertise:** Entrepreneurs develops expertise in some specialist technology. For example, Bill Gate's knowledge of computing is an example of the above.

5. **Credibility:** It is critical for leadership. If credibility can be built-up, then leadership becomes easier. If an entrepreneur loses credibility, then leadership is likely to be made more problematic if not lost altogether.

6. **Performance of the venture:** Credibility comes from the decisions which lead to successful outcomes. If credibility comes from being associated with success, it is not necessarily true that credibility is automatically lost as a result of the occasional failure.

7. **Leadership role:** The entrepreneur will usually be the most senior manager in the venture. They will be expected to take on a leadership role merely by virtue of being an entrepreneur.

8. **Desire to lead:** The thing which ultimately underpins leadership is the desire to lead. No one can be an effective leader unless he really want to take on the role of leader.

Entrepreneurial Vision and Mission

Entrepreneurial Vision

Entrepreneurs are typically strong in their vision. Vision exists between '**what is**' and '**what might be**'. A vision is a mental image which is created out of possibilities and not out of certainties. It defines where the entrepreneur wants to go, illuminates why he or she wants to be there and provides signposts for how they might get there. Vision is first and foremost, a communication with oneself. It is constructed personally and will vary from entrepreneur to entrepreneur. It is a starting point for giving a shape and direction to a venture.

An entrepreneur motivates to make their vision into reality. It specifies a destination rather than a route to get there. It is a picture into which the entrepreneur fits an understanding of why people will be better off, the source of the new value that will be created and relationships that will exist. Effective entrepreneurs understand how their vision can be used to motivate others as much as it can be used to motivate themselves. An entrepreneur must learn to challenge vision, it must be defined and shaped so that it is appropriate, viable and achievable, before it can be put to use. Vision includes the following:

(i) Helps an entrepreneur to define his/her goals.

(ii) Provides a sense of warmth and encouragement

(iii) Supports communication and leadership strategy

(iv) Provides a sense of direction

Entrepreneurial Mission

A mission is a formal statement which defines the purpose of the venture. It is a powerful communication tool which offers entrepreneurs a chance to articulate and give a form to their vision. Mission statement has two components i.e., strategic and philosophical. As a strategic statement, it aims to clarify – what the business aims at and as a philosophical statement it aims to clarify what value it will uphold. It is a powerful management tool which:

(i) Articulates the entrepreneur's vision: Developing a mission offers entrepreneurs a chance to articulate and give form to their vision. This helps them to refine and shape their vision, and it facilitates communication of the vision to the venture's stakeholders.

(ii) Encourages analysis of the venture: The purpose of developing a mission that entrepreneur and those that work with them stand back and think about their venture in some detail. If the mission is to be meaningful, then that analysis must be made in a detached way. Entrepreneurs must be able to subject their own vision to impartial scrutiny and consider how realistic and achievable it is.

(iii) Defines the scope of the business: An entrepreneurial venture exists to exploit some opportunity. Opportunities are most successfully exploited if resources are dedicated to them and brought to bear in a focused way. This demands that the opportunity be defined in a precise way.

(iv) Provides a guide for setting objectives: A mission is usually qualitative. It does not dictate specific qualitative outcomes. This is the role of objectives. The mission provides a starting point for defining specific objectives, for testing their suitability for the venture and for ordering of their priorities.

(v) Clarifies strategic options: A mission defines what the venture aims to achieve. In this it offers guidance on what paths might be taken. The mission provides a starting point for developing strategic options, for evaluating their consistency in delivering objectives and for judging their resource demands.

ENTREPRENEURS VS. MANAGERS

An entrepreneur and a manager are always considered as same and are used as interchangeable terms. When a person likes to control all aspects of a situation, then he is generally called as a manager, whereas if any person works through problems with people then he is more likely an entrepreneur. A manager is someone who directs a team and an entrepreneur is someone who organizes, manages, and assumes the risks of a business or enterprise. The main points of distinction between an entrepreneur and a manager are summarized below:

	ENTREPRENEURS	MANAGERS
1	An entrepreneur can be a manager.	A manager cannot be an entrepreneur.
2	An entrepreneur is the owner of an enterprise.	A manager is a salaried employee of an enterprise.
3	An entrepreneur is motivated by personal satisfaction and achievements.	A manager is motivated by promotion, recognition and pay revision.
4	An entrepreneur gets reward for the risk bearing role he is taking, i.e., profit, which is by nature, irregular and uncertain	A manager gets reward for the services rendered to the organisation i.e. salary, which is by nature, regular and certain.
5	An entrepreneur asks to himself, "Given what I want to achieve, what resources do I need to acquire.	A manager asks to himself "Given the resources under my control, what can I achieve."
6	An entrepreneur simply gets things through an entrepreneurial way.	A manager simply gets things done through others.
7	An entrepreneur always sets up a new enterprise.	A manager doesn't take a new venture.

Factors Affecting Entrepreneurship

Environment is the surrounding of the economy which influence the growth of entrepreneurship business. Environmental factors which affects the entrepreneurship has been classified into two categories:

1. Internal Environment
2. External Environment

Internal environment consists of the family background, kith and kin, social status, caste and religion, social mobility and social status of the entrepreneur. External environment consists of the political, economical, social, technological, legal, cultural and psychological. Political environment consists of the political atmosphere and quality of leadership in the economy greatly affecting the entrepreneurial business. Economical environment consists of the economic policies, trade tariffs, incentives and subsidies etc., available in the economy. Social environment consists of the consumer or labour attitude, opinions, motives etc. Technological environment consists of the competition, risk, technical know-how etc. Legal environment consists of the rules and regulation of the economy through different legislative policies. Cultural environment consists of the structure, aspiration, values and psychological environment consists of the motivation, attitude, perception etc. Below mentioned chart is clarifying the various internal and external environments which greatly affect the entrepreneurial business.

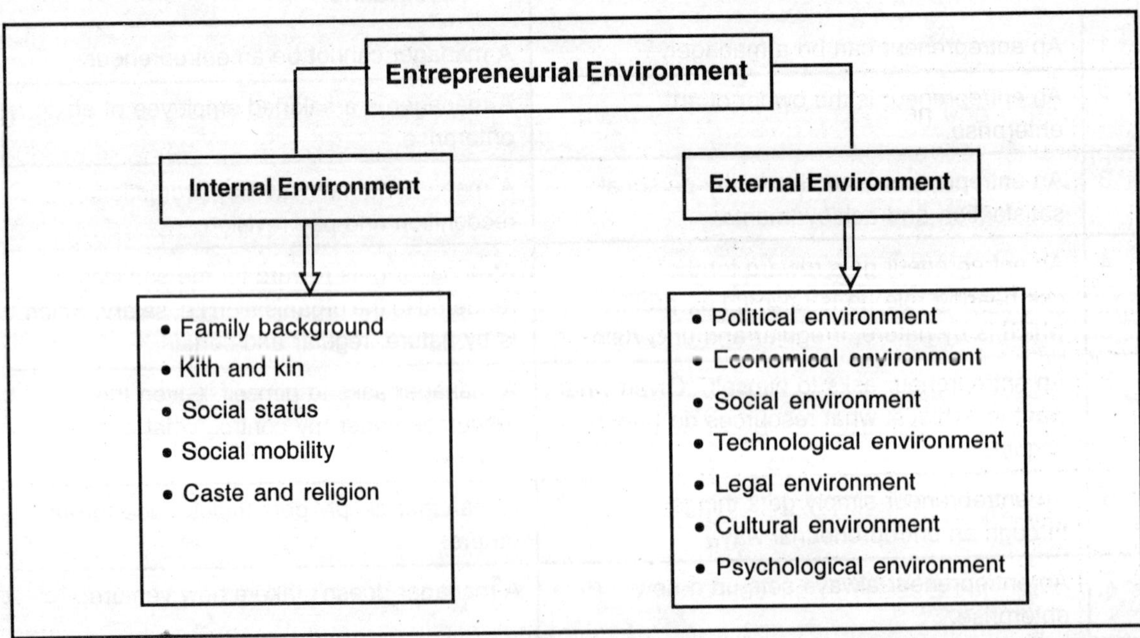

GROWTH OF ENTREPRENEURSHIP DEVELOPMENT IN INDIA

India has a long entrepreneurial tradition, which is helping the economy by utilizing the resources at micro level. An entrepreneur is the key figure in the process of economic growth in the country. He is an economic man who tries to maximize his profits by innovations. He is an organizer and speculator who is doing new things or doing things that is already being done, in a new way. In order to put ideas into practice, an entrepreneur requires certain qualities. The quality of entrepreneurship existing in any region determines to a large extent the development of that region. He is a key man who envisages new opportunities, new techniques and new line of production and coordinates all activities.

The liberalization of the Indian economy started by the P.V.Narasimha Rao government in 1991 and the Information Technology boom of the mid and late 90s have ushered in tremendous changes and set the stage for a wave of entrepreneurship taking India by storm. India, with its abundant pool of talent in the IT domain, management, manufacturing and pharmaceuticals, has become the choicest destination for outsourcing of services from all over the world. It is to India's credit that its corporate and legal systems have been operating with greater efficiency.

India's economy has been growing at a scorching pace. Today, its economy ranks above that of France, Italy and the United Kingdom. Its GDP is the third largest in Asia. The scene for Indian entrepreneur is ideal. An entrepreneur is the kingpin of the business who conceptualizes, builds and manages a business enterprise. Entrepreneurs are driving the growth of the Indian economy. They play a vital role in economic development as key contributors to technological innovation and new job growth. It has been stated that entrepreneurship is the process of opportunity recognition and implementation. It often begins with a vision or idea for a product or process coupled with a passion or zeal to make that idea a reality. An efficient entrepreneurship basically consists on setting goals to accomplish results in the shorter and longer run. Setting goals is the main step to start a project. Goals shuld be achievable, measurable and rated up into different stages so that you can monitor them more easily till the end of every stage.

The National Knowledge Commission (NKC) submitted its report on entrepreneurship to the government recently, stressing on the need to enhance entrepreneurship for employment generation and wealth creation. Mr. Sam Pitroda, Chairman, NKC had pointed out that India will probably have the largest set of young people in the world and Indian had the potential to become the workforce supplier to the world in the next few decades. The NKC study points out that if the local 'best business practices' as seen among today's entrepreneurs were implemented on nationwide scale, India could substantially improve its ranking as a business destination. Amongst the recommendations of the study are facilitation of information flow by developing handbooks on entrepreneurship, help in access to early-stage finance and establishment of secondary markets.

ENTREPRENEURS WHO HAVE CHANGED THE FACE OF INDIA

Indian entrepreneurs are making waves all across the world. Indian business firms are making acquisitions abroad and spreading their tentacles in various corners of the world. India has produced several famous personalities that have excelled in their field. These Indian heroes have battled against all odds and have reached the pinnacle of success by their courage, determination and perseverance. Their lives have inspired a whole generation of Indians and continue to inspire millions of Indians and others all around the world. Here are biographies of few such Indian heroes.

 **Dhirubhai Ambani**	Dhirajlal Harichanda Ambani (lovingly called Dhirubhai Ambani) was an Indian rags to riches, business tycoon who founded Reliance Industries Limited, India's largest private sector company. Reliance is the first Indian company to feature in Forbes 500 list. Dhirubhai Ambani was an ordinary man with extraordinary talent. He was a man with the uncommon capacity of seeing beyond, into the future. According to him, ***"Think Big, Think Fast, Think Ahead, Ideas Are No One's Monopoly."*** He was a visionary and a man who communicated with the rich and the poor with equal felicity, who was generous beyond the call of duty with those whom he liked and utterly ruthless with his rivals-a man of many parts, of irreconcilable contrasts and paradoxes galore.
 **Dr. Verghese Kurien**	Dr. Verghese Kurien is better known as the 'Father of the White Revolution' and the 'Milkman of India'. Dr. Varghese Kurien was the architect behind the success of the largest dairy development program in the world, christened as Operation Flood. He was the Chairman of the Gujarat Co-operative Milk Marketing Federation Ltd. (GCMMF) and his name was synonymous with the brand 'Amul-the taste of India'. The brand name AMUL sourced from the Sanskrit word Amoolya, means priceless and stands for Anand Milk Union Limited. Under Dr. Kurien's stewardship India became the largest producer of milk in the world.
 **Azim Hasham Premji**	Azim Hasham Premji, one of the richest Indians for the past several years and a businessman practices what he preaches. He is the Chairman and CEO of Wipro Technologies, today which is one of the largest software companies in India. He is an icon among Indian businessmen and his success story is a source of inspiration to a number of budding entrepreneurs. Azim Premji is credited with transforming Wipro, his family's vegetable oil business, into one of the world's foremost software company. According to him, "We believe this combination of excellence in operations and strong execution of our strategy is critical to achieve cur vision. We will continue to focus on both in future as well."

 **Ghanshyam Das Birla**	Ghanshyam Das Birla is considered as a doyen of Indian Industry. He was the man who laid the foundations of the Birla Empire; founder of the Federation of Indian Chambers of Commerce and Industry (FICCI). He was a multi-faceted personality. He is also popularly known as the builder of Birla Mandirs. Ghanshyam Das Birla also founded several educational institutions. Birla Institute of Technology and Sciences (BITS) Pilani has today evolved into one of India's best engineering schools.
 **Karsanbhai Patel**	Dr. Karsanbhai Khodidas Patel is the man behind the hugely successful brand, Nirma. His is a legendary rags to riches journey during which he shattered established business theories and rewrote new ones. Karsanbhai set up Nirma, (named after daughter Nirupama) selling detergent powder as an after-office business named the detergent powder. He offered a quality detergent powder, using indigenous technology, at a third of the prevailing price, without compromising on the product. After establishing its leadership in economy-priced detergents, Nirma's foray into the premium brand segment, in cakes and detergents was equally successful. It built up 30% market share in the premium detergent segment and achieved a greater than 20% share in the premium soaps market.
 **JRD Tata**	Jehangir Ratanji Dadabhoy Tata (lovingly called JRD Tata) was one of the most enterprising Indian entrepreneurs. He was the Chairman of Tata and Sons and a pioneer aviator and built one of the largest industrial houses of India. With this distinctive honour of being India's first pilot, he was instrumental in giving wings to India by building Tata Airlines (which ultimately became Air India), Tata Memorial Center for Cancer, Research and Treatment; Tata Institute of Social Sciences (TISS); Tata Institute of Fundamental Research (TIFR) and the National Center for Performing Arts etc. JRD Tata was also bestowed with the United Nations Population Award for his crusading endeavors towards initiating and successfully implementing the family planning movement in India, much before it became an official government policy.
 **Adi Godrej**	Adi Godrej is one of the icons of Indian Industry. He is the chairman of Godrej Group. Under Adi Godrej's leadership; the group is also involved in philanthropic activities. Godrej's were into manufacturing locks and vegetable-based soaps. The Godrej products were among the first indigenously manufactured products to displace entrenched foreign brands. Godrej is major supporter of the World Wildlife Fund in India, it has developed a green business campus in the Vikhroli township of Mumbai, which includes a 150-acre mangrove forest and a school for the children of company employees.

 **Kiran Mazumdar Shaw**	Kiran Mazumdar Shaw is the Chairman and Managing Director of Biocon Ltd, India's biggest biotechnology company. She had founded Biocon India in collaboration with Biocon Biochemicals Limited. Biocon's initial operation was to extract an enzyme from papaya.Under Kiran Mazumdar Shaw's stewardship Biocon transformed from an industrial enzymes company to an integrated biopharmaceutical company with strategic research initiatives. Today, Biocon is recognised as India's pioneering biotech enterprise. According to Kiran, "Don't seek jobs, create them."
 **Kumar Mangalam Birla**	Kumar Mangalam Birla is the Chairman of the Aditya Birla Group (named after his father, noted industrialist Aditya Birla). Under his leadership, the Aditya Birla Group, apart from consolidating its position in existing businesses, also ventured into sunrise sectors like cellular telephony, asset management, software and BPO. Major companies of Aditya Birla Group in India are Grasim, Hindalco, UltraTech Cement, Aditya Birla Nuvo and Idea Cellular. Aditya Birla Group's joint ventures include Birla Sun Life (Financial Services) and Birla NGK (insulators). He brought in radical changes, changed business strategies, professionalised the entire group and replaced internal systems. Kumar Mangalam reduced his group's dependence on the cyclic commodities sectors by entering consumer products.
 **M.S. Oberoi**	Rai Bahadur Mohan Singh Oberoi (named as M.S. Oberoi) was a renowned Indian hotelier, widely regarded as the father of 20th century India's hotel business, was the founder Chairman of Oberoi Hotels and Resorts, India's second-largest hotel company, with 35 luxury hotels in India, Sri Lanka, Nepal, Egypt, Australia and Hungary. He can be aptly termed as the father of the Indian hotel industry and founder of the Oberoi Group of Hotels.
 **Narayana Murthy**	Nagavara Ramarao Narayana Murthy ((lovingly called Narayana Murthy) is an Indian industrialist, software engineer, founder, Non-Executive Chairman and Chief Mentor of Infosys Technologies Limited. He is a living legend and an epitome of the fact that honesty, transparency, and moral integrity are not at variance with business acumen. He set new standards in corporate governance and morality when he stepped down as the Executive Chairman of Infosys.

 **Naresh Goyal**	Naresh Goyal is the founder Chairman of Jet Airways, India's largest domestic airline. Jet Airways presently operates over 320 flights daily to 48 destinations, of which five are international. Naresh Goel also figures in Forbes list of Indian billionaires. Today, Jet Airways has evolved into India's largest private domestic airline. Jet Airways8 has been voted India's "Best Domestic Airline" by several organisations of world-class repute. Jet Airways came up with an IPO and it was a huge success. Jet Airways was recently in controversy over its merger deal with Air Sahara. The merger was called off and the too airlines are currently considering arbitration.
 **Dr. Pratap Reddy**	Dr. Pratap Reddy is the founder of the Apollo Hospital Group, India's first corporate hospital group. He revolutionized the whole health care scenario of India and inspired others to follow the suit. Today, India has over 750 corporate hospitals all over the country. Dr. Pratap Reddy's latest initiatives are "Med Varsity"-a virtual medical university providing total access to experts in the field of medicine anywhere in the world- and "MEDNET" - Hospital Systems Management package. Both the initiatives are expected to transform health care sector in India.
 **Rahul Bajaj**	Rahul Bajaj is the Chairman of the Bajaj Group, which ranks among the top 10 business houses in India. The Bajaj Group has diversified interests ranging from automobiles, home appliances, lighting, iron and steel, insurance, travel and finance. Rahul Bajaj is one of India's most distinguished business leaders and internationally respected for his business acumen and entrepreneurial spirit. Rahul Bajaj created one of India's best companies in the difficult days of the licence-permit raj Bajaj Auto was top scooter producer in India and its Chetak brand had a 10- year waiting period.
 **Subhash Chandra**	Subhash Chandra is the founder of Zee TV, India's first private TV channel. He has launched Zee Telefilms Limited as a content supplier for Zee TV - India's first Hindi satellite channel. He was the first in India who sought to harness the huge business potential of satellite television channels. It was Subhash Chandra's vision that helped give birth to the satellite TV industry in India and inspired others to follow suit. Zee TV is the first service provider in India to launch Direct to Home (DTH) services. He has also launched many channels such as Zee News, Zee Cinema... In a short span of time Zee TV has become a big media and has give tough competition to international media moghuls such as Rupert Murdoch.

 **Brij Mohan Lal Munjal**	B.M. Munjal (Brij Mohan Lall Munjal) is the Chairman of the Hero Group. He is a first generation entrepreneur who started very small and through sheer hard work and perseverance made it to the top. Today, Hero Group is the largest manufacturer of two-wheelers in the world and Brij Mohan Lal Munjal is the man widely credited with its success. For his outstanding contribution to the success of Hero Group, Japan's Honda, the world's largest manufacturer of motorcycles, elicited interest in collaborating with the Hero Group to manufacture motor cycles in India in the name of Hero Honda.
 **Sunil Mittal**	Sunil Bharti Mittal is the Founder, Chairman and Managing Director of Bharti Group and runs India's largest GSM-based mobile phone service. Sunil Mittal can be called as originator of cellular phone revolution in India. Sunil Mittal founded Bharti Cellular Limited (BCL) to offer cellular services under the brand name AirTel. Bharti Cellular Limited also rolled out India's first private national as well as international long-distance service under the brand name IndiaOne.

SUMMARY

Entrepreneurship is a critical element in the growth of any economy. Today's knowledge based Indian economy is a fertile ground for entrepreneurs. It is rightly believed that India has an extraordinary talent pool with virtually limitless potential to produce entrepreneurs. By and large, the Indian society is averse to risk. People normally look for long-term and stable employment, such as government and public sector jobs. Social attitudes, lack of capital, inadequate physical infrastructure an, lack of government support are the major factors hindering entrepreneurship in India. Government needs to make efforts and encourage entrepreneurship by providing training and other facilities, especially in the rural areas. It is very much important to get committed to creating the right environment to develop successful entrepreneurs.

QUESTIONS

SHORT ANSWER QUESTIONS

1. Define entrepreneur and entrepreneurship.
2. Distinguish between entrepreneur and intrapreneur.
3. Distinguish between entrepreneur and manager.
4. Explain the evolution of entrepreneurship in India.

5. What are the characteristics of entrepreneurship?
6. What are the entrepreneurial vision and mission?
7. What is the entrepreneurial process? Explain in detail.

LONG ANSWER QUESTIONS

1. Who is an entrepreneur? How is it different from a manager? Discuss various skills of an entrepreneur?
2. Discuss various factors that influence the growth of entrepreneurship. State the steps to be taken to encourage entrepreneurship in the state of Orissa.
3. How will you define an entrepreneur? What are the distinguishing characteristics of an entrepreneurial person?

CHAPTER

ENTREPRENEURIAL BEHAVIOUR

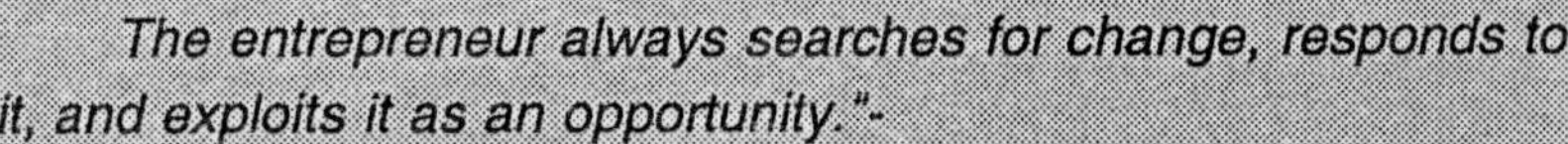

The entrepreneur always searches for change, responds to it, and exploits it as an opportunity."-

— Peter Drucker

Chapter Overview:

At the end of this chapter, you will be able to understand:

1. The entrepreneurial mind-set.
2. The information useful in profiling the entrepreneurial mind-set.
3. The most commonly cited characteristics found in successful entrepreneurs.
4. The "dark side" of entrepreneurship.
5. The entrepreneurial motivation.
6. The verbal and non-verbal communications.

Introduction

Managing the human dimension of the venture is critical to entrepreneurial success. People work best when they are motivated to do so. The entrepreneur cannot demand effort from someone; he must support the individual and encourage them to offer their efforts. An entrepreneur, before he sets up an enterprise, wants to satisfy himself that it is a profitable proposal. He wants to gather critical information and take decisions pertaining to various facets, i.e., technical arrangement, plant and machinery, market, location, statutory clearances in order that the tasks of establishing the project, and to some extent managing it later, become easy. A business plan is an outcome of an exercise meant to check the viability of an enterprise and analyse and firm up its essential parameters.

Innovation and Entrepreneur

Innovation is a very comprehensive term. One can bring innovations in products, services or one can innovate the way these are created, processed, packaged or better for the market efficiently in a cost effective manner. Today, competition is not the only issue bothering Indian small and medium enterprises, they are getting affected by the global economy, i.e., particularly in US economy either directly or indirectly. Today, the government too is encouraging the adoption of research and development amongst small and medium enterprises as ultimately it is knowledge, networking and innovation that will clearly define the standing of small enterprises in the global market. The road ahead with an entrepreneur and the growth of small and medium scale industries is based on innovations. Only innovations through research and development will pave way for the creation of local resources and at the same time adoption, absorption and diffusion of expertise for future expansion of entrepreneurial business.

The Entrepreneurial Mindset: Sources of Research on Entrepreneurs

Entrepreneurs are the growth engines of economics. They have pioneered most of what matters or have at least provided the world the tools. They are raw, real and revolutionary. They are the 'e' in the non-differential equation driven world of chaos in which we live and work. They drive the creative destruction process of transformation that economist Joseph Schumpeter recognised was key to radical innovation and sustained long-term economic growth. Growth of entrepreneurs is based on three dimensions such as research and popular publications, direct observations and speeches, seminars and presentations etc. Relationships among these three are given below:

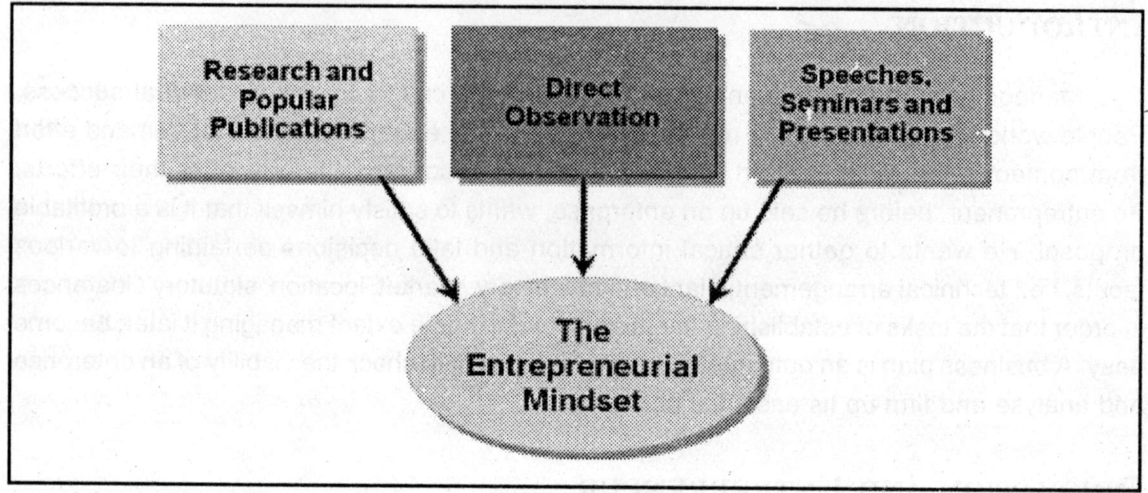

1. Publications
   - ✓ Technical and professional journals
   - ✓ Textbooks on entrepreneurship
   - ✓ Biographies or autobiographies of entrepreneurs
   - ✓ Compendiums about entrepreneurs
   - ✓ News periodicals
   - ✓ Venture periodicals
   - ✓ Newsletters
   - ✓ Proceedings of conferences
   - ✓ The internet
2. Direct Observation of practicing entrepreneurs
   - ✓ Interviews
   - ✓ Surveys
   - ✓ Case studies
3. Speeches, seminars, and presentations by practicing entrepreneurs.

Entrepreneurial Motivation

Entrepreneurship is an art or a skill to lead an endeavor or an enterprise. An entrepreneur is a person who has a vision, an ambition to initiate a new venture by accepting risks. Entrepreneurship requires motivation and inspiration at every stage and hence, business entrepreneur quotes are meant for such entrepreneurs. Finding Motivation is one of the biggest problems for an entrepreneur. Many time entrepreneurs complain that they cannot find it when they are carrying out a piece of work. Especially in workplaces where people are counting on you to deliver the best material you can output. Where do you find motivation? People tend to get motivated to carry out tasks and complete given work when they have something they want to achieve by doing the work, some people like to refer to these as goals or Incentives.

Entrepreneurial motivation is usually long term, and that's why it needs to be broken down into something shorter. Entrepreneurial motivation can be more difficult to find. Entrepreneurs create an innovative organization or network of organizations for the purpose of gain or growth, under conditions of risk and/or uncertainty (Dollinger, 2003). This includes the core elements of entrepreneurship, which can be found in the numerous definitions of the social sciences literatures. Even though academics have addressed a range of questions concerning both with the nature of the entrepreneurial process and the attributes and personality traits of entrepreneurs, research is still short of a consensus on some of the most important questions.

Types of Entrepreneurial Behaviour

Organizational behaviour is concerned with the understanding, prediction and control of human behaviour in any organisation. It is the study and application of knowledge about how people act within an organization. It seeks to shed light on the human factor and the study about the integrated behaviour like psychology, sociology and anthropology for the study of human behaviour in and around organization. Organizational behaviour involves three levels of analysis of behaviour:

1. Individual behaviour: Every individual is different from others. They are differing in physical characteristics, intelligence, aptitudes, attitudes, personality, skills etc. All these skills help an individual to interact with other fellow members in an organization. Various factors which influence the behaviour of individuals are ability, perception, motivation, organizational factors, socio-cultural factors etc.

2. Group behaviour: A group consists of two or more persons who interact with each other, consciously for the achievement of certain common objectives. Every job in the organization is interdependent and every task requires the cooperation from all the members in order to excel in the organization. Various factors which affect the group cohesiveness are nature, size, location, communication, status of the groups etc.

Motivation Theories, Motivating Factors

What comes first? The chicken or the egg? Motivation or action? The answer surprisingly is action. First, we have to prime the pump and the way is through action. People who tend to procrastinate, confuse motivation and action. The word "motivation" means different things to different people. One thing for sure is that one can't buy a jar of it: it has to come from within oneself. A person's brain needs constant motivational input just as muscles need exercise, engines need petrol and plants need water. People are the product of their thoughts and the aim of motivational material is to improve the quality of the thoughts. Motivation is nothing more than encouragement and we all perform better for it. Motivation comes by encouraging others.

Theories of Motivation

There are three main theories of motivation. They are:

1. Desire for achievement (a sense of significance),
2. Desire for power (a sense of strength) and,
3. Desire for affiliation (a sense of belonging).

1. Desire for achievement: Entrepreneurs think about individual capability in terms of skills and knowledge one has gained. However, the attitud of an individual is just as important as, his skill and knowledge. In business life, there are countless examples of executives who seem to have all the right skills, knowledge, technical or otherwise, and they still never seem to achieve results. It is because entrepreneurship is by practice of doing and not just by knowing or knowledge or logic. It is by the results and its authority is performance only.

2. Desire for power: Every entrepreneur has his/her own way of running an enterprise and ensuring its success and growth. An entrepreneur devotes all the time and energy to come up with innovative ways of ensuring success and profitability of a venture. Most entrepreneurs consider one particular business as their baby and nurture it throughout their lives. It is the desire of the entrepreneur to enjoy the power to establish the business.

3. Desire for affiliation: Entrepreneurial theories are linked to the concept of extrinsic and intrinsic rewards. Extrinsic motivation comes from outside, for example, the prospect of fame, recognition, monetary rewards, gaining power, respect or social approval, "Intrinsic rewards etc., come from the situations of motivation.

Factors/elements in the Process of Motivation

Motivation is the image or snapshot which encourage entrepreneur to achieve success. Self knowledge is the key to self-motivation. It is the inner belief as well as the attitude and views of strengths and weaknesses. Following are the various elements in the process of motivation:

1. Desire: Entrepreneurship is an asset that becomes even more valuable in a booming economy. An entrepreneur has the constant challenge to reach and sustain an optimum level of motivation which overcomes problems and brings results. To be motivated one must have an intense burning desire to get where or what one expects. If there is no challenge in what an individual is doing, motivation will soon wither and die.

2. Decision: An entrepreneur must make a conscious decision on what to aim for. He must understand why vision offers a picture of a more valuable world and how it will reward him. The vision will be a picture of the new world, the entrepreneur seeks to create. Motivation is an inner state which stimulates action or moves backed by drive. It can be the cause of an inner drive. The terms like wants, needs, desires, wishes, aims, goals, drives, motives and so on are related motivation.

3. Determination: It is the relationship between needs and goals which can make an integral part of motivation. Motivation implies goals toward which the movement occurs. Determination helps to climb mountains so that absolutely nothing will stop an entrepreneur.

4. Discipline: It is critical to pay the price whether one likes it or not. Motivation is strongest when it is the internalisation of the goals and dreams.

5. Focus: Motivation depends upon leadership skills. It is focused on communication skills and good employee management.

6. Direction: The respondent entrepreneurs were motivated primarily by the desire to create something new, the desire for autonomy, wealth and financial independence, the achievement of personal objectives and the propensity for action.

Entrepreneurial Mobility

The journey of an entrepreneur begins with innovation followed by invention and entrepreneurship. That is why the keen mobility is a story of innovation, invention and entrepreneurship. An entrepreneur focuses more on the development of new products through innovations only. A successful entrepreneur can be best defined as an innovative person with inherent capabilities and potential to initiate a business. It is based on the principle 'for those who dare to dream, there is a whole world to win.' Before starting any venture one has to know his/her skills and knowledge. One should have a taste to try something new and master it as quick as possible but first focus should be on the key areas. Entrepreneurship is a creative human act involving the mobilization of resources from one level of productive use to a higher level of use. "It is the process by which the individual pursues opportunities without regard to resources currently controlled. The journey of Reliance Company in India is the best example for the mobility of the venture of Dhirubhai Ambani. He was very optimistic about India and its young human resource. He used to say, 'My advice to young entrepreneurs is not to accept defeat in the face of odds; and challenge negative forces with hope, self-confidence and conviction. I believe that ambition and initiative will ultimately triumph. The success of young entrepreneurs will be the key to India's transformation in the new millennium."

MOTIVATION THEORIES AND ABRAHAM MASLOW'S HIERARCHY OF NEEDS

Abraham Maslow developed the hierarchy of needs model in 1940-50s USA, and the hierarchy of needs theory remains valid today for understanding human motivation, management training, and personal development. Indeed, Maslow's ideas surrounding the hierarchy of needs concerning the responsibility of employers to provide a workplace environment that encourages and enables employees to fulfil their own unique potential (self-actualization) are today more relevant than ever.

Motivation is the psychological feature that arouses an individual to action toward a desired goal. Motivation can also be the reason for an individual's action or that which gives purpose and direction to behaviour. In other words, motivation is an incentive that generates goal-directed behaviour. Over the last 80 years there have been many theories developed to describe how and why people are motivated to work. In the post-war period the key influence has been Maslow's hierarchy of needs theory developed in the early 1950s. This approach set the differing needs of all human beings in order of their importance, the first level needs having to be satisfied, at least to a minimum level, before one can proceed to the next stage. Maslow's Theory is based on the following premises:

- **Man is wanting being:** Human wants are unlimited. When one need is satisfied, another arises. This process is unending; it continues from birth to death.
- **Man's behaviour is motivated by unsatisfied needs:** The need which is satisfied no longer serves as a motivator of behaviour.
- **Man's needs are arranged in a hierarchy of importance:** As soon as needs at the lower level of hierarchy are satisfied, those at the higher level emerge and start demanding satisfaction. A graphical presentation of the hierarchy of needs postulated by Maslow is given below:

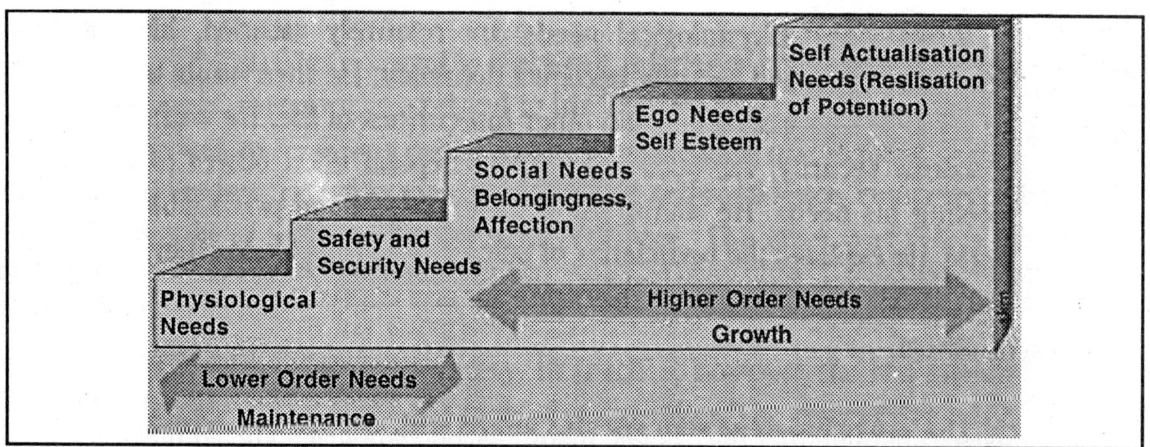

1. Physiological needs: These relate to the basic needs required to maintain life such as food, drink, oxygen, sleep, shelter and warmth. Obviously all human beings will seek to satisfy these at a basic level before proceeding upwards.

2. Safety and security needs: These are concerned with protection and security from external dangers. In the most basic sense, these relate to the protection of life although other elements become important in a work environment such as job security and physical safety. These latter needs are less categorical and do change from time to time.

3. Social needs: These relate to the feeling of belonging, being part of the work group with support and friendship from those one works with, or at home with one's family and friends.

4. Self-esteem or ego needs: These are the requirements for self-confidence such as competence in work and the desire to perform well and be seen to do so. Recognition from others is an important element of this need.

5. Self-actualisation needs: This area relates to intellectual needs which can include the knowledge and understanding of one's position, the need for self-development and for aesthetic requirements such as art and music. It can also be the satisfaction that people achieve in reaching their potential and knowing that they are undertaking good work.

Although Maslow believes that each level needed to be satisfied before moving onto the next level, this satisfaction may only be to a basic degree. For instance, a person's requirements for physiological needs may increase from peer pressure and through the ability to develop a higher standard of living.

Motivation Theories and Frederick Herzberg

In 1959, Frederick Herzberg proposed a development model based on Maslow's hierarchy covering maintenance and motivational factors relating to the work environment. He argued that basic maintenance factors such as salary, security and relationships with colleagues and superiors, needed to be satisfied to a level, but beyond that motivation was only achieved through recognition and the provision of additional responsibility so that the person could increase his or her self-esteem and self fulfillment.

Two-Factor Theory

According to Frederick Herzberg, there are two factors i.e., motivation and hygiene, which makes people to feel them about their jobs. Herzberg believed that businesses should motivate employees by adopting a democratic approach to management and by improving the nature and content of the actual job through certain methods. Some of the methods managers could use to achieve this are:

1. **Job enlargement:** Under this situation, workers being given a greater variety of tasks to perform (not necessarily more challenging) which should make the work more interesting.
2. **Job enrichment:** Under this situation, workers are given a wider range of more complex, interesting and challenging tasks surrounding a complete unit of work. This should give a greater sense of achievement.
3. **Empowerment:** Under this situation, delegation is given to the employees to make their own decisions over areas of their working life.

He surveyed workers, analyzed the results, and concluded that to understand employee satisfaction (or dissatisfaction), he had to divide work factors into two categories:

- Motivation factors. Those factors that are strong contributors to job satisfaction
- Hygiene factors. Those factors that are not strong contributors to satisfaction but must be present to meet a worker's expectations and prevent job dissatisfaction

Herzberg's Two-Factor Theory

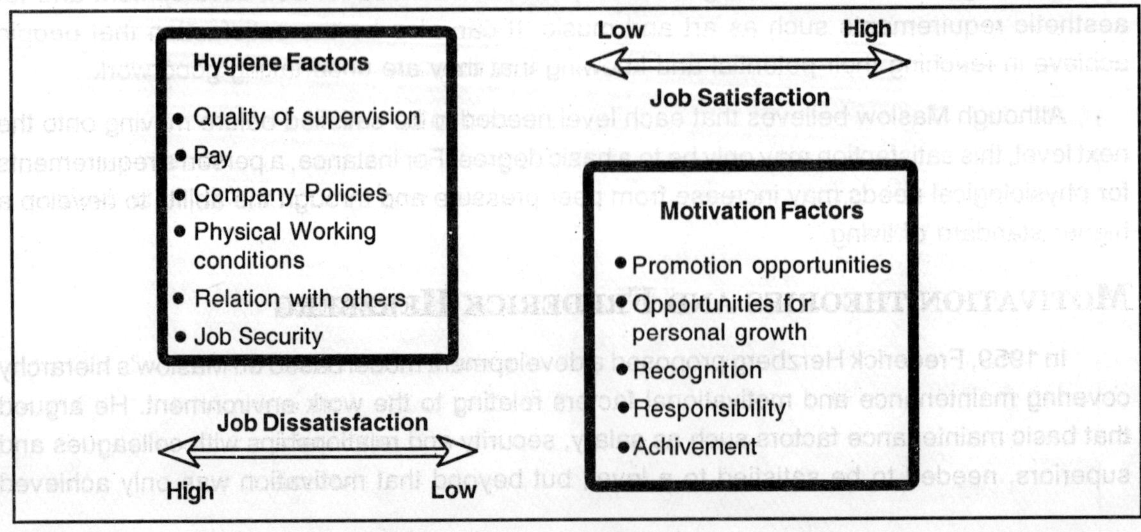

A comparison of Maslow and Herzberg models is given below:

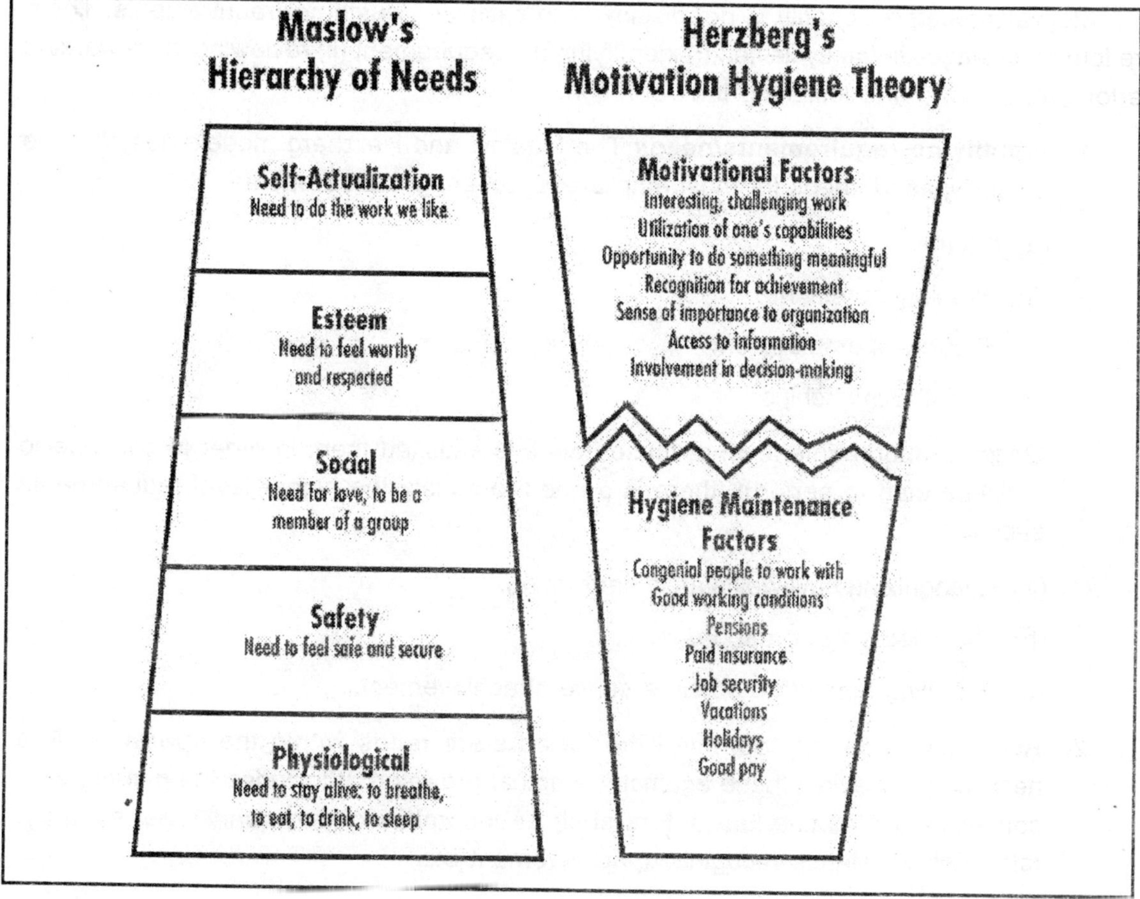

Maslow's and Herzberg's models provide useful ways of understanding the broad motivation of staff, but they give only a general indication. At any one time motivation will also depend on factors such as:

1. Changes in staffing, i.e., reductions or sudden influxes of new staff
2. Comparative salaries and benefits
3. Security of employment
4. Interest in the work

In applying these factors it is also important to understand how well staff believes they are being rewarded for their efforts.

What can be learnt from the theories?

Motivating staff for quality is not dissimilar to satisfying customer requirements. There are four main stages in the cycle i.e., (i) identifying the requirement (ii) reviewing (iii) rewarding performance, and (iv) redesigning the operation.

1. **Identifying requirements/needs:**The Maslow and Herzberg models describe the basic types of needs for most employees, covering such areas as:

   (a) Salary

   (b) Working conditions

   (c) Security of employment

   (d) Social relationships

   Once an appropriate level of these needs is satisfied then, in order to continue to motivate staff to perform, there is a need to satisfy the higher level requirements such as

   (a) Recognizing how well staff is performing.

   (b) The allocating of responsibility.

   (c) Enabling the staff to obtain a sense of achievement.

2. **Reviewing:** Having identified the broad staff needs within the operation, it is necessary to review these against the actual provision. It includes the primary staff concerns and motivation factors such as income, working conditions, security, relationships, status, recognition, achievement etc.

3. **Rewarding performance:** The amount of effort will depend on the degree to which this is recognized with a tangible reward such as a bonus or an intangible reward such as recognition by their supervisor or manager. Consideration must be given to both positive and negative reinforcement. Negative reinforcement i.e., 'punishment' for those not performing, should not be ignored. Within any group there is an acceptable level or peer performance of 'fair play'.

4. **Redesigning the operation:** To give staff pride in their work it is necessary to design it to provide the maximum satisfaction. There are three main elements of this development; staff needs to understand how the task relates to the overall process and their influence on achieving a good result. The task needs to be clearly defined and not confused with other tasks.

Entrepreneurial Behaviour and Psycho-theories:

Psychological approaches to entrepreneurship are fascinating both for entrepreneurship and psychology. Entrepreneurship can project from this interface between business and psychology because psychological variables are clearly related to entrepreneurial entry and success. Psychological variables (most notably action-related concepts) function as mediators in the process that leads to success (e.g., strategies). For psychology, entrepreneurship is interesting because it combines the following features:

(a) The level of analysis question is related to the dynamic of enterprise growth; in the beginning, a small scale enterprise is best described by looking at the owner. However, in somewhat more mature enterprises, the level of analysis has to change because more delegation, management, and implementation is necessary.

(b) Some interesting organizational hypotheses can better be studied with small-scale entrepreneurs than with large organizations. A good example is the study of contingency theories. Small-scale enterprises are more coherent than larger ones and therefore, contingency models can be tested better.

(c) There is no doubt that future workplaces will stress innovation and personal initiative more strongly and we need to know how small scale entrepreneurs act.

Role of Entrepreneur in the Socio-economic Environment

An entrepreneur, before setting up an enterprise, wants to satisfy himself that it is a profitable proposal. He wants to gather critical information and take decisions pertaining to various facets i.e., technical arrangement, plant and machinery, market location, statutory clearances in order that the tasks of establishing the project and to some extent managing it later, becomes easy. It is said that an economy is an effect for which entrepreneurship is the cause. Entrepreneurship development has therefore become a matter of great concern in all countries. But the real problem is how to develop entrepreneurship.

Role of Entrepreneur in the Industrial Development

Most important factors affecting manpower utilisation and unemployment are high rate of population growth unmatched by adequate investment to ensure new employment opportunities. This essentially reflects the structural imbalance in the process of development.

There are a number of financial institutions and programmes established by the Government to cater to the needs of small investors but unfortunately due to lack of knowledge and confidence they find it difficult to obtain the necessary guidance and assistance. If one has to analyse the needs of small entrepreneurs who have a marketable skills it would perhaps be:

- ✓ Development of skill levels to market standards
- ✓ Development of business skills
- ✓ Preparation of business feasibilities
- ✓ Financial assistance
- ✓ Marketing outlets, etc.

GOVERNMENT POLICIES TOWARDS PROMOTION OF ENTREPRENEURSHIP

Pandit Jawaharlal Nehru laid the foundations of modern India. His vision and determination have left a lasting impression on every facet of national endeavour since Independence. It is due to his initiative that India now has a strong and diversified industrial base and is a major industrial nation of the world. The goals and objectives set out for the nation by Pandit Nehru on the eve of Independence, namely, the rapid agricultural and industrial development of our country, rapid expansion of opportunities for gainful employment, progressive reduction of social and economic disparities, removal of poverty and attainment of self-reliance remain as valid today as at the time Pandit Nehru first set them out before the nation. Any industrial policy must contribute to the realisation of these goals and objectives at an accelerated pace. The present statement of industrial policy is inspired by these very concerns, and represents a renewed initiative towards consolidating the gains of national reconstruction at this crucial stage.

1. The New Small-Scale Sector Policy 1991: Industries are the backbone of any country. The progress and prosperity of any country largely depends upon the industrial development and no all round and balanced industrial growth is possible without an industrial policy. All industrially advanced countries have a national industrial policy of their own. It is determining a reasonable relationship between the state and the private enterprises, between industry and industry, regions and regions. The statement of industrial policy issued by the planning and development department of the then Government of India in April 1945. In 1948, immediately after independence, Government introduced the Industrial Policy Resolutions. This outlined the approach to industrial growth and development. It emphasized the importance to the economy of securing a continuous increase in production and ensuring its equitable distribution. After the adoption of the Constitution and the socio-economic goals, the Industrial Policy was comprehensively revised and adopted in 1956. The Industrial Policy Resolution of 1948 was followed by the Industrial Policy Resolution of 1956, which had as its objective the acceleration of the rate of economic growth and the speeding up of industrialisation as a means of achieving a socialist pattern of society. In 1956, capital was scarce and the base of entrepreneurship not strong enough. Hence, the 1956, Industrial Policy Resolution gave primacy to the role of the State to assume a predominant and direct responsibility for industrial development. The Industrial Policy statement of 1973, *inter alia,* identified high-priority industries where investment from large industrial houses and foreign companies would be permitted. The Industrial Policy Statement of 1977, laid emphasis on decentralisation and on the role of smallscale, tiny and cottage industries. The Industrial Policy Statement of 1980, focussed attention on the need for promoting competition in the domestic market, technological upgradation and modernisation. The policy laid the foundation for an increasingly competitive export based and for encouraging foreign investment in high-technology areas. This found expression in the Sixth Five Year Plan which bore the distinct stamp of Smt. Indira Gandhi. It was Smt. Indira Gandhi who emphasised the need for productivity to be the central concern in all economic and production activities. A number of policy and procedural changes were introduced in 1985 and, in 1986, under the leadership of Rajiv Gandhi aimed at increasing productivity, reducing costs and improving quality. The accent was on opening the domestic market to increased competition and readying our industry to stand on its own in the face of international competition. In July 1991, The Central Government announced a New Industrial Policy for the country.

A series of measures to liberalise the economy and to increase its competitiveness followed. The main ingredients of the new policy are de-regulation, scaling down of the public sector's role and encouragement of foreign investments through dilution of restrictions in foreign equity participation, repartriation of dividend dilution etc.

2. Industrial Licensing Policy: Industrial Licensing is governed by the Industries (Development and Regulation) Act, 1951. The Industrial Policy Resolution of 1956 identified the following three categories of industries: those that would be reserved for development in public sector, those that would be permitted for development through private enterprise with or without State participation, and those in which investment initiatives would ordinarily emanate from private entrepreneurs. Over the years, keeping in view the changing industrial scene in the country, the policy has undergone modifications. Industrial licensing policy and procedures have also been liberalised from time to time. A full realisation of the industrial potential of the country calls for a continuation of this process of change. The Industrial licensing in India can be read in the following stages:

- The Industries (Development and Regulation) Act, 1951
- Industrial Licensing Policy 1951-60
- Industrial Licensing Policy 1960-70
- Industrial Licensing Policy 1970
- Industrial Licensing Policy 1973

- Industrial Licensing Policy 1977
- Industrial Licensing Policy 1980-90
- Liberalisation of Industrial Licensing 1991

3. Foreign Investment: While freeing Indian industry from official controls, opportunities for promoting foreign investments in India should also be fully exploited. In view of the significant development of India's industrial economy in the last 40 years, the general resilience, size and level of sophistication achieved, and the significant changes that have also taken place in the world industrial economy, the relationship between domestic and foreign industry needs to be much more dynamic than it has been in the past in terms of both technology and investment. Foreign investment would bring attendant advantages of technology transfer, marketing expertise, introduction of modern managerial techniques and new possibilities for promotion of exports. This is particularly necessary in the changing global scenario of industrial and firms so that we can engage in purposive negotiation with such large firms, and provide the avenues for large investments in the development of industries and technology in the national interest.

Foreign Technology Agreement

There is a great need for promoting an industrial environment where the acquisition of technological capability receives priority. In the fast changing world of technology the relationship between the suppliers and users of technology must be a continuous one. Such a relationship becomes difficult to achieve when the approval process includes unnecessary governmental interference on a case to case basis involving endemic delays and fostering uncertainty. The Indian entrepreneur has now come of age so that he no longer needs such bureaucratic clearances of his commercial technology relationships with foreign technology suppliers. Indian industry can scarcely be competitive with the rest of the world if it is to operate within such a regulatory environment.

Social Responsibilities in Entrepreneurial Discipline

Small and medium sized enterprises (SMEs) play a key role in the modern market economy. The small businesses are the monolith fundamental of every prosperous and effectively functioning state. They possess a number of advantages, which place them into the centre of the economic and social goals of society. There is a variety of issues which the entrepreneur can accept as a part of the venture's social responsibility. Minimum standards in the treatment of employees, occupational health and safety and product liability will usually be subject to legal regulations. Entrepreneurs frequently take a positive attitude towards wider social issues such as treatment of the environment, relationships with developing nations.

The entrepreneurial business faces a choice in the way in which it approaches its social responsibilities. It may be defensive. The means that the business decides that its social responsibilities are a liability and that they hinder its performance. It may then try to avoid them and to minimize their impact. This may boost short-term profits but it can easily lead to a reaction by stakeholders, especially, but not exclusively, its employees and customers. Social responsibilities constrain the actions of a business. They often define what it cannot do, rather than what it can. This does not mean they are bad for business. They provide a sound and shared set of rules within which the business community can operate.

Factors in Developing Entrepreneurship: Cultural, Social and Economical

According to Peter Drucker, "One cannot make decisions for the future. Decisions are commitments to actions in the present, and in the present only. But actions in the present are also one and only way to make the future."

Entrepreneurship is reflected in all the major dimensions of civilization, *viz.,* social, political and economic. It involves creativity that is consistent with the healthy edge required to change the basis of competition. Entrepreneurship as in the past will determine technical innovations, status of social institutions and political management systems. On the basis of these factors, we can expect the future to be a place where basic needs will remain and only the wants will change. The economic innovation is common denominator of the economic theory. It is a process whereby factors on the supply side allow expanding output, while those on the demand side determine how far the growth will proceed. Economic innovation involves more than raising per capita output and income; it constitutes change in structure of production and society. Social development would give rise to improvement in overall quality of life, which leads to social innovation. The betterment of society will generate enough opportunities at the micro level for another economic innovation and thus the process continues. There must be a social attitude that views innovations with positive attitude and reject an innovation only when it is not acceptable.

Theories of Entrepreneurship

"He loves practice without theory is like the sailor who boards ship without a rudder and compass and never knows where he may case.'

Leonardo Da Vinci

There are four factors of production i.e., land, labour, capital and organization. Organization is the coordinating factor that brings together the other three factors and entrepreneurship is the element that powers and strengthens the organization. Many of the economists believe that entrepreneurship is itself the fourth factors of production that is the most important in driving a successful economy. Entrepreneurs are defined by their risk taking abilities and their intentions to fill in the void because of the existing lack of knowledge about a product. According to them, the entrepreneur ventures are carried out where there is a gap in the development of a product. The entrepreneurs work to fill the gap by introducing something that increases the effectiveness of the already existing product. The field of entrepreneurship continues to struggle with the development of a modern theory of entrepreneurship. In the past 20 years development of the current theories of entrepreneurship have centered on either opportunity recognition or the individual entrepreneur. At the same time many theoretical insights have come from economics, including a rediscovery of the work of Schumpeter. However because there is a lack of clarity about the theoretical assumptions that entrepreneurship scholars use in their work, assumptions from both individual opportunity recognition and economics, have been used as if they are interchangeable. This lack of theoretical distinction has hampered theory development in the field of entrepreneurship.

Throughout the theoretical history of entrepreneurship, scholars from multiple disciplines in the social sciences have grappled with a diverse set of interpretations and definitions to conceptualize this abstract idea. Entrepreneurship is an evolved thing. With the advancement of science and technology it has undergone metamorphosis change and emerged as a critical input for socio-economic development. Various writers have developed variety theories on entrepreneurship and popularized the concept among the common people. The theories of entrepreneurship that are propounded by many eminent theorists have been grouped under four categories. They are:

Cultural Theories	1. Theory of Imitating: Hoselitz
	2. Theory of Social Culture: Stokes
Economic Theories	1. Theory of Functional Behaviour: Casson
	2. Theory of Economic Incentives: Papanek and Harris
	3. Theory of Adjustment of Price: Kirzner
	4. Theory of X-Efficiency-Leibenstein
	5. Theory of Innovations-Schumpeter
	6. Theory of Harvard School
	7. Theory of High Achievement -McClelland
	8. Theory of Profit-Knight
	9. Theory of Market Equilibrium-Hayek
Psychological Theories	1. Theory of Psychology-Kunkal
	2. Theory of Personal Resourcefulness
Sociological Theories	1. Theory of Entrepreneurial Supply: Cochran
	2. Theory of Religious Belief: Weber
	3. Theory of Social Change: Hagen

1.CULTURAL THEORIES: Cultural theories pointed out that entrepreneurship is the product of the culture. Entrepreneurial talents come from cultural values and cultural systems embedded into the cultural environment. This theory supports two other theories i.e. (i) Hoselitz theory and (ii) Stokes theory.

(a) Theory of Imitating: According to Bert F. Hoselitz's theory, supply of entrepreneurship is governed by cultural factors and culturally minority groups are the spark-plugs of entrepreneurial and economic development. In many countries, entrepreneurs have emerged from a particular socio-economic class. Hoselitz reveals that in several countries entrepreneurial talents are found in persons having particular socio-economic background. He emphasized the role of culturally marginally groups like Jews and the Greeks in medieval Europe, the Chinese in South Africa and Indians in East Africa in promoting economic developments. Further he has emphasized on the theory through examples of Christians contributes to entrepreneurship in Lebanon, Halai Memon industrialists in Pakistan and Marwadis in India.

(b) Theory of Social Culture: According to David Stoke's theory, entrepreneurship is likely to emerge under specific social sanctions, social culture and economic action. According to Stokes, personal and societal opportunities and the presence of requisite psychological distributions may be seen as conditions for an individual movement to get changed into industrial entrepreneurship.

2. ECONOMIC THEORIES: According to these theories, entrepreneurship and economic growth take place when the economic conditions are favourable. Economic development takes place when a country is real rational income increases overall period of time wherein the role of entrepreneurs is an integral part. Economic incentives are the main motivators for entrepreneurial activities. Economic incentives include taxation policy, industrial policy, sources of finance and raw materials, infrastructure availability, investment and marketing opportunities, access to information about market conditions, technology etc.

(a) Theory of functional behaviour: According to Mark Christopher Casson theories, entrepreneurship can provide a synthetic theory of the business firm that provides an integrated framework for many partial theories of the firm. His theory deals with the functional behavior of entrepreneur and his qualities which are crucial for his success. Drawing on an institutional approach to entrepreneurship, it is argued that economic insights can combine with managerial perspectives to clarify and synthesize many strategic issues of firms. Four dimensions of environmental shock lead to different forms of entrepreneurship that leads, in turn, to different sizes and structures for firms. Entrepreneurs create firms that identify and monitor sources of volatility and channel information to key decision makers in the firm; entrepreneurial firms are located at nodes of information networks. The standard rational action model of neoclassical economics is generalized to an uncertain world of volatility and differential access to information, which generates differing perceptions of the business environment.

(b) Theory of economic incentives: According to G.F.Papanek and J.R.Harris Theory, economic incentives are the integral factors that have induced entrepreneurial initiatives. Main features of this theory are (i) Economic incentives, (ii) Link between economic gains and the inner urge and (iii) Economic gain.

(c) Theory of adjustment of price: According to M. Kirzner, the chief role of entrepreneur is based upon the adjustment of price in the market. The buyer may pay higher price or seller may accept a lower price, which gives rise to opportunities for profit. Further if different prices prevail in the same market, there in an opportunity for profitable arbitrage between two segments.

(d) Theory of X-efficiency: Harvey Leibenstein propounded the theory of X-efficiency which is popularly called Gap Filling Theory. According to Leibenstein, entrepreneurial functions are determined by the X-efficiency which means the degree of inefficiency on the use of resources within the firm. It includes routine entrepreneur, new entrepreneursip, and twin roles of entrepreneur, gap filling, input completing and X-efficiency factor. An example of Leibenstein's Thoery is Lalu Prasad Yadav, who is an entrepreneur for Indian Railways. He had turned around the Indian Railways by improving efficiency and innovation.

(e) Theory of innovation: This theory is developed by Joseph Schumpeter, who believes that entrepreneur helps the process of development in an economy. Schumpeter's theory of entrepreneurship is a pioneering work of economic development. Development in his sense implies that carrying out of new combinations of entrepreneurship is basically a creative activity. According to Schumpeter an entrepreneur is one who perceives the opportunities to innovate, i.e., to carry out new combinations of enterprises. He says that an entrepreneur is one who is innovative, creative and has a foresight. According to him, innovation occurs when the entrepreneur:

- Introduces a new product
- Introduces a new methods of production
- Opens new market
- Conquests of new source of supply of raw material
- Carrying out new organization.

The theory emphasizes on innovation, ignoring the risk taking and organizing abilities of an entrepreneur. Schumpeter's entrepreneur is a large scale businessman, who is rarely found in developing countries, where entrepreneurs are small scale businessmen who need to imitate rather than innovate. In view of the above, Schumpeterian theory of entrepreneurship has got the following features:

(i) **Distinction between invention and innovation:** Schumpeter makes a distinction between innovation and invention. Invention means creation of new things and innovation means application of new things onto practical use.

(ii) **Emphasis on entrepreneurial function:** Schumpeter has given emphasis on the role or entrepreneurial functions in economic development In his views development means basic transformation of the economy that is brought about by entrepreneurial functions.

(iii) **Presentation of disequilibrium situation through entrepreneurial activity:** The entrepreneurial activity represents a disequilibrium situation, a dynamic phenomenon and a break from the routine or a circular flow towards equilibrium.

Critical evaluation: Schumpeter's theory of innovation is criticized on the following ground:

1. The theory has the scope of entrepreneurism in the sense that it has included the individual businessman along with the directors and managers of the company.
2. Schumpeter's innovating entrepreneurs represents the enterprise with the R&D and innovative character. But developing countries lack these characters.
3. The theory emphasizes on innovation and excludes the risk taking and organizing aspects.
4. Schumpeter's entrepreneurs are large scale businessman who introduces new technology, method of production.
5. Schumpeter remained silent about as to why some economists had more entrepreneurial talent than others.

However, despite the above criticisms, this theory is regarded as one of the best theories in the history of entrepreneurial development.

(f) **Theory of harvard school:** Harvard school contemplated that entrepreneurship involves any deliberate activity that initiates, maintains and grows a profit-oriented enterprise for production or distribution of economic goods or services, which is inconsistent with internal and external forces. Internal forces refer to the internal qualities of the individual such as intelligence, skill, knowledge experience, intuition, exposure, etc. These forces influence the entrepreneurial activities of an individual to a great extent. On the other hand external forces refer to the economic, political, social, cultural and legal factors which influence origin and growth of entrepreneurship in an economy. This theory emphasizes on two types of entrepreneurial activities i.e., (i) Entrepreneurial functions like organization and combination of resources for creating viable enterprises, and (ii) The responsiveness to the environmental condition that influences decision making function besides the above mentioned activities, Harvard School also emphasizes on following points:

1. To search and evaluate economic opportunities
2. To master the process of mobilizing resources to accomplish the goal
3. To interconnect the different market segments for creating an absolutely ideal marketing environment
4. To create or expand the firm or business enterprise

(g) Theory of high achievement: This theory is developed by David McClelland. According to him entrepreneurship has been identified with two characteristics such as:

- Doing things in a new and better way, and
- Decision making under uncertainty.

He stressed that people with high achievement oriented (need to succeed) were more likely to become entrepreneurs. Such people are not influenced by money or external incentives. They consider profit to be a measure of success and competence. According to McClelland, a person has three types of needs at any given time, which are:

(i) Need for achievement (get success with one's one efforts)

(ii) Need for power (to dominate, influence others)

(iii) Need for affiliation (maintain friendly relations with others)

(h) Theory of profit: This theory is developed by Knight, Frank H. He points out that entrepreneurs are specialized group of persons who bears risk and deals with uncertainty. Main features of this theory are pure profit, situation of uncertainty, risk bearing capability, guarantee of specified sum, identification of socio economic and psychological factors, use of consolidation techniques to reduce business risks.

(i) **Theory of market equilibrium:** According to Hayek, the absence of entrepreneurs in Neo-classical economics is intimately associated with the assumption of market equilibrium. The elasticity of bank credit causes a disparity between the natural and market rate of interest. According to this theory, the postulate presupposes the fact that there is no need for further information to modify the decision.

3. PSYCHOLOGICAL THEORIES: Entrepreneurship gets a boost when society has sufficient supply of individuals with necessary psychological characteristics. The psychological characteristics include need for high achievement, a vision or foresight and ability to face opposition. These characteristics are formed during the individual's upbringing which stress on standards of excellence, self reliance and low father dominance.

(a) **Theory of psychology:** This theory is developed by John H. Kunkel. According to him psychological and sociological variables are the main determinants for the emergence of entrepreneurs. According to him, entrepreneurship can be dependent upon the following structures in the economy, i.e.,(i) Demand Structure (ii) Limitation Structure (iii) Labor Structure and (iv) Opportunity structure. Beginning with the premise that fundamental problems of economic development are non-economic, he emphasizes on the cultural values, role expectation and social sanctions as the key elements that determine the supply of entrepreneurs. As a society's model personality, entrepreneur is neither a supernormal individual nor a deviant person but is a role model of the society representing model personality. Model personality as a derivative of social conditioning, the role is partly shaped by the model personality that is a derivative of social conditioning of his generation. Further, innovation and invention go together with the type of conditioning in the society. Role expectations and entrepreneurial role: Primary cultural factor operating on the personality of the executive and the defining of his role by those involved must accommodate to some degree to the necessities of the operation to be carried out.

(b) **Theory of personal resourcefulness:** According to this theory, the root of entrepreneurial process can be traced to the initiative taken by some individuals to go beyond the existing way of life. The emphasis is on initiative rather than reaction, although events in the environment may have provided the trigger for the person to express initiative. This aspect seems to have been subsumed within 'innovation' which has been studied more as the 'change' or 'newness' associated with the term rather 'pro-activeness'.

4. SOCIOLOGICAL THEORY: Entrepreneurship is likely to get a boost in a particular social culture. Society's values, religious beliefs, customs, taboos etc., influence the behaviour of individual's in a society. The entrepreneur is a role performer according to the role expectations by the society.

(a) **Theory of entrepreneurial supply:** Thomas Cochran emphasizes on the cultural values, role expectation and social sanctions as the key elements that determine the supply of entrepreneurs.

(b) **Theory of religious belief:** Max Weber has propounded the theory of religious belief. According to him, entrepreneurism is a function of religious beliefs and impact of religion shapes the entrepreneurial culture. He emphasized that entrepreneurial energies are exogenous supplied by means of religious beliefs. The important elements of Weber's theory are discussed further:

1. **Spirit of capitalism:** In the Webbrian theory, spirit of capitalism is highlighted. We all know that capitalism is an economic system in which economic freedom and private enterprise are glorified, so also the entrepreneurial culture.
2. **Adventurous spirit:** Webber also made a distinction between spirit of capitalism and adventurous spirit. According to him, the former is influenced by the strict discipline whereas the latter is affected by free force of impulse. Entrepreneurship culture is influenced by both these factors.
3. **Protestant ethic:** According to Max Webber the spirit of capitalism can be grown only when the mental attitude in the society is favourable to capitalism
4. **Inducement of profit:** Webber introduced the new businessman into the picture of tranquil routine. The spirit of capitalism intertwined with the motive of profit resulting in creation of greater number of business enterprises.

(c) **Theory of social change:** This theory is developed by Everett E. Hagen. It explains how a traditional society becomes one in which continuing technical progress takes place. It exhorts certain elements which presume the entrepreneur's creativity as the key element of social transformation and economic growth. It reveals a general model of the society which considers interrelationship among physical environment, social culture, personality etc. According to Hagen, most of the economic theories of underdevelopment are inadequate. Hagen insisted that the follower's syndrome on the part of the entrepreneur is discouraged. This is because tho technology is an integral part of socio cultural-complex, and super-imposition of the same into different socio-cultural set-up may not deliver the goods.

The Kakinada Experiment

Conducted by McClelland in America, Mexico and Mumbai. Under this experiment, young adults were selected and put through a three month training programme. The training aimed at inducing the achievement motivation. The course contents were:

1. Trainees were asked to control their thinking and talk to themselves, positively.
2. They imagined themselves in need of challenges and success for which they had to set planned and achievable goals.
3. They strived to get concrete and frequent feedback
4. They tried to imitate their role models those who performed well.

Conclusions of the Experiment

- Traditional beliefs do not inhibit an entrepreneur
- Suitable training can provide necessary motivation to an entrepreneur.
- The achievement motivation had a positive impact on the performance of the participants.

It was the Kakinada experiment that made people realize the importance of EDP, (Entrepreneurial Development Programme), to induce motivation and competence in young, prospective entrepreneurs.

Drucker on Entrepreneurship

Peter F. Drucker opined that "an entrepreneur is one who always searches for change, responds to it and exploits it as an opportunity." He laid emphasis on two important factors – innovation and resource – that led to emergence of entrepreneurship. According to him, innovation is the real hub of entrepreneurship which creates resource. A thing is regarded as resource when its economic value is recognized. For example, mineral oil was considered worthless until the discovery of its use. Similarly, purchasing power was considered as an important resource by an American innovative entrepreneur who invented installment buying.

According to Drucker, successful entrepreneurship involves the following things:

1. Value and satisfaction obtained from resource by the consumer are increased.
2. New values are created
3. Material is converted into a resource or existing resources are combined in a new or more productive configuration.
4. Entrepreneurship is the practice which has a knowledge base.
5. Entrepreneurship is not confined to big businesses and economic institutions, i.e., equally important to small business and non-economic institutions.

6. Entrepreneurship behaviour rather than personality trait is more important to enhance entrepreneurship.
7. The foundation of entrepreneurship lies in concept and theory rather than intuition.

Thus, Drucker has given his views that 'an entrepreneur need not be a capitalist or an owner. A banker who mobilizes other's money and allocates it in areas of higher yield is very much an entrepreneur though he is not the owner of the money.

Decision Making Process of Entrepreneur

The strategic decisions of the entrepreneurs have to be perceived as the direct driving forces for the dynamics of the economy, hence, a study on their decision making process will enrich the knowledge of mechanisms that drive the companies to participate in the economy life of the state, thus creating growth and prosperity for society. A closer observation of the entrepreneurs' strategic behaviour and an inquiry on the managerial reasoning to perform in one way or another will broaden the vision of the policy makers of how to influence companies' environment and what concrete measures to introduce in their strategies of governance. Hence, it is important to acquire knowledge and conduct an in-depth study in order to identify the 'break' and 'pull and push' factors of growth. The difference between the entrepreneurial and the managerial styles can be viewed from five key business dimensions—strategic orientation, commitment to opportunity, commitment of resources, control of resources, and management structure. Managerial styles are called the administrative domain.

(i) **Strategic Orientation:** The entrepreneur's strategic orientation depends on his or her perception of the opportunity. This orientation is most important when other opportunities have diminishing returns accompanied by rapid changes in technology, consumer economies, social values, or political rules.

(ii) **Commitment to Opportunity:** In terms of the commitment to opportunity, the second key business dimension, the two domains vary greatly with respect to the length of this commitment. The entrepreneurial domain is pressured by the need for action, short decision windows, a willingness to assume risk, and few decision constituencies and has a short time span in terms of opportunity commitment.

(iii) **Commitment of Resources:** An entrepreneur is used to having resources committed at periodic intervals that are often based on certain tasks or objectives being reached. These resources, often acquired from others, are usually difficult to obtain, forcing the entrepreneur to maximize any resources used.

(iv) Control of Resources: Control of the resources follows a similar pattern. Since the administrator (manager) is rewarded by effective resource administration, there is often a drive to own or accumulate as many resources as possible. The pressures of power, status, and financial rewards cause the administrator (manager) to avoid rental or other periodic use of the resource.

(v) Management Structure: The final business dimension, management structure, also differs significantly between the two domains. In the administrative domain, the organizational structure is formalized and hierarchical in nature, reflecting the need for clearly defined lines of authority and responsibility.

BUSINESS COMMUNICATIONS

Communication is the lifeblood of an organization. In today's competitive business world, effective communication is more essential than ever before. It is the foundation on which companies and careers are built and a crucial component of lasting success. It is used to promote a product, service or organization, with the objective of making sale. Communication is the exchange of ideas, opinions and information through written or spoken words, symbols or actions. It is a dialogue, not a monologue. In fact, communication is more concerned with a dual listening process. For communication to be effective, the message must mean the same thing to both the sender and the receiver.

According to **Keith Davis,** "Communication is the process of passing information and understanding from one person to another. It is essentially a bridge of meaning between the people. By using the bridge, a person can safely cross the river of misunderstanding"

According to **Robert Anderson,** "Communication is an interchange of thoughts, opinions, or information, through speech, writing or signs". Written Communication means communication by means of written symbols (either printed or handwritten).

In business, communication is considered as core among business, interpersonal skills and etiquette. Communication is any act by which one person gives to or receives from another person, information about that person's needs, desires, perceptions, knowledge, or affective states. It is used to promote a product, service, organization; relay information within the business; or deal with legal and similar issues. It is also a means of relaying between a supply chain, for example the consumer and manufacturer. In business communication, message is conveyed through various channels including internet, print (publications), radio, television, outdoor, and word of mouth. When communication stops, organized activity ceases to exist. Individual uncoordinated activity returns in an organization. So, Communication in an organization is as vital as blood for life.

Important Characteristics of Communication

- It is a two-way process.
- Communication process happens between or among two or more parties i.e., the sender and the receiver.
- Communication involves exchange of ideas, feelings, information, thoughts and knowledge.
- Communication involves mutuality of understanding between the sender and the receiver.

TYPES OF BUSINESS COMMUNICATION

There are two types of business communication in an organization:

1. Internal Communication
2. External Communication

1. **Internal Communication:** Communication within an organization is called internal communication. Effective internal communication is a vital means of addressing organizational concerns. Good communication may help to increase job satisfaction, safety, productivity and profits and decrease grievances and turnover. Internal communication may be formal or informal. Good communication helps to raise job satisfaction, safety, productivity, profits and decrease complaints. Internal business communication is further classified into:

   (i) Upward communication,

   (ii) Downward communication and

   (iii) Horizontal or lateral communication.

Upward communication is the flow of information from downward level to the upward level i.e. from subordinates to superiors or from employees to the management. Upward communication helps management to know whether messages have been received properly or not. It is used as a means for staff to exchange information, offer ideas, provide feedback, express enthusiasms etc.

Downward communication is the flow of information from upward level to the downward level i.e., from top of the organizational management hierarchy and it is about the mission and policies. Downward communication comes when upward communication has been successfully established. It is used as a means to transmit vital information, give instruction, encourage two way discussion, provide motivation, increase efficiencies etc.

Horizontal or lateral communication involves coordinating information and allows people with the similar rank or designation in an organization to cooperate or collaborate. When communication exists among the employees for mutual understanding and resulting increase of efficiency and productivity of organisation, it is a case of horizontal or lateral communication. It helps them to solve problems, improve team work, accomplish tasks, build goodwill and above all boost efficiency.

2. **External Communication:** When communication takes place with people outside the company it is called external communication. For example, communication with vendors and customers are the external communication. It will lead to better operational efficiency, increasing sales volume, public credibility and profits.

Forms of Communication

There are two forms of communication i.e., Verbal and Non-Verbal.

Verbal Communication

Verbal communication is an inseparable part of business communication. Business deals with variety of people from various ages, cultures and races. Fluent verbal communication is essential to deal with those people in business. Self-confidence with fluent communication can lead to a business success. It includes words, language, speaking etc. Language is originated from sounds and gestures. Public speaking is another verbal communication which will address a group of people. Before delivering public speech, one must be prepared according to the type of audience. The contents of the speech should be authentic. It must include the main points in which the speech has been highlighted.

(a) Oral Communication: Oral communication is information spoken by mouth, the use of speech which consists of face to face communication, telephonic communication, public address system, audio and visual (Radio, TV) lecturers, conference etc.

- ✓ **Advantages:** It is quick, cheap, time-saving, immediate feedback is obtained, quick solutions and effective.
- ✓ **Disadvantages:** It has a temporary appeal, cannot provide legal evidence, quickly forgotten, cannot be preserved.

(b) Written Communication: Written communication is writing the words one can communicate. Good written communication is very much essential for business either printed or handwritten. Some of the ways of using written communication in business are e-mail message, reports, articles, memos, proposals, letters, bulletins, minutes, orders, quotations, contracts, forms, enquiries etc. Written communication is used not only in business but also for informal communication purposes. Mobile SMS is an example of informal written communication.

✓ **Advantages:** It is permanent and can be preserved, can be carefully drafted and corrected if necessary, has a legal value, can be referred frequently and helps to fix the responsibility of a person.

✓ **Disadvantages:** It is costly, time consuming and no immediate feedback etc.

Non-verbal Communication

Non-verbal communication is the communication without the use of written or spoken words. It involves physical way of communication like, tone of the voice, touch, smell and body motion. Creative and aesthetic non-verbal communication includes singing, music, dancing and sculpturing. Symbols and sign language are also included in non-verbal communication. Although people are generally not aware of it, may send and receive non-verbal signals all the time. These signals may indicate what they are truly feeling. Non-verbal communication includes body language, para language, space and time language, sign language etc.

1. **Body Language:** It refers to any kind of bodily movement or gesture instead of words. It includes facial expression, which transmits a message to the observer. Body posture and physical contact convey a lot of information. Body posture matters a lot when one is communicating verbally to someone. Folded arms and crossed legs are some of the signals conveyed by a body posture. Physical contact, like, shaking hands, pushing, patting and touching expresses the feeling of intimacy. According to the expert, communication can be broken into the following data, i.e., verbal communication (7%), body-movements/gestures (55%) and voice tone (38%).

2. **Para Language:** It is a very close ally to verbal communication but it is a non-verbal communication. 'Para' means 'like' hence para-language means like-language. It is a non verbal communication because it does not consist of the words but shows how the words are spoken. It is based on the voice.

3. **Space and Time Language:** It is sending signals which are mutually understood by the sender and the receiver. These signals may originate in various sources. One such source is the space around us which communicates in a unique way. It includes surroundings (design and language). It communicates social status also.

4. **Sign Language:** A sign language is a language which, instead of conveyed sound patterns, uses visually transmitted sign patterns.

People that want to work in a big corporation need to have complete control of their communication skills. Communication is the mainstay of businesses. It is how organizations get their message across to educate their prospects, to effect their buying decisions, and to service their customers. With the advent of technology, virtually any kind of communication can be re-purposed or re-used in a different way to try new marketing and content approaches.

SUMMARY

It is said that etiquette and manners stop advising and start pursuing. Good manners are not a sign of weakness. They indicate strength of character. Widely and incorrectly considered a social barrier, good manners are what keep society intact. In business and in the workplace, on the domestic front and in our social lives, we all stand to benefit from more effective communication skills.

The concept of entrepreneurship is understood as a combination of creativity and innovation. It is a stance taken within the business applying inherent creativity as the act of 'thinking of' new things. It involves coming up with innovative Ideas and trying out new methods within the operations. The concept of entrepreneurship is also concerned with new ways of looking at opportunities and identifying a new approach towards solving problems. Entrepreneurship requires the entrepreneur to shift paradigms and do away with old assumptions and perspectives. The entrepreneur basically adopts techniques to stimulate creativity amongst employees.

The concept of entrepreneurship involves the consideration of a number of opportunities to enhance employee performance and business profits. The entrepreneur is expected to imply strategic planning to assess if the opportunities provided for growth are worthwhile and how they could be successfully exploited. Strategic planning is an essential part of the concept of entrepreneurship and effective application helps to ensure successful operation. It is a useful tool within the sphere of influence of entrepreneurship and serves a market for improving the business performance. The concept of entrepreneurship involves the owner, taking absolute responsibility of empowering the employees and in turn, affecting sales and profitability of the business.

QUESTIONS

SHORT ANSWER QUESTIONS

1. Discuss the basic factors of different theories of entrepreneurship.
2. What do you mean by innovation?
3. What do you mean by decision making process of entrepreneur?
4. What are the various types of communication usually found in an entrepreneurial business?
5. What are the various forms of communications?

LONG ANSWER QUESTIONS

1. Define entrepreneurial behaviour. Discuss various factors affecting the entrepreneurial behaviour in emerging country like India.
2. Discuss the relevance of motivational theories of entrepreneurs.
3. Explain the Maslow's hierarchy needs and identify the needs which are most relevant for the entrepreneur's motivation.
4. Explain the motivational theories of Frederick Herzberg. What are the various factors based on the above theories.
5. What do you mean by entrepreneurial behaviours and psycho theories? Explain the role of entrepreneurs in the socio-economic environment.
6. What do you mean by business communications? Explain the important characteristics of communications.

CHAPTER

BUSINESS OPPORTUNITY IDENTIFICATION

"Vision without action is a daydream. Action without vision is a nightmare."

— Japanese Proverb

Chapter Overview:

At the end of this chapter, you will be able to understand:

1. The landscape of entrepreneurship.
2. The environmental analysis.
3. Preparation of feasibility report.
4. Franchise and their responsibilities.

INTRODUCTION

Entrepreneurial activity is essentially person-oriented. The strengths, weaknesses, preferences and values of the entrepreneur will affect his choice of business opportunity. An entrepreneur is therefore advised to be aware of his own self all the time. Business opportunity and entrepreneurial response to it together form the foundation on which the super structure of a new venture rests. If the foundation is weak or defective, the super structure may well collapse or require extensive and support efforts in course of time. So, all the care and efforts, time and trouble taken to select right business opportunities will repay themselves multi-fold in course of time.

THE LANDSCAPE OF BUSINESS OPPORTUNITY

An opportunity is the chance to do something in a way which is both different to, and better than, the way it is done at the moment. It offers the possibility of delivering new value to the customer. Every opportunity is different, but there are some common patterns in the way in which opportunities take shape. Entrepreneurship is increasingly recognized as an important driver of economic growth, productivity, innovation and employment, and it is widely accepted as a key aspect of economic dynamism: the birth and death of firms and their growth and downsizing. As firms enter and exit the market, theory suggests that the new arrivals will be more efficient than those they displace. Existing firms that are not driven out are forced to innovate and become more productive in order to compete. Many studies have given empirical support to this process of "creative destruction" first described by Joseph Schumpeter. However, while academic studies have long recognized the importance of entrepreneurship, policy makers have only recently explicitly discovered it. Indeed, entrepreneurship was long considered an exogenous factor in government policies, and policy efforts were often directed simply towards the large population of very small firms rather than aimed at stimulating entrepreneurs able to introduce new products, processes or organisational forms in order to exploit new markets and grow. The types of opportunities available in the business are:

1. **New product:** The new product offers the customer a physical device which provides a new means to satisfy a need or to solve a problem. A new product may be based on existing technology or it might exploit new technological possibilities. It might also represent a chance to add value to an existing product by using an appropriate branding strategy.

2. **New service:** A new service offers customers a series of acts, which satisfy a particular need or solve a particular problem. Many new offerings have both 'product' and 'service' dimensions.

3. **New means of production:** Producing an existing product is not an opportunity in itself. It will offer an opportunity if it can be used to deliver additional value to the customers.

4. **New distribution route:** A new way of getting the product to the customer which means the customer finds it easier, more convenient or less time consuming to get to the product or service.

5. **Improved service:** In order to enhance the value of a product for the customer, adequate services have to be provided with it. The service often involves maintaining the product in some way but it can also be based on supporting the customer in using the product or offering them training in its use.

6. **Relationship building:** Business relationships are built on trust and trust adds value by reducing the cost needed to monitor contacts. Trust can be providing a source of competitive advantage and can be used to build networks which competitors find it hard to break into.

Problems Before Starting a New Business

India has always been in the limelight in terms of the business opportunities available. Indian business opportunity is huge in possibly every sector - financial services, telecom, IT, automobiles, media, real estate and alike. India is still considered to be one of the most enviable destinations for doing business. Presently it is counted among those nations which has been least affected by the global recession? Thus it clearly proves that India's business potential is huge. India's extensive band of engineers, scientists, technicians, managers and skilled manpower are among the best in the world.

The Indian business market is large and bubbling with newer opportunities. Increased purchasing power and consumerism is what drives the business scenario in India. Thus, there is an opportunity for competitive advantage (low cost sourcing of products and services). It has been observed that investments in India have been capable of yielding lucrative returns and thus companies have started to capture the domestic market business opportunities. The India business opportunity is getting quite exciting and innovative with the passing of every year. People are infusing new opportunities such that international investments might flow into the country. There are a lot of business ideas for entrepreneurs who are interested to set up business in India through Internet ventures, outsourcing technology, e-commerce opportunities, and software development opportunities. Following are the various problems to start a new business in India:

(1) Selection of business: One of the most important decisions before engaging oneself in any business activity is to focus on the proper selection of business. Detailed investigation and utmost care should be taken up in the selection of business. Once a decision is taken and a business is established, it then becomes difficult to change it.

(2) Demand for the product: The stability of a product in the market depends upon the future trend of demand. It should not be taken up on the basis of current demand only. Future trend in demand should be carefully examined. If the demand for a product is irregular, seasonal, uncertain and the margin of profit earned by existing firms is very low, it is no use in starting such a business. For examples, a beauty parlour in fashionable area can do more business than such a parlour in a locality where people of low income are living.

(3) Size of business unit: Business involves production or purchase of goods and services. The size of business unit means the scale of business. The size of business unit depends upon the demand for the commodity in the market, the availability of resources, technical and organizational ability of the entrepreneur etc. if the business is carried on a large scale; it brings economies in expenses determination of the scale of business is an important factor to be considered before establishing a business unit.

(4) Provision of capital: Capital is the life blood of business. Before starting a business, the capital needs of the business is to be assessed. The capital needs depend upon its fixed and working capital requirements. After considering the financial requirements, the sources for raising funds for the business should be taken up. In case the full amount of capital required for establishing and operating business cannot be met from owned capital, (own resources) then arrangements shall have to be made for the availability of raising of borrowed capital from banks and financial institutions.

(5) Location: The location of a project is decided by comparing the relative cost advantages of setting up the project at various places. The selection of a suitable place for the establishment of a business is of utmost importance for the success of a business. Normally, it is the nearness to the source of the raw materials, trained labour, banking facilities; telephone gas, cheap transport, nearness to market for finished products etc., are the important considerations in the selection of a site for business.

(6) Selection of physical facilities: The selection of physical facilities depends upon the nature of a new business. In case of a manufacturing concern, the decisions acquiring land, building, machinery, godown etc., through purchase or on rent basis or on lease are to be carefully undertaken, In case of trading concern, the purchase/hire of shop in the shopping centre, provision and proper display of goods, etc., need proper consideration.

(7) Plan layout: Every business needs a plan. The success of a business particularly manufacturing depends greatly on its plan layout. The plan layout is the setting up of machines and equipment of the factory. If the plan layout is good, it facilitates the flow of work. There is an effective utilization of men, materials and machines.

(8) Selection of staff: Every business has to acquire adequate number of staff (both skilled and unskilled) for the operation of a business. Utmost care should be taken on the selection of right persons for the right jobs.

(9) Technology and selection of office equipment: Technology is the process of converting inputs into outputs. The provisions of office equipment, tables, chairs, telephones, calculators, duplicating, air-conditioners etc., are essential for a business house. These equipment improve the working and efficiency of the staff.

(10) Fulfillment of legal requirements: Every business unit needs certain legal formalities for smooth running. An entrepreneur before starting a business has to fulfill the conditions and rules enforced by the state. Legal formalities help an organisation to keep the document upto date as per the demand of the government.

Innovation and Exploitation of Opportunity

A business opportunity is a chance to do something differently and better. An innovation is a way of doing something differently and better. Innovation is a means of exploiting a business opportunity. It has a definite meaning in economics. All goods and services are regarded as being made up of three factors such as natural raw materials, physical and mental labour. Innovation is a new combination of these three things. Entrepreneur acts as innovators, who are people, who create new combinations of these factors and then present them to the market for assessment by consumers. Innovations includes new products, new services, new production techniques, new operating practices, new ways of delivering the product or service to the customers, new means of informing the customer about the product etc.

Search for Business Ideas, Sources of Ideas, Idea Processing

Business ideas are come from a careful analysis of the market trends and the consumer needs. If anybody wants to start a new business, he has to investigate the ideas before launching his idea into a product. Following are the few points which will help a person to explore business ideas:

1. **Examining own skill set for business ideas:** Before starting any business one needs to ask variety of questions to himself/herself such as What can I do?, What have I done? Will people be willing to pay for my products or services? Answer to all these questions will help an individual to explore the information about the business ideas.

2. **Keeping current events ready:** An individual needs to identify the market trends at a regular basis with the conscious intent of finding business ideas, industry news and ideas of business possibilities. Upto date information about the current market will strengthen a person to explore the opportunity to launch a product in the market.

3. **Invent a new product or service:** Invention of new product or service may exploit an established technology or it may be the outcome of a whole new technology. The new product may offer a radically new of doing something or it may simply be an improvement on an existing theme. Products are not only simply a physical tool for achieving particular ends. They can also have a role to play in satisfying emotional needs.

4. **Add value to an existing product:** Customers can only use products and services they can access. Adding value to an existing product is just as easy as finding leaves on trees. In order to add the value, one might also add services or combine the product with other products.

5. **Investigate other markets:** Some business ideas are not confined to local consumption rather it provides an outlook to the other markets. Finding out about other cultures and investigating other market opportunities is an excellent way to find business ideas.

6. **Improve an existing product or service:** An entrepreneur is said to be an opportunity seeker. Improvement in the existing product or services requires a chance to do something differently and better. An entrepreneurial venture does not have to restrict itself to just one innovation or even one type of innovation. Success can be built on a combination of innovations for example, a new product delivered in a new way with a new message.

7. **Getting on the bandwagon:** It is an effect which is created by larger social trends. Sometimes markets surge for no apparent reason; masses of people suddenly want something and which cannot be fulfilled immediately. Search for business ideas will be achieved when an entrepreneur wants to discover the idea that is best suited to the skills and desires. One should believe that transformation of ideas into the business needs three steps i.e., Dream, Think and Plan.

Business Plan: Elements

A business plan is an essential tool for the entrepreneur. It is a plan which works for a business to look ahead, allocate resources, focus on key points and prepare for problems and opportunities. It is a formal statement of a set of business goals. It conveys the goals and the strategies of the business. It may also contain background information about the organization or team attempting to reach those goals. A business plan is a document that shows how a business is going to achieve its objectives. Many people think of business plans only for starting a new business or applying for business loans. But they are also vital for running a business, to know whether or not the business needs new loans or new investments. A successful business plan is a living roadmap to the future and not just a document in a desk drawer. Its need plans to optimize growth and development according to priorities.

Any business plan consists of three parts:

1. **Business concept:** It consists of the business structure, product or service and planning to make the business a grand success.
2. **Market place:** It consists of the potentiality of customer for whom the product is meant for. While studying the market place, one has to study the position of the competitors before launching the product.
3. **Financial:** It includes the statement of income and expenses, position of assets and liabilities. It is very much essential to study the basic financial statements.

Elements of a Business Plan

There are no hard and fast rules about what a business plan should include since a business plan must be shaped to reflect the needs and requirements of the venture it represents. The following list indicates the type and scope of information and themes that might be included in a fairly exhaustive business plan.

1. **Mission:** The formal mission statement that defines the business.
2. **Overview of key objectives:** It has two parts i.e., financial objectives (turnover and profit) and strategic objectives (market position).
3. **The market environment:** It has several parts such as background to the market (size of the market, overall growth rate), competitors, product offerings etc.
4. **Strategy:** It has several parts such as product strategy, pricing strategy, distribution strategy, promotional strategy, networking etc.
5. **Financial forecast:** It includes income, routine expenditure, capital expenditure, cash flows etc.
6. **Activity:** it includes the new product development, advertising campaigns etc.
7. **People:** It includes the key persons, skills, experiences etc., required.

Format of a Business Plan

BUSINESS PLAN FORMAT

The following format should provide a good overview of a prospective investment.

1. Business
   - ✓ Company's business (description short enough to fit on a business card)
   - ✓ Mission statement
2. Products
   - ✓ Product description
   - ✓ Development schedule
   - ✓ Differentiation
   - ✓ Price point
3. Market
   - ✓ Trends
   - ✓ Historic and projected sizes in dollars
   - ✓ Product match to market definition
4. Distribution
   - ✓ Sales channels
   - ✓ Partnerships
   - ✓ Customers
5. Competition
   - ✓ Competitors
   - ✓ Competitive advantages
6. Team
   - ✓ Background of management
   - ✓ Board composition

7. Financials

   ✓ Historic and projected Profit & Loss (first two years by quarters)

   ✓ Projected cash flow (first two years by quarters)

   ✓ Current balance sheet

   ✓ Projected head count by functional area (R&D, sales, marketing, G&A)

   ✓ Capitalization schedule

8. Deal

   ✓ Amount raised

   ✓ Valuation asked

   ✓ Use of proceeds

Forms of Business Organizations

A business may be defined as an institution organized and operated to provide goods and services to the society with the objective of earning profit. One of the most important decisions to be made is choosing the structure of a business organization. It refers to all necessary arrangements required to conduct a business. According to **L.R. Dickson,** "business as a form of activity pursued primarily with the object of earning profit for the benefit of those on whose behalf the activity is conducted." It refers to all those steps that need to be undertaken for establishing relationship between men, material, and machinery to carry on business efficiently for earning profits.

While establishing a business, the most important task is to select a proper form of organization. This is because the conduct of business, its control, acquisition of capital, extent of risk, distribution of profit, legal formalities, etc., all depends on the form of organization. While taking a decision about the various forms of business organizations, an entrepreneur has to carefully analyse the long-term implications to select the form of ownership. The choice of an entrepreneur will base on the following conditions:

1. The vision regarding the size and nature of the business.
2. The level of control one wish to have.
3. The level of structure one is willing to deal with.
4. The tax implications of the different ownership structures.
5. Expected profit (or loss) of the business.
6. The risk of the personal assets from business liabilities

Following are the various forms of business organizations:

1. Sole Proprietorship
2. Joint Hindu Family Business
3. Partnership
4. Joint Stock Company
5. Co-operative Society

(I) SOLE PROPRIETORSHIP

Meaning

The sole proprietorship is the oldest, most common and simplest form of business organization. When the ownership and management of business are in control of one individual, it is known as sole proprietorship or sole tradership. It is based on the principle of "One man control is the best in the world, if that man is big enough to manage everything."

The sole proprietorship is an extremely common business organizational strategy where a business is owned exclusively by a single individual on his or her own without the use of a separate and distinct business form. A sole proprietorship is a business entity owned and managed by one person. The sole proprietorship can be organized very informally, is not subject to much country or state regulations, and is relatively simple to manage and control. The law does not regard the sole proprietorship business as a different entity from its proprietor (or owner). With little government regulations, they are the simplest business to set up.

To start a sole proprietorship, one has to create a business name and decide on a location for the business and file for a business license and get permission from the local authorities if someone wants to operate business from home. In sole proprietorship business, one person usually owns the business and manages the day-to-day responsibility for running the business. The proprietor assumes complete personal responsibility for all of its liabilities or debts. A sole-proprietorship business will cease when the proprietor either dies or otherwise ceases to carry on business. All rights that the business has, belongs to the proprietor. Similarly, all liabilities or debts that are incurred by the business are in law, the liabilities or debts of the proprietor. The assets and profits that the business generates are owned by the proprietor who is personally liable to pay whatever tax is payable in respect of these assets and profits. The sole trade business ceases to exist or terminates on the owner's death or withdrawal. However, an owner can sell the business, but can no longer remain the proprietor. For example, shops or stores which are available in every locality such as the grocery store, the vegetable store, the sweets shop, the chemist shop, the paanwala, the stationery store, the STD/ISD telephone booths etc. come under sole proprietorship. It is not that a sole tradership business must be a small one. The volume of activities of such a business unit may be quite large. However, since it is owned and managed by one single individual, often the size of business remains small.

CHARACTERISTICS OF A SOLE PROPRIETORSHIP

1. Individual ownership: A sole proprietorship is wholly owned by an individual, who supplies the total capital, required for the business, from his own source or from borrowed sources. The entire profit arising out of the business goes to the proprietor and he also bears the entire risk or loss of the business.

2. Individual management and control: The owner of the enterprise is generally the manager of the business. He alone takes all the decisions pertaining to the business. He has got absolute right to plan for the business and execute them without any interference from anywhere. Ownership and management are vested in the same person.

3. Unlimited liability: The liability of the sole proprietor is unlimited. It means in case the business assets are not sufficient to meet the business liabilities, his private assets are to be used to discharge the liabilities of the business.

4. Minimum government regulations: A sole proprietorship concern is free from Government regulations. No formalities are to be observed in its formation, management or in its closure. However, a few legal restrictions may be there in setting up a particular type of business such as to open a restaurant, the sole proprietor needs a license from the local municipality; to open a chemist shop, the individual must have a license from the government.

5. Stability: The stability and continuity of the sole trade business depends upon the capacity, competence and the life span of the proprietor.

Advantages of Sole Proprietorship

1. **Easy to form and dissolve:** The biggest advantage of a sole trader business is its easy formation. Since no legal formalities need to perform to start a sole proprietary business, it is most easy to start a business. Sometimes, a few restrictions are placed by local bodies such as municipalities, etc., from the view point of maintenance of health and sanitation. It is also equally convenient to dissolve a sole proprietorship concern.

2. **Better control:** The sole proprietor is the supreme judge of all matters pertaining to his business. He is free to prepare any plans and policies and execute them for the success of his business without any interference. He is free to direct and control the operations of his business.

3. **Promptness in decision making:** A sole proprietor being a single owner is not required to consult anyone while taking decisions. Quick decisions and prompt actions improve the efficiency of the business operations. As the proprietor takes all the decisions himself, decision making becomes quick.

4. **Flexibility in operations:** A sole proprietor can easily bring about changes in the size and nature of activities according to the changing conditions in the market without causing least of unsought consequences. Sole proprietorship offers the scope for flexibility in business operations by allowing the business to adopt and adjust itself to changing times and situations.

5. **Retention of business secrets:** A sole proprietor is not required to publish his accounts. He maintains absolute secrecy regarding his business activities. Business secrecy provides an edge to the firm over its rival firms. The degree of retention of business secrecy is the highest in this form of organization.

6. **Direct motivation:** In sole proprietorship there is a direct relationship between efforts and rewards. He enjoys the entire profits and hence is inspired, induced and motivated to make the best possible use of his skills and resources to maximize profits.

7. **Personal attention to consumer needs:** As the size of a sole proprietary business being small, the owner maintains a personal touch with his employees and customers. Personal attention to consumers results in increased sales and individual attention to employees brings in efficiency and motivation on the part of employees thereby reducing the cost of production.

8. **Creation of employment:** A sole proprietorship business facilitates self-employment and also employment for many others. It encourages and promotes entrepreneurial skill among the individuals.

9. **Social benefits:** Since a sole proprietor has to face all kinds of problems and challenges single handed, he has absolute freedom in taking decisions. This gives him high self-esteem and dignity in the society and gradually he acquires several social virtues like self-reliance, self-determination, independent thought and action, initiative, hard work etc

10. **Equitable distribution of wealth:** A sole proprietorship business is generally a small scale business, there is opportunity for many individuals to own and manage small business units. This enables widespread dispersion of economic wealth and diffuses concentration of business.

11. **Credit standing:** A sole proprietor is the master of his own business; he is liable to pay the debts of his business out of his private property. As the credit worthiness or standing of the sole property concern is greatly enhanced, the creditor does not hesitate to lend to a sole proprietor.

Disadvantages of Sole Proprietorship

1. **Unlimited liability:** In sole proprietorship, the liability of the business is unlimited. It restricts the sole trader to take more risk and his private assets are being utilized to pay the liabilities of the business.
2. **Limited financial resources:** Since the capital Is contributed by one individual only, the business operations have necessarily to be on a limited scale. The ability to raise and borrow money by one individual is always limited. The inadequacy of finance is a major handicap for the growth of sole proprietorship and limited availability of capital do not allow the business to expand.
3. **Limited managerial skill:** An individual has limited knowledge and skill. Whoever may be a person, his resourcefulness and business management will be less effective beyond a certain stage. Thus his capacity to undertake responsibilities, his capacity to manage, to take decisions and to bear the risks of business is also limited, which ultimately affect the growth of the business.
4. **Uncertainty of duration:** The existence of a sole trading concern is linked with the life of the proprietor. A personal quality of the proprietor, Illness, death or insolvency brings an end to the business. The continuity of business operation is, therefore, uncertain.

Suitability of Sole Proprietorship

Sole proprietorship business is suitable where the product cannot be standardized and has to be made to order. This form of organization is suitable where the nature of business is simple and requires quick decision. For business where the production technology is simple and the capital required as well as the risk associated with it is not heavy, this type of firm is suitable. It is also considered suitable for the production of goods which involve manual skill e.g., handicrafts, filigree works, jewellery, tailoring, hair cutting, etc., where the customers give importance to personal attention.

(II) JOINT HINDU FAMILY BUSINESS

Meaning

The Joint Hindu Family (JHF) business is a form of business organization in which the family possesses some inherited property and usually found in India. In this form of business, all the members of a Hindu undivided family own the business jointly. A Joint Hindu Family business comes into existence as per the Hindu Inheritance Laws of India Ltd. In a Joint Hindu Family business only the male members get a share in the business by virtue of their being part of the family. It comes into existence by the operation of Hindu Law and not out of contract between the members. The membership is limited up to three successive generations. Thus, an individual, his son(s), and his grandson(s) become the members of a Joint Hindu Family by birth. Members are called as coparceners. Following the Hindu Succession Act, 1956, a female relative of a deceased male coparcener will have a share in the co-parcenary interest after the death of the coparcener. The affairs of business are managed by the head of the family, who is known as the "KARTA."

Characteristics

1. **Legal status:** The membership of the Joint Hindu Family business is the result of status which is arising from birth in the family. There is no discrimination in terms of minority and majority on the basis of age. It is governed by Hindu Law.
2. **Membership:** Only the male person's can claim co-parcenery interest in the Joint Hindu Family business.
3. **Karta:** The rights of the Joint Hindu Family business vests in Karta alone (Head of the family). He has the implied authority to obtain loans through mortgage, etc., for the purpose of the business.
4. **Profit sharing:** All co-parceners have equal share in the profits of the business. In the event of death of any of the co-parcener, his wife can claim share of profit.
5. **Management:** The management of a Joint Hindu Family business is in the hands of the senior-most family member who is known as the Karta. He has the authority to manage the business and his ways of managing cannot be questioned by the co-parceners.
6. **Liability:** The liability of all members of the Joint Hindu Family business, except that of the Karta is limited to the value of their individual interests in the joint property. The liability of the Karta is unlimited which may extend to his personal property.
7. **Fluctuating share:** The share of each member's interest keeps on fluctuating. This is because, every birth of a male child in the family adds to the number of co-parceners and every death of a co-parcener reduces the number.

8. **Continued existence:** A Joint Hindu Family business is not affected by the death or insolvency of a co-parcener or even that of the Karta. However, a Joint Hindu Family business can be dissolved any time either through mutual agreement between members or by partition.

Advantages of Joint Hindu Family Business

1. **Share in Profits:** In Joint Hindu Family business, each co-parcener is assured a share in the profits irrespective of his contribution to the successful running of the business. It safeguards the interests of every member whether he is minor, sick, disabled or widow.
2. **Freedom in Management:** The head of the Joint Hindu Family business is known as Karta, who enjoys full freedom in conducting the family business and takes quick decisions without much interference.
3. **Sharing of Knowledge and Experience:** A Joint Hindu Family business helps the young members of the family to gain experience from the elder members about the discipline, self-sacrifice etc., which helps them to monitor their family business in future.
4. **Unlimited Liability:** The liability of the co-parceners is limited whereas for the Karta is unlimited. Unlimited liability helps Karta to operate the business in most efficient way.

Disadvantages of Joint Hindu Family Business

1. **Limited resources:** A Joint Hindu Family business has limited resources in finance and managerial capabilities. It is very much difficult for the Karta to undertake a risky business.
2. **Lack of motivation:** Members in a Joint Hindu Family business lacks motivation to work hard. It is because the fruits of their hard word is not given individually rather they are shared among all the co-parceners.
3. **Freedom of karta :** In a Joint Hindu Family business, Karta has the absolute freedom to manage the business for which he has got all the freedom to misuse it for his personal gain.

Suitability of Joint Hindu Family Business

The success of a Joint Hindu Family business is mostly depends upon the efficiency and capability of the Karta and the mutual understanding between the co-parceners. Due to the decline in the Joint Hindu Family business, gradually it is losing its ground

PARTNERSHIP

Meaning

A partnership form of organization is one where two or more persons combine their skill, capital and managerial abilities to run a business with a view to earn profit. Persons from similar background or persons of different ability and skills, may join together to carry on a business. Each member of such a group is individually known as 'partner' and collectively the members are known as a 'partnership firm'. These firms are governed by the Indian Partnership Act, 1932. All the partners share the profit or losses and have control and liability for business operations. The taxes are paid by the partners on their personal tax returns, in proportion to their share of ownership. In a partnership business each person contributes something to the business i.e., ideas, money and property. The law does not treat a partnership as a separate legal entity from its partners. The partners collectively own the assets of the partnership and are each individually liable for the debts and liabilities of the business. Each partner is personally liable for the full amount of debt owing by the partnership without any limit. A partnership business dissolves on the death or withdrawal of a partner unless the partnership agreement provides otherwise. For smooth functioning of the partnership business, a partnership deed usually made among the partners forms a legal agreement.

Characteristics of a Partnership

1. **Number of partners:** There must be at least two persons to form a partnership business. The Indian Partnership Act, 1932 fixes no maximum limit on the number of partners in a partnership firm. However the maximum limit on the number of partners is ten in case of banking business and twenty in case of all other types of business. But the Companies Act, 1956 lies down that any partnership or association of more than the above limit is illegal unless registered as a Joint Stock Company.
2. **Contractual relationship:** The relation between the partners of a partnership firm is created by contract and not by status as in case of Joint Hindu Family. There must be an agreement between two or more persons to enter into partnership. The agreement may be verbal, written or implied. If the agreement is in writing it is known as a 'Partnership Deed'.
3. **Competence of partners:** All partners must be competent to enter into a contract. Minors, lunatics, insolvent and other persons incompetent to enter into a valid contract cannot enter into a partnership agreement. However, a minor can be admitted to the benefits of partnership, i.e., he can have a share in the profits.

4. **Sharing of profit and loss:** There must be an agreement to share the profits and losses of the business of the partnership firm. In order to avoid the disputes which may arise in future, the partnership deed is clarifying the share of profits and losses. In the absence of an agreement, they share it equally.
5. **Unlimited liability:** Partnership is a contractual relationship among the partners of a firm. They are liable jointly and severally for the debts and obligations of the firm. That means if the assets of the firm are not sufficient to meet the obligations of creditors of the firm, the private assets of the partners can be attached to satisfy their claims. Even a single partner may be called upon to pay the debts of the firm. Of course, he can get back the money due from other partners. The liability of a minor is, however, limited to the extent of his share in the profits, in case of dissolution of a firm.
6. **Principal-Agent relationship:** There is a principal and agent relationship exists in the partnership business. Partnership firm may be carried on by all the partners or any one of them acting for all. This means that every partner is acting as an agent on behalf of others and he is a principal when others act on his behalf. It is, therefore, essential that there should be mutual trust and faith among the partners in the interest of the firm.
7. **Transfer of interest:** A partner cannot transfer his proprietary interest to any person (except those who are already the partners) without the unanimous consent of other partners.
8. **Legal status:** A partnership firm is just a name for the business as a whole. The firm means partners and the partners mean the firm. Law does not recognize the firm as a separate entity distinct from the partners.
9. **Voluntary registration:** The registration of partnership is not compulsory. Registration is considered as desirable because it helps a firm to avail several benefits. For example, if it is registered, any partner can file a case against other partners, or a firm can file a suit against outsiders in case of disputes, claims, disagreements, etc.
10. **Dissolution of partnership:** Dissolution of the partnership firm implies not a complete closure of partnership business. When any change occurred in the existing agreement or in the number of partners, the partnership is dissolved.

Advantages of Partnership Firm

1. **Ease of formation:** A partnership can be formed without many legal formalities in terms of its formation. Every partnership firm need not be registered.

2. **Larger resources:** In comparison to the sole proprietorship, a partnership firm can pool larger resources. The credit worthiness is also greater in this form than in case of sole proprietorship. This enables a partnership firm to undertake operations on a relatively larger scale and thereby reaping the economies of scale.
3. **Flexibility in operation:** Partnership business is not regulated by any law so it imports flexibility in its operation. The partners can change their operations and amend objectives if necessary. It can change its business whenever the partners like. However, it is easier to change the line of business if the firm is not successful in one line of business because of its small scale operations.
4. **Better management:** As there is a direct relationship between ownership, control and profit, partners can take more interest in the affairs of business. Partners can take prompt decision as and when business needs which ultimately helps for better management.
5. **Sharing of risk:** In partnership, partners share their profits and losses as per the agreement made by them before commencement of the business. In the absence of any partnership agreement, they share the profits or losses equally.
6. **Protection of minority interest:** Every partner has an equal say in the decision making of the business. As minor partners are taken into the partnership firm, their interests are protected by all other partners.
7. **Better human or public telations:** In a partnership firm, every partner can made to develop healthy and cordial relations with employees, customers, suppliers and citizens, etc. The fruits of such a relationship may be reflected in higher accomplishments and larger profits for the business.

Disadvantages of Partnership Firm

1. **Instability:** A partnership firm comes to an end with the death, retirement or insolvency of partners. The life of the partnership firm is highly uncertain. Hence the business does not have stability to continue to exist indefinitely.
2. **Unlimited liability:** From this stand-point, the liability of partners is jointly and severally liable to an unlimited extent. Any one of the partners can be called upon to pay all the debts even from his personal properties. This may have more dangerous effect of curbing entrepreneurship because the partners may be afraid of venturing into new areas of business.
3. **Lack of harmony:** The partnership business works steadily as long as there is harmony and mutual understanding among the partners. There is an equal right and

greater possibilities of friction and quarrel among the partners. Differences of opinion among partners may lead to distrust and disharmony which may ultimately result in disruption and closure of the firm.

4. **Limited capital:** As the maximum number of partners cannot exceed 10 in banking business and 20 in ordinary business, the amount of capital resources is limited to the contribution to be made by the partners. As there is a restriction on the maximum number of partners, the firm can raise limited capital.

5. **Social losses:** When a partnership firm dissolved due to the lack of harmony among the partners, it creates a loss to the society both in terms of supply of goods and services and in terms of source of employment.

Suitability of Partnership Firm:

In a partnership firm, persons having different abilities, managerial talent and skills join together to carry on a business. Partnership business is suitable for small business such as wholesale and retail trade, professional services, medium sized mercantile houses etc. Many organizations are initially started as partnership firms and when it is economically viable, it is converted into a company.

(III) JOINT STOCK COMPANY

Meaning

A Joint Stock Company is an artificial person created by law, having a separate legal entity, with a perpetual succession and a common seal. The companies are governed by the Indian Companies Act, 1956. The main purpose of the company is to earn profit. The capital of the company is divided into a number of shares and the holders of these shares are known as shareholders. They are the real owners of the company. Companies like Tata Iron & Steel Co. Limited, Hindustan Lever Limited, Reliance Industries Limited, Steel Authority of India Limited, Ponds India Limited etc., are few examples of Joint Stock Company.

In the words of **Lord Justice Lindley,** "A Joint Stock Company is an association of many persons who contribute money or money's worth to a common stock and employs it for a common purpose. The common stock so contributed is denoted in money and is capital of the company. The persons who contribute it or to whom it belongs are members. The proportion of capital which each member is entitled to his share. Shares are always transferable, although right to transfer them is often more or less restricted."

Characteristics

1. **Artificial legal person:** A Joint Stock Company is an artificial person in the sense that it is created by law and has its own identity in the eyes of law. It can sue and be sued in its own name and does not possess physical attributes of a natural person. However, it has a legal status.
2. **Separate legal entity:** Being an artificial person, a company has a legal entity distinct from its members. It is an artificial person having an independent existence. A shareholder cannot be held responsible for the acts of the company.
3. **Common Seal:** Every company has a common seal by which it is represented while dealing with outsiders. The common seal with the name of the company engraved on it and is used as a substitute for its signature.
4. **Perpetual existence:** A company once formed continues to exist as long as it fulfils the requirements of law. It is not affected by the death, lunacy, insolvency or retirement of any of its members.
5. **Limited liability:** The liability of a member of a Joint Stock Company is limited by guarantee or the shares he owns. In other words, in case of payment of debts by the company, a shareholder is held liable only to the extent of his share.
6. **Transferability of shares:** The shareholders are full liberty to dispose of their shares to any person of their choice. Transferability of shares enables a shareholder to increase or decrease his investment in a company at any time.
7. **Membership:** A Joint Stock company having a minimum membership of two persons and maximum fifty is known as a Private Limited Company. But in case of a Public Limited Company, the minimum is seven and the maximum membership is unlimited.
8. **Management:** A Joint Stock Company has a democratic management and control. Even though the shareholders are the owners of the company, all of them cannot participate in the management process. The company is managed by the elected representatives of shareholders known as Directors.
9. **Separation of ownership and management:** A Joint Stock Company is not managed by all the members as the members may be large. The whole affairs of a company are conferred to elected representatives of members known as Directors, who is the hands and brains of the company. Because of the diffused ownership of company, the real owners of the company are not in a position to take part in the management of the company.

Advantages of Joint Stock Company

1. **Limited liability:** In a Joint Stock Company the liability of its members is limited to the extent of shares held by them. This attracts a large number of small investors to invest in the company. It helps the company to raise huge capital. Because of limited liability, a company is also able to take larger risks.
2. **Continuity of existence:** The continuity and stability of the company is not affected by the death, insolvency and insanity of any of the partners. A company is an artificial person created by law and possesses independent legal status.
3. **Large capital:** It is much easy to generate capital in case of companies than in case of sole proprietorship or partnership. The company can anytime subscribe its shares and raise its capital.
4. **Limited liability:** The liability of each shareholder is limited. This feature of company encourages more investment in the company as the shareholders are liable to the extent of their investments in the company.
5. **Transferability of shares:** This feature of the company provides liquidity to the funds invested. The shareholders can any time sell their shares for cash in stock exchange.
6. **Democratic set up:** A company elected representatives of shareholders to manage and control the working of the company. They are fully accountable to the shareholders of the company.
7. **Social benefit:** Due to the existence of the company form of business, every society is benefited in respect of employment opportunities, facility of huge capital formation which ultimately improves the standard of living.

Disadvantages of Joint Stock Company

1. **Difficult and costly formation:** The formation of a company requires fulfillment of a number of legal formalities. Provisions of the Companies Act are to be complied with and large amounts have to be spent to fulfil the preliminaries.
2. **Lack of personal touch:** There is a divorce between ownership and management of the joint stock company. The affairs of the company are managed by the professional managers. This lacks personal touch of the shareholders.
3. **Bureaucratic control:** Quick decisions and prompt actions are absent in the management of a company. As a result, the decision making process are delayed.

4. **Excessive government control:** A company is expected to comply with the provisions of several Acts. Non-compliance of these invites heavy penalty. This affects the smooth functioning of the company.
5. **Social abuses:** A joint stock company is a large scale business organisation having huge resources. It is very much difficult to maintain cordial relationship between the management and the employees. Lack of cordial relations may sometimes lead to strikes, lockouts, retrenchments, closure etc.
6. **Lack of secrecy:** As it is mandatory for a public company to publish its annual accounts, it is very much difficult to maintain the secrecy in the company form of organization.

Suitability of Joint Stock Company

A joint stock company is suitable where the volume of business is quite large, the area of operation is widespread, the risk involved is heavy and there is a need for huge financial resources and manpower. It is also preferred when there is need for professional management and flexibility of operations. In certain businesses like banking and insurance, business can only be undertaken by joint stock companies.

CO-OPERATIVE SOCIETY

Meaning

A co-operative society is a form of business organization which is primarily established to protect and safeguard the economic interest of the relatively weaker sections of the society. The main purpose of the society is to render services to its members in particular and to the society in general. It functions under the Cooperative Societies Act, 1912 and other State Co-operative Societies Acts. Minimum ten persons can form a co-operative society. The functions of the co-operative society are entirely different from all other forms of organization. The main objectives of co-operative society are: (a) rendering service rather than earning profit, (b) mutual help instead of competition, and (c) self help in place of dependence. On the basis of nature of services rendered by cooperatives they may be classified into the following categories:

(i) **Producers' Co-operatives:** These co-operative societies are formed to help and strengthen small producers who cannot stand up in the competition offered by the organized large scale producers. Small producers face problems in collecting inputs and marketing their products. The Weavers co-operative society, the Handloom Owners co-operative society are examples of such co-operatives.

(ii) **Consumers' Co-operatives:** These societies are formed for the main purpose of protecting the interests of ordinary consumers of society by making consumer goods available at reasonable prices. For this purpose, consumers' buy their goods from wholesale prices and sell them to members and often to non-members as well at prices slightly lower than the market prices. For example, Kendriya Bhandar in Delhi, Alaka in Bhubaneswar etc., are few examples of consumer co-operatives.

(iii) **Marketing Co-operatives:** These societies are set up for the selling of manufactured products or agricultural commodities to eliminate exploitation by the middlemen while marketing their products. There are two broad categories of marketing co-operatives such as (a) Industrial marketing co-operatives, and (b) Agricultural marketing co-operatives. For example J&K Handicrafts, Utkalika etc., are few examples of marketing co-operatives.

(iv) **Housing Co-operatives:** These societies are formed by those people who strive to own a flat or a piece of land for constructing their own house. They are usually formed to provide housing facilities to its members. These societies are formed both in rural and urban areas mostly in urban areas and in big cities where the problem of housing is acute.

(v) **Credit Co-operatives:** These societies are formed to provide financial help to its members on favourable terms of interest, security and re-payment. Such co-operatives are organized both in urban and rural areas. In urban areas they are called Co-operative Banks and in rural areas they are called as Rural Credit Societies.

(vi) **Farming Co-operatives:** These societies are formed by small farmers to carry on work jointly and thereby share the benefits of large scale farming. Few examples are construction co-operatives, transport co-operatives etc., falls under this category.

Characteristics

1. **Voluntary association:** Co-operatives are voluntary association of members. Any person may become a member of such an organization irrespective of his caste, creed, religion, colour, sex etc.

2. **Service motive:** The primary objective of establishing any co-operative organization is to render services to its members in particular and to the society in general. The emphasis is on service and not on profit.

3. **Sources of finances:** The capital of the co-operative organization is procured from its members in the form of units called shares. However the share capital constitutes only a limited source of business finance.

4. **Democratic management:** The management of the co-operative organisation vests in a management committee which is elected by the member in the annual general meeting. Each member has one vote and members elect a committee known as the Executive committee to look after the day to day administration of the co-operative society.

5. **Separate legal entity:** Co-operative organisation enjoys a separate and independent legal entity which is distinct from that of its members. As such, it has a perpetual life and is not affected by the entry and exit of members. It can enter into business contracts in its own name and also can sue and be sued in its own name.

6. **Distribution of surplus:** The profits earned by a cooperative organization after meeting its trading expenses and paying a fixed rate of dividend and bonus are not distributed among the members. As per the co-operative law some part of the profits is to be transferred to general reserve and some amount may be utilized for the general welfare of the locality in which the society is functioning.

Advantages of Co-operative Society

1. **Easy formation:** It is easy and simple to form a co-operative society. Any ten adult persons can voluntarily form an association and get themselves registered with the Registrar of Co-operative Societies.

2. **Limited liability:** The liability of its members are limited to the extent of capital contributed by them. They are not personally liable for the debts of the society.

3. **Open membership:** There is no restriction on any individual to be a member of any co-operative. Any person having common interest can become its members.

4. **Management:** A co-operative society functions a democratic manner, i.e., each member has only one vote.

5. **Winding up:** The co-operative society has a stable life. The dissolution of a co-operative firm is quite difficult. It does not cease to exist in case of death, or insolvency or resignation of a member.

Disadvantages of Co-operatives

1. **Limited capital:** Co-operative societies have limited capital because of the membership remaining confined to a locality or particular section of the people. Members do not invest much in its shares due to low rate of return on capital invested by them.

2. **Inefficient management:** The affairs of the co-operative society are not managed in efficient manner because of the member who manages do not have business experience. Lack of managerial expertise greatly affects the day-to-day management of the co-operative societies.

3. **Absence of motivation:** As there is no direct link between effort and reward, members of the co-operatives are not motivated to put in their best effort for the betterment of the society.

4. **Lack of Co-operation:** Co-operatives are formed with the very idea of co-operation from each and every member. Due to lot of friction and bickering among the members due to personality differences, ego clash, etc., the co-operative becomes inactive in its operations.

5. **Lack of secrecy:** Maintenance of business secrecy is very much important for the smooth functioning of the co-operatives.

6. **Dependence on government:** Excessive government rules and regulations over co-operatives may adversely affect the flexibility of its operations. The inadequacy of capital and lack of grants make co-operatives dependent on the government for support and patronage.

Suitability of Co-operatives: The main purpose of every co-operative society is to provide service than to earn profit. Its prime objective is to promote common economic interest. It is very much easier to raise capital and through assistance from financial institutions and government. It is suitable for small and medium sized organizations. However the large sized IFFCO (Indian Farmers and Fertilizers Cooperative), the Kaira Co-operative Processing Milk under the brand name of AMUL-the tacto of India are the illustrious exceptions.

CHOICE OF AN APPROPRIATE FORM OF BUSINESS ORGANISATION;

One of the important tasks for the entrepreneur is to select a suitable form of business organisation. Once a form of organization is chosen, it is very difficult to switch over to another form. There are a number of factors to be considered while selecting an appropriate form of business organisation.

1. **Nature of business:** The selection of a particular form of organisation is dependent on the nature of the business. For any service activity, sole proprietorship is very much suitable upon the nature of business activity. For service activity it can be ideally done through sole proprietorship or partnership. But if it is a manufacturing business then a partnership or company is preferable.

2. **Volume of business:** If the volume of business or scale of operation is small, a sole proprietorship or partnership form is ideal. But if the volume of business is on a large scale, company form is the best.
3. **Area of operation:** If the business is spread over a wide area, the company form is better suited, but if it is confined to a particular locality or region, other forms may be suitable.
4. **Finance:** If the requirement of finance is less, sole proprietorship or partnership business is suitable. But if the initial as well as the working capital required for carrying on the business is very large, one has to opt for a company form.
5. **Ownership and control:** When the business is owned and controlled by few persons, partnership business is most suitable where as the ownership and control lies with the many persons, company form of ownership is desired.
6. **Liability:** If the business is based on unlimited liabilities, sole proprietorship or partnership form is suitable, whereas where the liabilities are limited, one may opt company form of business.

FRANCHISE: FACTORS, ADVANTAGES AND DISADVANTAGES

All of us have heard of booming franchisé business. Every other day we witness increasing number of franchise food chains or retail chains in malls or popular marketing hubs. A franchise is a right granted to an individual or group to market a company's goods or services within a certain territory or location. In other words, when a company decides to distribute its products or services to an independent third party operator on a contract basis, it is known as franchise business. In today's cut-throat competition market everyone wants to stay ahead in the race. One of the ways to get an advantage over the competitors is by indulging in franchise business.

Franchisee is the independent third party operator using registered products and services whereas the company that grants the rights to the franchisee to use its products and techniques. The best contribution of franchises is in developing independent entrepreneurs who want to be their own boss. There are plenty of franchise businesses available worldwide which are being operated by self-driven individuals. However, before one decides to buy a franchise business, he must be aware of all the pros and cons involved with it. He must have proper understanding of franchise business. Franchise business is no doubt lucrative, but its success is very much dependent upon the strength of the brand and how it is being operated.

Meaning and Definition of Franchise

Franchise is one form of exclusive retailing. It in fact, is not just a method of retailing. It is a method of marketing which is lying between entrepreneurship and employment. A franchiser is an independent business person who abides by the marketing plan of the financier and pays him a fee for the use of his brand and known-how. Franchise is a form of business organization in which a firm which already has a successful product or service (the franchisor) enters into a continuing contractual relationship with other businesses (franchisees) operating under the franchisor's trade name and usually with the franchisor's guidance, in exchange for a fee. The franchising concept can be understood as license type transactions. In India, all the contracts come under the purview of the Indian Contract Act, 1872, which is based mainly on the English Law Principles. The agreement to the franchise is a standard printed agreement which deals with rights and obligations of the licensor and licensee. The term 'franchise' has its origin in the French word 'affranchir' which means to 'to free'. In its simplest terms a franchise can be considered a license from owner of trademark or trade name permitting another to sell a product or service under that name or mark. The usefulness of franchising lies in the fact that it helps the mega corporations to expand their business and popularize their brand names without investing large amounts of money. These corporations act as 'franchisers'. It is the local dealer who acts as a 'franchisee' and operates at a lesser cost by using his local market knowledge. The franchisee will be able to do business successfully without risks by utilizing the good-will attached to the brand name of the franchiser.

According to the **International Franchise Association (IFA)** of America, "A franchising operation is a contractual relationship between the franchiser and franchisee in which the franchiser offers or is obligated to maintain a continuing interest in the business of the franchisee in such area as know-how and training; wherein the franchisee operates under a common trade name, format and procedure owned and controlled by the franchiser, and in which the franchisee has or will make a substantial capital investment in his business from his own resources".

Brand visibility is one of the important activities of every company. Today, competition in every field has become cut-throat and everyone wants to stay ahead in the race. One can remain ahead or get an advantage over the competitors is by indulging in business. One of the best techniques to make the business survive in today's competitive environment is to grab onto one of the numerous franchise business opportunities. Indian has emerged as a major economy with consistent economic growth is truly impressive. Even the global meltdown of 2008 did not hurt India the way it hit western countries. That indicates resilience of the economy.

India is one of the biggest emerging markets for various goods and services, ranging from bare necessities to expensive luxuries. Until 1991, due to the archaic Foreign Exchange Regulation Act, 1973 (FERA), almost all sectors of goods and services relating to the consumer markets in India were secure from the grasp of foreign investors. After the repeal of FERA and the coming into force of the Foreign Exchange Management Act, 1999 (FEMA), foreign investors found their passage into India with rules for entry becoming far more favourable.

Entrepreneurship Through Franchising

India holds the opportunity of being one of the biggest entrepreneurial resource, and significantly contributors to the economic growth. India has also become a prime destination for Western franchise operators looking to expand their business. Today, franchising is the latest and most profitable buzzword in the SME (Small and Medium Enterprises) sector, with almost all leading companies considering franchising their products and services. Especially with a boom in the retail sector, franchising has further emerged as a catalyst for growth in the sector. Franchising, globally contributes to 20 per cent of the GDP, whereas in India, it is growing at a pace of 25-30 per cent and is estimated at Rs. 50 billion currently. Indian retail industry consisting of over 15 million outlets provides employment to over 7% of the population. Today, the Indian retail industry is estimated at about US$ 200 billion and it is expected to grow at a compounded 30% over the next 5 years.

In India, buying a franchise business is a better option as compared to starting your own business from scratch. There are different platforms where one can look for a franchise business. One can check out details in local newspapers or browse the Internet to look for information about companies or brands interested in expansion of their business. However, websites are also the best ones to find information about the best franchise business in India.

Major Factors Influencing Franchising

Franchise investment is one of the safest businesses that involves less cost and more revenue. India is also fast gaining reputation for its new breed of entrepreneurs who are looking for available franchise opportunities. Following are the various factors which influence the growth and expansion of franchising.

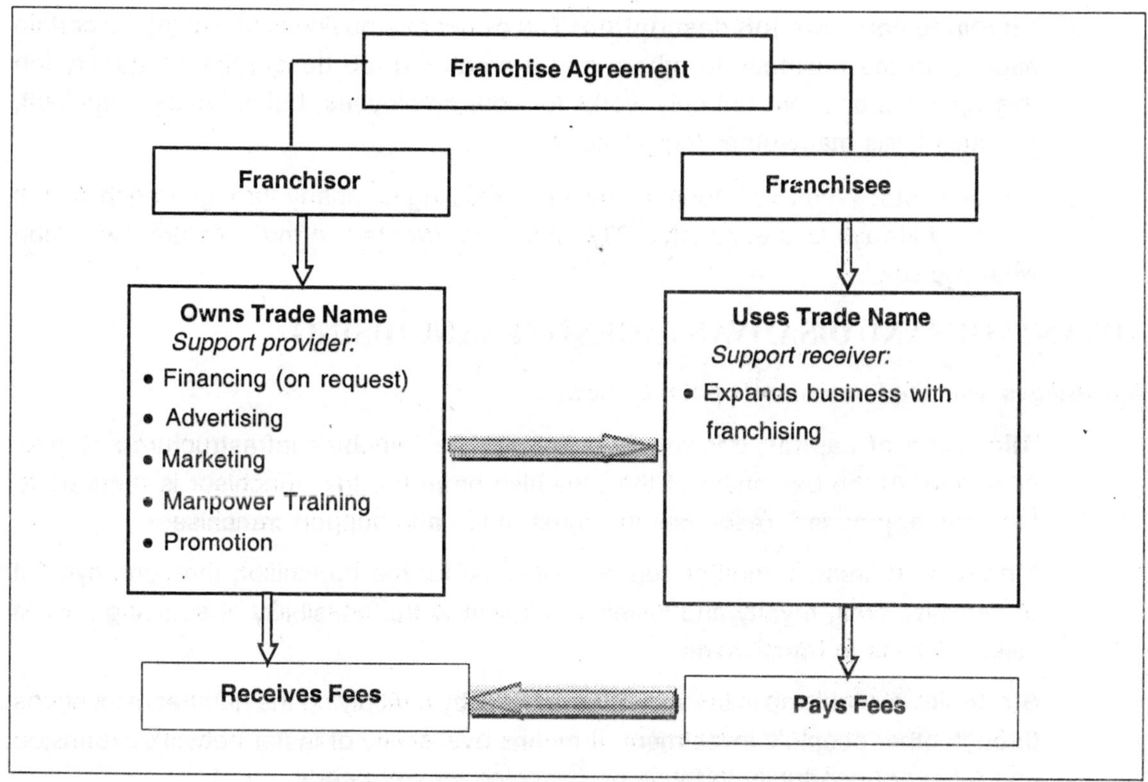

Importance of Franchising

There are various points which will help a company to go for franchising. Following are the important points of franchising.

1. **Market growth:** Franchise is the key to rapid market expansion. It helps a company to growth rapidly and expands the range of markets in quick time and without incurring large investments. The computer education network of NIIT is a good example of rapid growth through franchising. It has able to build a network of over 100 branches across the country through franchising.

2. **Helps in brand building:** Brand building is indeed a journey. Building a brand has everything to do with capturing the hearts and minds of consumers. A brand incorporates and conveys the values and traits that a company wants associated with their product or service. Establishing a strong brand can have significant value, and truly is a journey that companies should embark upon in their quest to be successful.

3. **Choosing your own job description:** The owner of a business can delegate certain aspects of the business to others and it creates a job description. A quality job description is one that not only works for your employees, but is legally compliant, and also fulfils many other requirements.

4. **Lower costs:** When someone is buying an existing company through franchising, it is almost always less expensive. The business owners live the scripture, "you reap what you sow".

ADVANTAGES AND DISADVANTAGES OF FRANCHISING

Advantages from the Franchisor's point of view:

1. **Allocation of capital:** It is required to build the franchise infrastructure and pilot operation. At the beginning of the franchise program, the franchisor is required to have the appropriate resources to recruit, train, and support franchisees.

2. **Financial:** It creates another source of income for the franchisor, through payment of franchise fees, royalty and levies in addition to the possibility of sourcing private label products to franchisees.

3. **Strategic:** Franchising is the spreading of risks by multiplying the number of locations through other people's investment. It means availability of faster network expansion and a better opportunity to focus on changing market needs

4. **Operational:** Franchising also means uniformity of procedures, which reflects on consistency, enhanced productivity levels and better quality. It creates and maintains an effective quality control.

Disadvantages from the Franchisor's point of view

1. In the beginning of the franchise programme, there is a fear of risk that trade name may be spoiled by the franchisee until the franchisor is capable of selecting the right candidate for the business.

2. The franchisor has to disclose the confidential information in connection with the franchising before giving power for use.

Advantages from the Franchisee point of view:

1. **Business plan:** In almost all the franchisee business, the franchisors provide help to the franchisee to develop the business plan.

2. **Lower risks:** Franchise operation has a lower risk of failure than an independent business.

3. **Marketing assistance:** Franchisor usually provides marketing assistance to popularize the parent company through professional advertising campaigns.

4. **Established product or service:** A franchisor offers a product or service which are already available in the market and that has sold successfully.

Disadvantages from the Franchisee point of view:

1. The payment made by the franchisee as fees and royalty to the franchisor in some cases can be exaggerated.

2. The transfer of all goodwill built in the local market to the franchisor upon expiration or termination of the franchise contract.

3. The franchisees provide the capital for expansion, which allows you a high degree of financial leverage.

4. Because the franchisees contribute to an advertising fund, which you control, you can expand brand awareness without financial commitment on your part.

5. The franchisees provide the capital for expansion, which allows you a high degree of financial leverage.

Legal Aspects in Franchising

Franchising is a popular way to start a new business yet like everything else in life it also has some pros and cons. One must be aware of all the concerning features of franchising business. There are plenty of lucrative franchising business opportunities. But the first thing one need to figure out is the type of business that he wants to get into.

The laws relating to franchising are excellent so far as western countries are concerned. In India the concept of franchising is in its nascent stages. So the rights and liabilities of the franchiser and the franchisee have not been dealt with elaborately under any law. Generally the law of contracts is applicable to franchise agreements. The franchise agreement must be lawful and not against the public policy in India. The franchising agreement is considered licensing contract in India with a single difference relating to the territorial operation of the business. Some of the laws that indirectly cover the area of franchising in India are:

1. **Intellectual Property Law and Franchising in India:** Intellectual Property rights should be protected very carefully in any country so as to make the franchising system successful. Otherwise when the franchiser enters into new territory with its products, its product may be copied, and brand name may be misused which in turn affects goodwill of the franchiser.

2. **The Trademarks Act, 1999:** This Act has been enacted to provide for the registration and better protection of trademarks and for the prevention of the use of fraudulent marks on merchandise. The best way to protect a trademark must get it registered in India. India has made a step towards fulfilling its international obligations.
3. **The Designs Act, 2000:** Design has now been defined as only the features of shape, configuration, pattern, ornament or composition of lines or colours applied to any article whether in two dimensional or 3D or in both forms. Application for design registration can be made in any class by the proprietor of the design. Registration is granted only in one class. The proprietor of the Design shall have copyright in the Design for 10 years from the date of registration.
4. **The Copyright Act, 1957:** The Copyright Act can be used successfully by the franchiser when he wishes to protect his franchising manual. The manual contains the entire technique of running the franchise business. The manual should not be used unauthorized or improperly by any other person without having the permission of the franchiser as it amounts to violation of copyright being held by the franchiser.
5. **Labour Laws and Franchising:** There are various enactments concerning labourers in India. All franchising contracts are amenable to labour laws in India. Labour laws govern the day-to-day conditions of employment in a franchising system. When a franchise outlet is closed or shut down, then the labour laws play a vital role in determining the compensation to be paid to the employees of that franchise outlet by the master franchisee, franchiser or franchisee.

SUMMARY

A business plan is a tool with three basic purposes: communication, management, and planning. As a communication tool, it is used to attract investment capital, secure loans, convince workers to hire on, and assist in attracting strategic business partners. As a management tool, the business plan helps you track, monitor and evaluate your progress. As a planning tool, the business plan guides you through the various phases of your business. India is one of the biggest emerging markets for various goods and services, ranging from bare necessities to expensive luxuries. The purpose of business goes beyond earning profit.

QUESTIONS

SHORT ANSWER QUESTIONS

1. What factors are taken into account while selecting any form of entrepreneurial business?

2. What are the various categories of co-operative societies?
3. Who is a Karta? What are the characteristics of Joint Hindu Family business?
4. What are the limitations of a Joint Stock Company form of business?

LONG ANSWER QUESTIONS

1. What do you understand by business opportunity identification? What are the various types of opportunities are available in entrepreneurship development?
2. What are the various problems which are encountered before starting a new business? Explain them in detail.
3. "*One man control is the best in the World, if that man is big enough to manage everything* ". Elucidate the above statement.
4. What is a partnership business? What are the various characteristics and advantages of partnership business?
5. Define a Joint Stock Company? What are the various characteristics of a Joint Stock Company?

VENTURE CAPITAL FINANCE

"A carelessly planned project takes three times longer to complete than expected; a carefully planned project takes only twice as long."

— Golub's Law

Chapter Overview:

At the end of this chapter, you will be able to understand:

1. The concept of venture capital financing.
2. Salient features of venture capital.
3. Various stages of venture capital financing.
4. Venture capital in India,opportunity analysis and competitive factors.
5. Future of venture capital.

Introduction

Every business needs sufficient amount of capital to start and grow. There are a number of alternative methods to fund growth. These include the owner or proprietor's own capital, arranging debt finance, or seeking an equity partner, as is the case with private equity and venture capital. The concept of venture capital was coined in the United States in the 40's. It is a term still to have an encashed definition. Venture Capital is a long term equity capital invested in new or rapidly expanding enterprises. The venture capital fund needs two inputs namely, pool of capital and management skills. Private equity is a broad term that refers to any type of non-public ownership equity securities that are not listed on a public exchange. Private equity encompasses both early stage (venture capital) and later stage (buy-out, expansion) investing. Venture capital (VC) is funding invested, or available for investment, in an enterprise that offers the probability of profit along with the possibility of loss. Indeed, venture capital was once known also as risk capital, but that term has fallen out of usage, probably because investors do not like to see the words "risk" and "capital" in close conjunction. Venture capitalists often do not tend to think that their investments involve an element of risk, but are assured a successful return by virtue of the investor's knowledge and business sense.

Financing Small Scale Industries: The 4 Fs of Initial Finance:

Initial investment usually arises from 4 Fs:

1. Founders' own savings and assets
2. Family money and contributions
3. Friends' money or assets
4. Foolhardy investors' sums handed over as a result of silver-tongued persuasion.

Three forms of initial finance: That start-up capital takes one of three main forms

1. **Personal savings:** The simplest form, their own cash reserves or assets.
2. **Debt:** Borrowing from a lender, paying interest but retaining control.
3. **Equity:** Selling shares for capital, no interest but losing partial control.

The objective of the VC scheme is to provide a window to entrepreneurs who have thought of ventures having special characteristics to be innovative but at the same time may not qualify for assistance through the conventional route of loans and financing. Projects involving new and untried/untested processes and technologies which have scope for commercial application with characteristics of high risk and high return are one example of the type of projects which a VC looks for.

Venture capital is a sophisticated equity finance designed for funding high-risk and high reward projects. It mobilizes and pools the management skills in order to encourage the entrepreneurs to establish a new venture. The viability of the venture capital investments largely depends on the quality of the management because their expertise is the key consideration in selecting a project. It is an alternative source of finance where the industry is technology based, the entrepreneur is inexperienced and investment carries high risk of loss. The development of venture capital is the response to the demand created for more risk bearing funds to finance commercialization of new technologies and innovative market solutions. The success of venture capital financing based on the risk analysis, project evaluation and assessment of integrity of the entrepreneur. Venture capital agencies would have to scout around for innovative technology schemes and translate them for viable returns.

Venture capital financing plays an active role, which provides equity and long term loan capital to the business, which does not have easy access to the capital market. It involves a small amount of investment in a new and relatively untried technology, initiated by relatively new or professionally or technically qualified entrepreneurs with inadequate funds. It is a financing institution, which joins entrepreneur as a co-promoter in a project, involving high risk. It normally pools the resources including managerial abilities and assists the entrepreneurs in the early stage of the project. It plays a crucial role by exploring vast untapped potentialities and overcoming threats. The main objectives of venture capital financing are:

(i) Developing the technological aspect of the industry and

(ii) Import technologies, which are widely applied to the industries.

The Small and Medium Enterprises (SMEs) deserves special treatment because it is quite difficult to raise funds from the capital market due to high transaction costs, fear of loss or control and increased disclosure requirements. Venture capital is the most appropriate mechanism of financing SMEs. It is an equity investment in highly potential business promoted by innovative entrepreneurs, small firms invariably have difficulty in securing adequate capital either to begin operations (start-up capital), to expand existing operations (development capital) or to sustain existing operations in the event of financial hardship venture capital and entrepreneur are the two essential components for a vibrant and dynamic economy. Venture capital is boosting force and entrepreneur is the driver of economic growth. The concept of venture capital is:

Your Brain + My Money = Venture Capital i.e., combination of entrepreneur's idea and banker's money.

Salient Features of Venture Capital

1. **Entrepreneurial promoter:** Venture capital undertakings are usually run by those people who are professionally and technically qualified but facing scarcity of funds to invest therein. They are competent and capable technocrats who are looking forward to invest their money in the risk projects.
2. **Innovative technology:** All investments are made in innovative projects with new technology. The high risk investment in the project may not be acceptable to the market. Many technocrats choose the new path where they can invest their money in order to earn good amount of profit.
3. **Longer gestation period:** Venture capital funds are invested for a long period of time. The benefits from the investment will start after a stipulated period of time. So the gestation period is long. It is an active form of investment with high degree of involvement in the management of the venture.

Venture Capital Investment Process

The Paradigm shift in Venture Capital

	The Old	The New
Seed and start-up capital	• Conditional loans • Equity support from financial institution • Social development funds • Informal sources	• Conditional loans • Equity support from financial institutions • Social development funds • Informal sources
Expansion financing	• Term loans	• Venture leasing • Equity support from financial institutions • Private equity • Convertible debentures • Cumulative preference share
Bridge financing		• Bank loans • Special purpose vehicles.

Various Stages of Venture Capital Financing

The main objective of venture capital financing is to support the venture capital undertaking at an early stage and capital gains at later stages. The various stages of venture capital financing include start-up, first-round, second-round, third-round, and fourth-round financing. The degree of risk associated with a business gradually diminishes in every subsequent stage of business development. The various stages of venture capital financing are:

1. **Seed-money stage:** Small amount of financing needed to prove a concept or develop a product. Marketing is not included in this stage.
2. **Start-up:** Financing for a firm that started up in the past one year. Funds are paid for marketing and product development.
3. **First-round financing:** Additional money to begin sales and manufacturing after a firm has spent its startup capital.
4. **Second-round financing:** Funds marked for working capital for a firm that is selling its product but is still losing money.
5. **Third-round financing:** Financing for a firm that is breaking even and is contemplating an expansion project.
6. **Fourth-round financing:** Money provided for firms that are likely to go public soon. It is also known as bridge financing.

Venture Capital in India, Opportunity Analysis and Competitive Factors

Venture capital is playing a innovative and developmental role which is greatly helping the small and medium enterprises. There are broadly six categories of venture capital companies in India. They are:

1. Specific funds promoted jointly by Indian private sector companies, all India financial institutions.
2. VCCs/VCFs set-up by foreign banks/foreign institutions/NRIs investors, such as ANZ Grindlays Investment Services Ltd.
3. VCCs/VCFs promoted by All India Financial Institutions *viz.,* RCTC, TDICI, IL&FS-VCF.
4. VCCs/VCFs promoted by commercial banks like Canbank Venture Capital Fund.
5. VCCs/VCFs promoted by State Level developmental financial institutions like APIDC Venture capital fund.

6. VCCs/VCFs promoted jointly by Indian private sector companies *viz.*, GVCF, IVCF, IFB-VCF and 20th Century VCF.

7. VCCs/VCFs setup by foreign banks/foreign institutions /NRIs investors such as ANZ Grindlays Investment Services Ltd.

Sources of Venture Capital Finance, Capital Structure, Capitalization

Business finance is concerned with the acquisition and utilization of funds in meeting the financial needs of any entrepreneurial business. It may be defined as the planning, acquiring, utilizing, managing and controlling of funds of any kind used in connection with business. Finance is said to be the life-blood of any business. The prosperity, day-to-day working and future of a business unit mainly depend on the availability of adequate finance. It should be available in adequate amounts to face trade cycles, recessions and other critical times.

Availability of funds will be the main attraction for an entrepreneur, the terms and procedures involved in procuring these funds should be carefully examined in deciding the effectiveness and usefulness of getting this loan. While considering the financial assistance for an entrepreneurial business one must consider the following:

(a) Cost of borrowings

(b) Time factors (i) period for which funds are needed and (ii) Time taken to obtain money.

(c) Purpose for which funds are needed

(d) Norms of financial institutions or govt. regulations

(e) Repayment capacity and pattern.

Sources of Venture Capital Finance

The sources of finance can be divided into two major heads:

(i) Internal sources, and

(ii) External sources

(i) Internal sources: Internal sources of funds includ the following:

(a) Own savings and investments

(b) Personal loans from Provident Funds/Life Insurance Corporations/Cooperative Banks etc.

(c) Personal borrowings from friends and relatives.

(d) Capital raised through mortgage of personal assets like shares, land, buildings etc.

(e) Profit earned or transferred from existing business or investment or trade.

(ii) External sources: An entrepreneur makes his decision considering all the pros and cons of available sources. Information on some of the external sources of funds available to the entrepreneur includes the following:

(i) Long term loan: In order to purchase fixed assets for setting up an enterprise, finance requirements will be for long time. Financial institutions and banks are usually give loans for such purposes depending upon the type or assets and amount desired.

(ii) Short term loan: When finance requirement is temporary, banks and other financial companies give finance for temporary period varying from 2 days to one year.

(iii) Plant leasing: One of the recent popular sources of external finance is the leasing of plant. The finance companies or leasing companies provides the needed equipment or plants on lease basis. Clients pay some nominal deposit and monthly rent for the equipment taken on lease.

(iv) Hire-purchase: Sometimes fixed assets are given on hire purchase basis to the clients on the basis of some initial down payment of deposit. However the ownership is not transferred to the owner until the final repayment of the requisite amount.

(v) Working capital loan: For day to day management of the business, an entrepreneur takes working capital loans from the concerned banks or financial institutions, which is normally available for a period of one year. It can be renewable every year and is given against hypothecation or mortgage of assets.

Forms of Capital: Capitalization, Capital Structure and Financial Structure

Finance plays an important role in the management of any organisation. Every business needs funds from the promotional stage up to the winding up process. It is very essential for the business to estimate the capital requirement well in advance. The term capitalisation, capital structure and financial structure are not same. Capitalisation refers to the funds of the business for which securities are issued to the public. For example, equity and preference shares, debentures etc. are issued to the public to raise funds. Capital structure refers to the portion of the total funds available to the company except current liabilities. It consists of equity shares, preference shares, debentures, reserves and surpluses. Financial structures refer to the total of liabilities in the Balance Sheet.

Financial structure = Capital structure plus current liabilities

SIGNIFICANCE OR IMPORTANCE OF BUSINESS FINANCE

Adequate finance provides the following benefits to an entrepreneur:

(i) It helps the firm to carry out its operations smoothly and successfully.

(ii) It is required for the purchase of fixed and current assets.

(iii) It helps the firm to replace its fixed assets in time.

(iv) It helps the firm to face the recession, trade cycles.

TYPES OF CAPITAL: DEBT VS. EQUITY

Every entrepreneur must ask themselves, how much financial risk they can tolerate and how much control they are willing to give up in their venture. An entrepreneur should consider risk and control when deciding between debt (personal loans, business loans) and equity (investments by others for partial ownership). Equity will help to grow quicker but will result in sharing of wealth and control with other investors. Debt is less expensive than equity and quicker and easier to find. Gonorally one will have to pledge assets that are personal and in a small business the owner personally pledges assets, but requires regular payments of principle and equity.

Stages of venture financing

Stages	Name	Descriptions
Stage-I	Seed	Conceptualisation/planning
Stage-II	Start-up	Operational/production
Stage-III	Expansion	Expansion in production/marketing
Stage-IV	Mezzanine	Last stage befor public offering
Stage-V	Buy-out	Acquisition of a product line/business
Stage-VI	Turnaround	Re-establishment of business

The Paradigm Shift in Venture Capital

Money being the most important component in any business often is a problem for an entrepreneur and especially if a person has no prior experience or means to secure finance to start his venture the problem becomes acute. In this situation a venture capital comes to the rescue. A typical venture capital is a legal entity that provides money to a person who has an idea and wants to commercialize it. In return the VC takes equity or stake in the company along with the promoters. Now the company commences its operation and reaches breakeven and finally makes profit, then the VC sells its equity either to promoter as buy back or to a third party. Normally a VC invests in new unproven technologies that are highly risky. In order to be eligible for such VC funds one has to demonstrate that the idea is new, novel or innovative and is in clear departure from the existing, if any.

Legal Issues for Establishing a New Unit

The biggest problem faced is the use of idea by an unauthorized or undesired entity. Since an entrepreneur is a relatively inexperienced person he is unaware of unethical practices and hence is a soft target for shrewd persons who can deprive the right person from the credit. So a person should try to protect his idea under some law and obtain some evidence that would be recognized by courts.

Some of the Legal Protections are

1. **Patents:** The best way is to look for the innovation and file a patent application, this is best way as a the patent office gives a formal receipt of the patent application along with the date, name of the inventor this evidence is recognized by courts or arbitration tribunals;
2. **Design:** This is another way to protect ornamental or external design of the product. This is same as patent and legally recognized evidence is generated;
3. **Copyright:** Though it is a weak protection nonetheless if no legal remedy depending on the case it is advised to go for copyright protection;
4. **Arbitration:** Insert an arbitration clause in the non-disclosure agreement. So any authority named in the clause can adjudicate upon any dispute so referred;

Documentation Required for Promotion of New Units

As per the practice followed in India by Venture Capital Financing, the following are the legal documents which are generally executed between parties.

1. **In the case of Loan:**
   - Investment agreement
   - Promissory note
   - Pledge of movables by promoter/director
   - Hypothecation agreement
   - Agreement between the VCF and the promoters
   - Undertakings covering special stipulations
2. **In the case of Equity:**
   - Investment agreement
   - Equity buy-back agreement with promoter/director
   - Any other agreement warranted by terms and conditions of sanction
   - Undertakings covering special stipulations
3. **In the case of Joint facility:**
   - All the above documents with suitably modified clauses Each of the above documents has specific objectives and covers separate grounds to govern the legal relationship between the parties.

Confidence Building Measures

The very thought of disclosing the idea is not easily acceptable with an Entrepreneur and a VC will not put his money at stake without going through the entire idea. These issues are the blocks in the mindset are the main impediments in the whole process. So need arise for some confidence building measures. Possible confidence building measures can be a carefully drafted non-disclosure agreement with the dealing VC. First step is to ascertain the legal nature of the entity and whother the person dealing is the true and legally authorized person to enter into contract or deal in such transactions. It is always advisable to ask for the Articles of Association and memorandum of the company, its registration and affiliations with Securities Exchange Board of India.

Positioning of Venture Capital Investment Process

The idea of positioning provides a very powerful tool to aid entrepreneurial decision making. Positioning provides a framework for locating the venture in relation to its competitors. Existing suppliers to a market do not serve its customers as completely as they might. They leave gaps in the market which a new venture can attempt to fill, to gaining a foothold in that market. Identifying the window of opportunity, a new start-up will signal its presence, in these gaps. A new venture is at face value, in a weak position relative to established competitors. Even if the established players had not previously spotted the window of opportunity, a new start-up will signal its presence to them. Identifying a strategic position is a fundamental element of the strategic planning process.

VENTURE CAPITAL FUNDS IN INDIA

Venture capital is playing a innovative and developmental role which is greatly helping the small and medium enterprises. Some of the important venture capital funds in India are listed below:

1. APIDC Venture capital limited, 1102, Babukhan Estate, Hyderabad-500001.
2. Canbank Venture Capital Fund Limited, IInd Floor, Kareem Towers, Bengaluru.
3. Gujarat Venture Capital Fund 1997, Ashram Road, Ahmedabad-380009.
4. Industrial Venture Capital Limited, Thyagaraya Road, Chennai-600017.
5. Auto Ancillary Fund, Opp. Signals Enclave, New Delhi-110101.
6. Gujarat Venture Capital Fund, 1995, Ashram Road, Ahmedabad-380009.
7. Karnataka Information Technology Venture Capital Fund Cunningham Road, Bengaluru.
8. India Auto Ancillary Fund , Nariman Point, Mumbai-400021.
9. Information Technology Fund, Nariman Point, Mumbai-400021.
10. Tamilnadu Infotech Funds, Nariman Point, Mumbai-400021.
11. Orissa Venture Capital Fund, Nariman Point, Mumbai-400021.
12. Uttar Pradesh Venture Capital Fund, Nariman Point, Mumbai-400021.
13. SICOM Venture Capital Fund, Nariman Point, Mumbai-400021.
14. Punjab Infotech Venture Fund, 18, Himalaya Marg, Chandigarh-160017.
15. National Venture Fund for Software and Information Technology Industry.

Venture Capital: Strengths and Weakness

Strengths:

- Industry crossed learning curve
- Matured capital market system
- Electronic trading – NSE, BSE and OTCEI
- Offshore funds have strong foreign ties
- Growing number of foreign trained professionals
- Better awareness among entrepreneurs and intermediaries
- Irreversible reforms.

Weakness:

- Limited exit options
- Beaurucratic meddling and rigid official attitude
- Too many regulators – SEBI, RBI.
- Policy maker's attention toward capital market reform
- Lack of level playing in taxation policy
- Acute shortage of professionals
- Normal investing cycle getting compressed
- Rapid oxohange rate devaluation.

The Future of Venture Capital

In the year of globalization, there is high scope for technological innovations. India has a wide spectrum of growth industries where operational and organizational challenges will become more apparent to the fund managers. Following suggestions may be considered to make the guidelines more effective:

1. The management of the concerned organization should be strong in their skills and commitments.
2. Ideas should be generated about the future demand of the products comparing to the competitors position.

3. Financial institutions should take quick decisions, identifying and appraising projects, provide good management assistance and systematically monitor the projects.
4. VCCs and VCFs should be given flexibility with regard to investment of short-term funds.
5. Reserve Bank of India should clarify its position with regard to investment by Indian banks and foreign banks.
6. Necessary legislative measures should be completed for the tax concessions.

All suggestions outlined above are indicative and not exhaustive propositions.

SUMMARY

Though in India venture capital financing is in the infancy stage, it is likely to progress if the entrepreneur gets encouragement from the Central and State Government by way of patronizing the products manufactured and giving tem rate contract. Venture capital agencies would have to scout around for innovative technology schemes and translate them for viable returns. Venture capital could be an effective scheme if adequate services are provided for fostering the development of rapid industrialisation in order to promote entrepreneurship.

The venture capital investment helps for the growth of innovative entrepreneurships in India. Venture capital has developed as a result of the need to provide non-conventional, risky finance to new ventures based on innovative entrepreneurship. Venture capital is an investment in the form of equity, quasi-equity and sometimes debt-straight or conditional, made in new or untried concepts, promoted by a technically or professionally qualified entrepreneur. Venture capital means risk capital. It refers to capital investment, both equity and debt, which carries substantial risk and uncertainties. The risk envisaged may be very high may be so high as to result in total loss or very less so as to result in high gains

QUESTIONS

SHORT ANSWER QUESTIONS

1. What are the 4Fs of initial finance?
2. What do you understand by the term capital structure?
3. What are the various categories of venture capital companies in India?
4. What are the factors taken into consideration while considering the financial assistance for an entrepreneurial business?
5. What are the various legal issues connected with the venture capital financing?

LONG ANSWER QUESTIONS

1. What are the different sources of finance? Explain each of them in detail.
2. What are the measures taken by government to provide venture capital to the entrepreneurs in India?
3. What do you understand by venture capital? Explain salient features and the paradigm shift in venture capital?
4. What are the various stages of venture capital financing? Explain each of them in detail.
5. What are the various informal sources of capital found in entrepreneurial venture?
6. What are the various advantages and disadvantages of venture capitals in India?

CHAPTER

ENTREPRENEURSHIP DEVELOPMENT PROGRAMMES (EDPs)

"The biggest mistake anyone can make is to focus on the competitor. You focus on the consumer and you will get it right."

— K.B. Dadiseth

Chapter Overview:

At the end of this chapter, you will be able to understand:

1. Objectives of entrepreneurship development programme.
2. Need for entrepreneurship development programme.
3. Phases of entrepreneurship development programme.
4. Role of Government in entrepreneurship development programme.

Introduction

Entrepreneurship is recognized as the heart of all industrial developments particularly in the small and medium enterprises. Development of policies and programmes will succeed only if they help to generate and sustain entrepreneurship of the right kind. It is the task of promotional agencies to identify and sustain entrepreneurship in order to sustain industrial growth. Most people think of an 'entrepreneur' as something very glamorous. But entrepreneurship is far from being a glamorous occupation. It takes lot of effort and commitment to succeed as an entrepreneur.

An Entrepreneurship Development Programme (EDP) may be defined as a programme which is designed to help a person in strengthening his entrepreneurial skills, motives and capabilities for playing his entrepreneurial role more effectively and efficiently. Entrepreneurship is regarded as one of the important determinants of the industrial growth of the country. There is a cause and effect relationship between entrepreneurship and the economy.

Entrepreneurial Education and its Importance

Entrepreneurship education is the practice of starting new organizations, particularly new businesses generally in response to identified opportunities. Entrepreneur is the person who is willing to take the risks involved in starting and managing a business. Entrepreneur education is not only about creating business plans and starting new ventures; it is all about creativity, innovation and growth. Entrepreneurial education requires while starting a new venture, financing new venture, growing and managing an emerging venture and business plan development. All the above skills provide the developmental curriculum opportunities that enable individuals to operate in competition with the world and context to experiences related to becoming an entrepreneur.

Objectives of Entrepreneurship Development Programmes

Entrepreneurship Development Programme is an organized, ongoing and continuous activity through which new class of entrepreneurs are promoted and produced to accept the current business challenges. The main purpose of EDP is to motivate the persons to opt entrepreneurship as a career who are capable of perceiving and exploiting business opportunities. The main objectives of Entrepreneurship Development Programme (EDP) are:

1. To bring the awareness and enhance capabilities of the person to take up entrepreneurship as a profession.

2. To develop and strengthen the entrepreneurial quality, to motivate them for achievement and to enable participants to be independent, capable, promising entrepreneurs.
3. To enhance the motivation, knowledge and skills of potential entrepreneurs to take up a new project.
4. To formulate new projects and familiarization for the process of starting enterprises.
5. To identify persons with entrepreneurial quality and motivate them through a structured training course to became entrepreneur.
6. To identify, select and motivate the potential entrepreneurs through intensive campaign and seminars to take up risky projects.
7. To make the trainees prepared to start their own enterprise after the completion of the training programme.
8. To motivate the first generation entrepreneurs and build competence in them to set up their own unit.
9. To promote the concept of self employment among young generation.
10. To strengthen entrepreneurial ability, interest and to develop entrepreneurial skills.

Flow Chart of Entrepreneurship Development Programmes (EDPs)

The flow chart of EDP process is as follows:

Step-1	Selection of the area
Step-2	Techno-economic survey of selected area
Step-3	Preparation of project feasibility studies for selected types of industries
Step-4	Design of curriculum and revision to meet the specific target group needs.
Step-5	Publicity and advertisement of EDP course
Step-6	Symposium about EDP at training site to aspirants and local businessman
Step-7	Selection of the participants for the EDP
Step-8	EDP training
Step-9	Follow up
Step-10	Post training assistance

NEED FOR ENTREPRENEURSHIP DEVELOPMENT PROGRAMME (EDP):

Entrepreneurship Development Programme is very much essential for the first generation entrepreneurs because proper training and guidance will help them to get success. It is promoted to help alleviate the unemployment problem, to overcome the problem of stagnation and to increase the competitiveness and growth of business and industries. The thrust of entrepreneurship development programme is to motivate people to accept entrepreneurship as a career. Training and successful entrepreneurs becomes ideal for other. Following are the various needs for EDPs:

(i) **Eliminates poverty and unemployment:** One of the important problems of any developing country is unemployment. The problem of poverty is severe and of long-standing duration in India, and is at its most acute in rural areas. In recent years central and state governments have started a number of schemes aimed at reducing rural poverty but they cannot solve the problem completely because of their shortcomings and inadequacies. India needs to return to the syndrome of high growth rate quickly and sustain it for at least eight years to eradicate poverty, illiteracy, unemployment and backwardness. Entrepreneurship development programmes help people towards self employment and provide entrepreneurship as a career. Government of India has introduced various programmes to eliminate the poverty and solve the unemployment problem through National Rural Employment Programme (NREP), Integrated Rural Development Programme (IRDP) etc.

(ii) **Balanced regional development and growth:**One of the objectives of setting up of public enterprises is to promote balanced regional development. It can be possible through the expansion of the employment opportunities in backward regions. The pace of economic development of different States and Regions in the country has not been uniform over the years owing to historic reasons and a number of other factors. Industrialisation plays an important role in correcting the regional imbalances and accelerating the industrial growth. In order to remove regional inequalities and encourage balanced industrial growth of different states/regions, subsidies to industries set up in backward districts. Successful EDPs help in faster industrialisation and reduce the concentration of economic power. It is because the small scale industries can be set up in remote areas with little financial resources which help in achieving balanced regional development.

(iii) **Prevents industrial slums:** The Indian economy, which has over the last six decades passed through various phases of growth, is now all set to enter an altogether different orbit marked by a high rate of expansion, combined with 'inclusive growth.' Slums are an outcome of imbalanced urban growth resulting from over-concentration of economic activities. As per the census 2001, 42.6 million of India's population lives in slums. This constitutes about 15 % of the total urban population of the country. The urban cities are highly congested and leading to industrial slums. Decentralisation of industries is very much require by fot locating the industries. EDPs help in removal of industrial slums as the entrepreneurs are provided with various schemes, incentives, subsidies and infrastructural facilities to set up their own enterprises in all the regions.

(iv) **Harnessing locally available resources:** Human beings have inhabited the earth; they have used the earth's resources and have continuously transformed it. Each landscape is the upshot not only of natural processes but of the actions throughout history of human beings whose responsibility is to organize, protect and manage the environment they share. People use many of the earth's natural resources. All of the products we use have a natural resource base. Minerals, forest products, water, and soil are just a few of the natural resources humans use to produce energy and make things people use. Since abundant resources are available locally, proper use of these resources will help to carve out a healthy base for sound economic and rapid industrialisation. The EDPs can help in harnessing these resources by training and educating the entrepreneurs.

(v) **Defuses social tension:** Self-employment and entrepreneurship become increasingly important in our modern economies. Many people have an ambition to "run their own business", and these days more people than ever are starting up their own businesses. With redundancies on the increase in the recession, many people will take the chance of "working for themselves" and will relish the opportunity of being their own boss and not being answerable to anybody else. It is, of course, admirable, but they could be digging a hole for themselves. Every young person feels frustrated if he does not get employment after completing his education. The talent of the youth must be diverted towords self-employment careers to help the country in defusing social tension and unrest among youth is possible by EDPs.

(vi) **Capital formation:** It is one of the most critical activities in getting a business started. Business creation has moved a lot from the days of Marco Polo and Schumpeter. The biggest hurdle the entrepreneurs face is in raising the initial capital needed for the new venture. Getting equity from family and friends has many advantages over other types of financing. Entrepreneurship development programmes helps an individual to raise capital to start a business or to grow an existing business.

(vii) **Improvement in per capita income:** Entrepreneurs play a vital role in achieving a higher rate of economic growth. Entrepreneurs are able to produce goods at lower cost and supply quality goods at lower price to the community according to their requirements. When the price of the commodities decreases, consumer gets the power to buy more goods for their satisfaction. All this are possible through entrepreneurship development programmes.

(viii) Facilitating overall development: Entrepreneurship development programmes are great and successful in India. If everything goes in proper channel with proper judgment, it will flourish to fill up the sky. Entrepreneurship development programmes inspires innovations, creative ideas and provide new solution to the problems.

WHO NEEDS EDPs?

(i) Business executives: Entrepreneurship Development Programmes (EDPs) explores each facet of business enterprise from an executive's top-level view. EDP is designed for people who are excited about learning from other experienced leaders who come from a variety of industries and cultures. It examines fundamental management topics and focuses on practical business applications. It helps the business executives:

- ✓ Create, identify and evaluate new venture opportunities
- ✓ Interpret customer needs and quantify the value proposition
- ✓ Navigate the venture capital investment process
- ✓ Understand how the process of starting new ventures may vary geographically and culturally.
- ✓ Obtain critical feedback on business plans.
- ✓ Start and build a successful technology-based company
- ✓ Develop the skill to create totally new industries
- ✓ Leverage new science and technologies from corporate or university laboratories
- ✓ Enhance and expand their networks.
- ✓ Learn to drive performance in a fast-changing global environment
- ✓ Discover how to build a better business: gain skills, create networks, inspire others

(ii) Technical and other qualified group: The Entrepreneurship Development Programmes (EDPs) are designed for aspiring entrepreneurs, corporate venturing officers, and persons who would like to develop or strengthen a climate of entrepreneurship in their corporations, and regions.

(iii) Women entrepreneur: Women play a very important role in the economic development of India. They are involved in business activities at all levels, making important contributions to economic growth. Indian women are increasingly active in parts of the economy that were previously considered as male domain. Women are succeeding in business; they are still constrained by the gender values, norms and stereotypes in the environment in which they operate.

(iv) Ex-serviceman: An ex-service man may be retired or released from such service at his or her own request or has been released on medical grounds or released from such service after completing the specific period of engagement. EDP training is also essential for the ex-service man who are again joined in any business undertaking.

(v) Weaker sections of the society: Special attention is being given for the welfare of weaker sections of the society. Weaker sections consist of backward classes, scheduled tribe, scheduled caste, etc. Government is providing various financial assistance to provide training facilities to upgrade themselves as per the requirement of the particular business unit.

PHASES OF ENTREPRENEURSHIP DEVELOPMENT PROGRAMMES (EDPs)

Entrepreneurs can be developed through systematically designed training programmes. There are three phases of entrepreneurship development programmes. They are:

1. Pre-Training Phase
2. Training and Development Phase
3. Post Training Phase (Follow-up)

1. Pre-training phase: It is the first phase of entrepreneurial development. The main objective of pre-training phase is to identify and select the entrepreneurs and includes the following:

(i) Arrangement for inauguration of program

(ii) Creating of infrastructure for training

(iii) Designing the course curriculum or contents.

(iv) Designing tools and techniques for selection of trainees

(v) Exploring and selecting appropriate faculty and resource persons.

(vi) Formation of selection committee

(vii) Insertion of advertisement.

(viii) Publicity campaign for the programme

(ix) Screening and selection of potential entrepreneurs.

2. Training and development phase: It is the second phase of entrepreneurial development. The main objective of training and development phase is to bring desirable change in the behaviour of trainees and includes the following:

(i) Bringing desirable changes in behaviour of trainees

(ii) Developing a goal directed behaviour pattern.

(iii) Developing a high degree of self confidence.

(iv) Developing a strong sense of perseverance and commitment.

(v) Developing motivational skills

(vi) Raising the motivation level of entrepreneurs.

3. Post training phase (Follow up): It is the third and final phase of entrepreneurial development. The main objective of post training phase is to judge how far the objectives have been achieved and includes the following:

(i) Framing future policy

(ii) Monitoring and follow up of drawbacks.

(iii) Review past training approach.

(iv) Review the pre-training work.

(v) Review the process of training programme.

Course Contents and Curriculum of EDPs

Entrepreneurship education is a lifelong learning process, starting as early as elementary school and progressing through all levels of education, including adult education. The standard and their supporting performance indicators are a framework for teachers to use in building appropriate objectives, learning activities, and assessments for their target audience. The course contents may be followed as per the points mentioned below:

- ✓ Introduction to entrepreneurship
- ✓ Motivation training
- ✓ Essentials of management
- ✓ Fundamentals of project feasibility study
- ✓ Organizing the business
- ✓ Plant visit

Using this framework, students will have progressively more challenging educational activities, experiences that will enable them to develop the insight needed to discover and create entrepreneurial opportunities.

Factors of Choice in Assessing the Right Course Curriculum:

Following are the various factors which are taken into consideration while framing the course curriculum of entrepreneurship development programmes. There are three aspects while assessing the potentialities of the entrepreneur. They are:

(i) Pedagogical choices:

- ✓ Case studies
- ✓ Business plans judged by outsiders
- ✓ Mentoring
- ✓ Entrepreneur lectures
- ✓ Projects
- ✓ Conceptual lectures

(ii) Selection of entrepreneurs for EDP:

- ✓ Selection of top 25 to 30 applicants only
- ✓ Applications screened for demographics and socio-cultural data – age, education, work etc.
- ✓ Financial resources and types of business etc.
- ✓ Motivational factors – pull factors
- ✓ Source of encouragement, credibility, endurance, concreteness of plan
- ✓ Psychological test results – traits like risk taking need for achievement.

(iii) Methods of training:

- ✓ Individual instruction
- ✓ Group instruction
- ✓ Lecture method
- ✓ Demonstration method
- ✓ Written instruction method
- ✓ Conference
- ✓ Meeting

EDP – Role, Relevance and Achievement

Entrepreneurship development programmes has been designed with an aim of encouraging self-employment. Regular EDP training encourages and motivates potential and existing entrepreneurs to start a new business or diversify and expand the existing one. It also provides employment opportunities among the unemployed youth. Through regular training, they are well equipped to face the risks and challenges as an entrepreneur. It also ensures availability of skilled manpower at all managerial levels.

Entrepreneurship development programmes enhancing the abilities, potential among entrepreneurs, increase efficiency, minimizes wastages in production process, minimizes accidents on the job, increases speed of work etc.

Role of Government in Organizing Entrepreneurship Development Programme

(I) Prime Minister's Employment Generation Programme (PMEGP): Government of India has introduced a new credit linked subsidy programme called Prime Minister's Employment Generation Programme (PMEGP) by merging the two schemes that were in operation till 31.03.2008 namely Prime Minister's Rojgar Yojana (PMRY) and Rural Employment Generation Programme (REGP) for generation of employment opportunities through establishment of micro enterprises in rural as well as urban areas under the central sector scheme to be administered by the Ministry of Micro, Small and Medium Enterprises (MoMSME). The scheme was launched on 15th August, 2008. Khadi and Village Industries Commission (KVIC), a statutory organisation under the administration of Ministry of MSME is the nodal agency at national level for implementation of the scheme. At state level the scheme is implemented through KVIC, KVIB and District Industries center.

PMEGP = PMRY + REGP

Objectives of PMEGP

(i) To generate employment opportunities in rural as well as urban areas of the country through setting up of new self-employment ventures/projects/micro enterprises.

(ii) To bring together widely dispersed traditional artisans/rural and urban unemployed youth and give them self-employment opportunities to the extent possible, at their place and also to increase their income.

(iii) To provide continuous and sustainable employment to a large segment of traditional and prospective artisans and rural and urban unemployed youth in the country, so as to help arrest migration of rural youth to urban areas.

(iv) To increase the wage earning capacity of artisans and contribute to increase in the growth rate of rural and urban employment.

(II) Educational and Training Institutions involved in Entrepreneurship Development Programmes in India: All Entrepreneurship Development Programmes (EDPs) are conducted by specialized institutions. The question that arises is whether these characteristics are inborn in the entrepreneurs or whether they can be induced and developed. A list of few educational and training institutions which are imparting entrepreneurship development programmes in India is given below:

Educational Institutions:

(i) **The Wadhwani Centre for Entrepreneurial Development (WCED), Indian School of Business (ISB), Hyderabad:** The Wadhwani Centre for Entrepreneurial Development (WCED) at Indian School of Business, Hyderabad launched in the year 2000 by Dr. Romesh Wadhwani, an IT entrepreneur in Silicon Valley, California. The Wadhwani Foundation is a not-for-profit organization aims to create entrepreneurs by encouraging direct contact with successful entrepreneurs in India and abroad.

(ii) **Centre for Innovation Incubation and Entrepreneurship (CIIE), Indian Institute of Management, Ahmedabad:** Centre for Innovation, Incubation and entrepreneurship was set up at the Indian Institute of Management Ahmedabad (IIMA) in collaboration with Government of India and Gujarat Government to promote innovation and entrepreneurship in India. Experience and expertise at IIMA in the areas of management, innovation, technology networks along with entrepreneurship provide the necessary impetus and intellectual basis for this initiative.

(iii) **Entrepreneurship Development Institute of India (EDII), Ahmedabad:** The Entrepreneurship Development Institute of India (EDII) is a non-profit organisation dedicated to promote entrepreneurship that is based in Ahmedabad, Gujarat, India. It was founded in 1983, with the sponsorship of the Industrial Development Bank of India (IDBI), the Industrial Finance Corporation of India (IFCI), the Industrial Credit and Investment Corporation of India (ICICI) and State Bank of India (SBI).

(iv) **Indian Institute of Entrepreneurship(IIE), Guwahati:** It is an autonomous National Institute was established in the year 1993, in Guwahati by the erstwhile Ministry of Industry (now the Ministry of Micro, Small and Medium Enterprises), Government of India set up at Guwahati. The main aim of the institute is to be the leading provider of quality professional development programmers, research and consultancy activities in small and micro enterprises focusing on entrepreneurship development.

(v) **Xavier Institute of Management and Entrepreneurship (XIME):** XIME is the first B-School in Bengaluru to have received the coveted 5 year accreditation by AICTE (All India Council for Technical Education) in the year 2004. It is a leading business school in Bengaluru, Karnataka, which has as its mission to provide value-based management education, not only to those seeking careers in the corporate sector, but also to entrepreneurs, small scale industrialists and those working in public (state) sector industry and services.

(vi) **Xavier Institute of Management and Research (XIMR), Mumbai:** XIMR is a premier management institute offering quality education in the state of Maharashtra. The management institute is ranked among the top B-schools not only in the state of Maharashtra, but also in the country. XIMR, the successor to the erstwhile XIM, is the youngest member of the Jesuit Education Network, the oldest and largest in the world, spread over 5 continents.

(vii) **Entrepreneurship and Management Development Institute (EMDI), Rajasthan:**

Entrepreneurship and Management Development Institute has been set up by the Government of Rajasthan and Government of India in association with National and State Level Financial Institution. EMDI acts as a facilitator and a resource institution to motivate and help prospective and existing entrepreneurs in their entrepreneurial endeavors/efforts through positive training interventions.

(viii) **Xavier Institute of Social Service (XISS), Ranchi:** The Xavier Institute of Social Service (XISS) was established as an extension department of St. Xavier's College, Ranchi in 1955, with the objective of training young men and women in rural development, personnel management and industrial relations. XISS over the last years has treaded the path of glory and success. Today, it has become one of the premium management schools of India in the fields of personnel management, rural development, information management and business management.

(ix) **Society for Innovation and Entrepreneurship (SINE), Indian Institute of Technology, Bombay:** IIT Bombay, known as one of the best sources of technology innovation and research excellence in India, was an early adopter of the concept of business incubation in India. It has hosted Society for Innovation and Entrepreneurship, (SINE) an umbrella for promotion of entrepreneurship at IIT Bombay. It administers a business incubator which provides support for technology based entrepreneurship.

Training Institutions

Apart from the university level educational institute on entrepreneurship development, there are number of other institutes both government and private which actively participate in promoting entrepreneurship education.

(i) **National Institute for Entrepreneurship and Small Business Development (NIESBUD):** The National Institute for Entrepreneurship and Small Business Development (NIESBUD) was established in 1983, by the Ministry of Industry (now Ministry of Small Scale Industries), Govt. of India, as an apex body for coordinating, training and overseeing the activities of various institutions/agencies engaged in entrepreneurship development particularly in the area of small industry and small business.

(ii) **National Institute for Micro, Small and Medium Enterprises (NIMSME) (formerly known as National Institute of Small Industries Extension Training (NISIET):** It is an organisation of the ministry Ministry of Small Scale Industries and Agro and Rural Industries, Government of India. It is a pioneer Institute in enterprise promotion and functions through the six activities of training, consultancy, research, education, information and extension services. NIMSME (National Institute for Micro, Small and Medium Enterprise) was originally set up as National Institute of Small Industry Extension Training (NISIET) and was established in 1960, under the Ministry of Small Scale Industries, located at Hyderabad.

(iii) **Federation of Indian Women Entrepreneurs (FIWE):** It is a National-level organization, founded in 1993, is one of India's premier institutions for women thoroughly devoted towards entrepreneurship development, having a large membership base of 15,000 individual members/professionals and more than 28 member associations spread throughout the country. The objective of the organization is to foster the economic empowerment of women, particularly the SME segment, by helping them to become successful entrepreneurs and become a part of the mainstream industry.

(iv) **Asian Society for Entrepreneurship Education and Development(ASEED):** It is an Institute that has evolved its own identity as an autonomous non-profit body registered under 1860 Societies Act, working in the field of development management. ASEED started its mission in early 90s and since then it has been contributing in the area of livelihood creation and sustainable development. A multi-dimensional novel institution dedicated to making sustainable development a reality in the Asia Pacific region. Presently, ASEED has two main divisions named as ASEED-GRAMEEN and ASEED-IDMAT.

(v) **Entrepreneurship Development Cell:** The Entrepreneurship Development Cell was initiated to develop entrepreneurial culture in the institute and to foster techno-entrepreneurship for generation of wealth and employment. Considering performance and activities in this field entrepreneurship cell has been sponsored by AICTE, Delhi. The ED cell organizes entrepreneurship awareness camps, entrepreneurship development programmes, conduct research works and survey for identifying entrepreneurial opportunities and guide and assist prospective entrepreneurs on various aspects such as preparing project reports, obtaining project approvals, loans and facilities from agencies of support system, information and technologies etc.

(vi) **Indian Investment Centre (IIC):** The Indian Investment Centre is a registered society functioning under the administrative control of the Ministry of Finance, promoting foreign private investment including NRI investment. Indian Investment Centre Chief

Commissioner (Investment and NRIs) is also the ex-officio Chairman of the Organisation. It is a nodal agency for investments by NRIs and Persons of Indian Origin (PIOs).

(vii) **Science and Technology Entrepreneurship Parks (STEP):** The Science and Technology Entrepreneurs Park programme was initiated to provide a re-orientation in the approach to innovation and entrepreneurship involving education, training, research, finance, management and the government. The major objectives of STEP are to forge linkages among academic and Reaserch and Development (R&D) institutions on one hand and the industry on the other hand.

(viii) **Technical Consultancy Organisations (TCOs):** Technical Consultancy Organisations provide a complete set of consultancy services to small and medium enterprises, individual entrepreneurs, government departments and agencies, various state level institutions, commercial banks and other various institutions. Over the years they have diversified with variety of services which includes (i) Project conceptualization and other related services (ii) Credit syndication, (iii) Documentation of project reports, (iv) Restructuring of projects.

(ix) **Commercial Banks:** The commercial banks usually provide short-term finance for setting up industrial estates meant for small scale industries. Commercial banks in India are now holding entrepreneurship development programmes in collaboration with specialized institutions.

(i) State Bank of India launched EDP in 1978

(ii) Punjab National Bank – Merchant banking division

(iii) Indian Bank – Entrepreneurship Development Cell

(iv) Bank of Baroda – Entrepreneurship Banking Service

(v) Bank of India – Entrepreneurial clinic-cum-guidance service

(vi) Canara Bank – Industrial information and guidance service

(vii) Grindlays Bank – Merchant banking service

(viii) Central Bank of India – Cent-Kalyani Yojana for women

Critical Evaluation of EDPs

It is an important task for the organisation to evaluate the post training skills of the entrepreneurs who have undergone training in entrepreneur development programmes.

Problems in the Conduct of EDPs

1. Absence of faculty awareness, opportunities and interest
2. Lack of entrepreneurship education evaluation to measure the effects and impact of learning attitudes and behaviours.
3. Lack of qualified faculty members to teach entrepreneurship conducive environment-financial, political, economical and social
4. Lack of skills and knowledge in interested faculty
5. Lack of teaching staff management and development

Summary

Entrepreneurship development programme (EDP) and small and medium enterprises are the obverse and reverse of the same coin. Small and medium enterprises (SMEs) are the breeding ground for entrepreneurship. EDP means a programme designed to help a person in strengthening his entrepreneurial motive and in acquiring skills and capabilities necessary for playing his entrepreneurial role effectively EDP has been recognized as an effective human resource development tool. Government and various financial institutions are in the forefront in entrepreneurship development. These entire developmental programmes are aimed at training people to take up self-employment or to acquire gainful employment. It is very essential for stimulating innovation and the entrepreneurial spirit to support the development of new ideas through new and latest programmes.

Questions

SHORT ANSWER QUESTIONS

1. What are the various National Level Entrepreneurial Development Institutes in India?
2. What are the different stages of Entrepreneurship Development Programmes?
3. What are the objectives of Entrepreneurship Development Programmes?
4. What are the phases of Entrepreneurship Development Programmes?
5. What are the various steps taken by the government of India in organising Entrepreneurship Development Programmes?
6. What is Entrepreneurship Development Programmes?

LONG ANSWER QUESTIONS

1. Do you consider that Entrepreneurship Development Programmes will help an overall development of an economy? Explain.
2. What are the needs for Entrepreneurship Development Programmes in India?
3. What do you mean by Entrepreneurship Development Programmes? Explain the various phases of Entrepreneurship Development Programmes?
4. What is an EDP (Entrepreneurship Development Programmes)? How should an Entrepreneurship Development Programmes be designed to pave the path for budding entrepreneurs? Exemplify your answer.
5. What is Entrepreneurship Development Programmes? What are the prerequisites and essentials of Entrepreneurship Development Programmes?
6. What is Entrepreneurship Development Programmes? Who are the persons required for Entrepreneurship Development Programmes?

ROLE OF ENTREPRENEUR

"The entrepreneur always searches for change, responds to it, and exploits it as an opportunity."

— Peter F. Drucker

Chapter Overview:

At the end of this chapter, you will be able to understand:

1. Role of entrepreneur in economic growth.
2. Generation of employment opportunities.
3. Personnel management and labour laws.
4. Export market and foreign exchange earnings.
5. Socialisation of entrepreneurship.

Introduction

Entrepreneur is a person who habitually creates and innovates to build something of recognized value around perceived opportunities. It means it is a process of creating value through unique resource combinations to exploit the various opportunities. Entrepreneurs play a central role in the economy by establishing firms, which in turn create markets and organizations. The entrepreneurial process results from the actions of the entrepreneur. It can only occur if the entrepreneur acts to develop an innovation and promote it to customers. The entrepreneurial process is dynamic. Success comes from the contingencies of the entrepreneur, the opportunity, the organisation and resources coming together and supporting each other.

Role of Entrepreneur in Economic Growth

An entrepreneur is an individual who lies at the heart of the entrepreneurial process. Entrepreneurs often act singly but in many instances entrepreneurial teams are important. Different members of the team may take on different roles and share responsibilities. Economic growth is defined in economic terms as the increase in value of goods and services produced by an economy and conventionally measured by the increase in real gross domestic product (GDP). Entrepreneurship is a major contributing factor to the economic well being of a country, both in terms of economic growth and job creation. There are four attributes which develop entrepreneurial abilities such as initiative, decision making, innovations and risk taking. The entrepreneur takes the initiative to bring together the economic resources of land, labour and capital to produce a commodity with the hope that such production will create a profitable venture. An entrepreneur makes the basic business policy decisions through innovation and rick.

Entrepreneur – as an Innovator

An entrepreneur posses many unique characteristics. He/she is known as an innovator, who constantly comes up with new products and services. Innovations start with good ideas ,and good ideas start in the mind of a creative individual. Creativity is one of the characteristics that make us human, but sometimes we think some people are more creative than others. Innovation has been defined as 'the introduction of something new'. It is being rightly said by **Charles Darwin,** 'It's not the strongest of the species that survive, nor the most intelligent, but the one that is most responsive to change." Innovation is the development process which translates an idea into an application. It requires persistence in analytically working out the details of product design or service, to develop marketing, obtain finances and plan operations. If the entrepreneur is going to manufacture a product, the process includes obtaining materials and technical know-how, manufacturing capabilities, staffing, operations to establish an organisation.

Every business has fairly a predictable life cycle. They start with an innovation, search for a repeatable business model, build the infrastructure for a business, then grow by efficiently executing the model i.e., Search-Build-Grow. Entrepreneurs need to search purposefully for the sources of innovation, the change and their symptoms that indicate opportunities for successful innovations. Uncertainty is a classic characteristic of the innovation process. Most innovations have some level of technical, market, resources and organization uncertainty associated with the process. There are six categories of innovations such as architectural innovations, discontinuous innovations, disruptive innovations, radical innovations, sustaining innovations and incremental innovations. As an innovator, an entrepreneur is attempts to introduce new products and new ways of doing things.

Generation of Employment Opportunities

The entrepreneur contributes ideas to the startup enterprise and is concerned with the personal dimensions of intellectual property. The entrepreneur is a party who contracts with venture capitalists and others who help form the startup enterprise. An entrepreneur plays a pivotal role in economic equilibrium. Starting a small business requires a good idea, a sound plan and initial investment capital. The entrepreneur contributes to the financing of the startup enterprise and faces the risk of personal bankruptcy. The entrepreneur contributes effort and management to the startup enterprise which affects his labor market decisions, personal income, and tax liability. In entrepreneurship, the individual is the most important element. Entrepreneurship is not limited to any class, community, gender or religion. There is no age bar. Any person who possesses certain traits and attitudes can become an entrepreneur.

Personnel Management

It can be defined as obtaining, using and maintaining a satisfied workforce. It is concerned with employees at work and with their relationship within the organization. According to **Flippo,** "Personnel Management is the planning, organizing, compensation, integration and maintenance of people for the purpose of contributing to organizational, individual and societal goals." According to Brech, "Personnel management is that part which is primarily concerned with human resource of organization."

Nature of Personnel Management

1. It includes the function of employment, development and compensation.
2. It is concerned with promoting and stimulating competent workforce to make their fullest contribution to the concern.
3. It exists to advise and assist the line managers in personnel matters.

4. It is based on the human orientation and tries to help the workers to develop their potential fully to the concern.
5. It also motivates the employees through its effective incentive plans so that the employees provide fullest cooperation.

FUNCTIONS OF PERSONNEL MANAGEMENT

Following are the four functions of Personnel Management:

1. Manpower Planning
2. Recruitment
3. Selection
4. Training and Development

(I) Manpower Planning: It is an important task in personnel management. It is otherwise known as human resource planning. It consists of putting right number of people, right kind of people at the right place, right time, doing the right things for which they are suited for the achievement of goals of the organization. Understaffing loses the business economies of scale and specialization, orders, customers and profits. Overstaffing is wasteful and expensive, if sustained, and it is costly to eliminate because of modern legislation in respect of redundancy payments, consultation, minimum periods of notice, etc. Manpower Planning is making a decision in advance what is to be done. It is the willpower of course of action to achieve the desired results. Manpower Planning includes coordinating, motivating and controlling of the various activities within your organization.

The productivity of any organization is usually calculated by using the formula i.e., Productivity = Output/Input. In order to calculate the rough index of employee productivity the formula can be modified as: Employee productivity = Total production/Total number of employees.

Steps in Manpower Planning

1. **Analysing the current and future manpower inventory:** It is the forecasting of the future manpower and the status of current manpower. This can be measured through the various techniques such as trend analysis, workload analysis, workforce analysis etc.
2. **Developing employment programmes:** On the basis of the analysis of current and future requirements of the manpower, the employment programme can be framed and developed accordingly.

3. **Designing training programmes:** On the basis of the employment programmes such as recruitment, selection and placement, training programmes have to be developed on the basis of skills, capabilities and knowledge of the workers.

Advantages of Manpower Planning

1. It ensures optimum use of available human resources.
2. It provides smooth working even after expansion of the organization.
3. It opens possibility for workers for future promotions, thus providing incentive.
4. It creates healthy atmosphere of encouragement and motivation in the organization.

(II) Recruitment: Recruitment is a process of identifying the need for a job, defining the requirements of the position and the job holder, advertising the position and choosing the most appropriate person for the job. It is an important part of an organization's human resource planning and their competitive strength. Competent human resources at the right positions in the organisation are a vital resource and can be a core competency or a strategic advantage for it. The objective of the recruitment process is to obtain the number and quality of employees that can be selected in order to help the organization to achieve its goals and objectives. There are two types of recruitments.

Internal Recruitment	External Recruitment
(i) Transfer	(i) Press advertisements
(ii) Promotions	(ii) Employment at factory level
(iii) Re-employment of ex-employees	(iii) Educational institutions
	(iv) Placement agencies
	(v) Employment exchanges
	(vi) Recommendations
	(vii) Labour contractors
	(viii) Unsolicited applicants
	(ix) E-recruitment

(III) Selection: It is the procedure of matching organizational requirements with the skills and qualifications of people. Effective selection can be done only when there is an effective matching. The process of personnel selection involves collecting information about individuals for the purpose of determining suitability for employment in a particular job. This information is collected using one or more selection devices or methods which are categorized below:

1. Preliminary interview (screening)
2. Personality test

3. Biographical data
4. Cognitive abilities tests
5. Physical abilities tests
6. Medical examination
7. Appointment letter

(IV) Training and Development: Training is a crucial for organizational development and success. It is fruitful to both employers and employees of an organization. Training is a problem solving tool and development is a decision making tool. A trained person is developed for trouble shooting and decision making. Development is educating the educated. The various benefits of training are given below:

- **(i) Improves morale of employees:** Proper training helps the employees to get job security and job satisfaction. The more satisfied the employee is and the greater is his morale and more he will contribute to organizational success.
- **(ii) Less supervision:** A well trained employee will need less supervision which will be less wastage of time and efforts.
- **(iii) Chances of promotion:** Employees acquire skills and efficiency during training is more eligible for promotion.
- **(iv) Increased productivity:** Training improves efficiency and productivity of employees.

Methods of Training

There are two methods of training:

(i) On the job training (Coaching, job rotation, understudy, multiple management etc.)

(ii) Off the job training (Sensitivity training, case study, simulation exercises, management grid, incident method, in basket method, conference, lecturers, programmes by academic institutions, transactional analysis, management games etc.)

Out of the various training methods, management games occupy a major place in the effectiveness of various training programmes.

Industrial Relations and Labour Laws

Industrial Relations

Industrial relations has become one of the most delicate and complex problems of modern industrial society. Industrial progress is impossible without cooperation of labours and harmonious relationships. Industrial relations are the relationships between employees and employers within the organizational settings.The field of industrial relations looks at the relationship between management and workers, particularly groups of workers represented by a union. Industrial relations are basically the interactions between employers, employees and the government, and the institutions and associations through which such interactions are mediated. Industrial relations are the major force which influences the social, political and economic development of a country. Managing industrial relations is a challenging task which deals with a highly complex, fast developing, ever-changing, and expanding field.

Objectives of Industrial Relation

1. To safeguard the interest of labour and management by securing the highest level of mutual understanding and goodwill among all sections in the industry.
2. To avoid industrial conflict and develops harmonious relations among the workers and the management for higher productivity and industrial progress.
3. To raise productivity to a higher level and high turnover.
4. To establish and promote the growth of an industrial democracy based on labor partnership in the sharing of profits and of managerial decisions.
5. To minimize industrial disputes like strikes, lockouts and gheraos.

Labour Laws

According to **Mahatma Gandhi,** 'A nation may do without its millionaires and without its capitalists, but a nation can never do without its labour'. In India, a number of labour legislation has been enacted to promote the condition of the labour keeping in view the development of industry and national economy. The law relating to labour and employment in India is primarily known under the broad category of "Industrial Law". The prevailing social and economic conditions have been largely influential in shaping the Indian labour legislation, which regulate various aspects of work such as the number of hours of work, wages, social security and facilities provided. These laws may broadly be classified as follows:

(I) Laws on Consumption:

✓ The Payment of Wages Act, 1936

The main objective is to ensure regular and prompt payment of wages and to prevent the exploitation of a wage earner by prohibiting arbitrary fines and deductions from his wages.

✓ The Minimum Wages Act, 1948

The main objective is to determine the minimum wages in industry and trade where labour organizations are non-existent or ineffective.

✓ The Payment of Bonus Act, 1965

The main objective is to provide statutory obligations for payment of bonus to persons employed in certain establishments on the basis of profits or productivity.

✓ The Equal Remuneration Act, 1976

The main objective is to provide for the payment of equal remuneration to men and women workers and for the prevention of discrimination, on the ground of sex, against women in the matter of employment and for matters connected therewith or incidental thereto.

✓ The Sales Promotion Employees (Conditions of Service) Act, 1976

The main objective is to regulate certain conditions of service of sales promotion employees in certain establishments.

(II) Laws on Working Conditions

✓ The Factories Act, 1948

The main objective is to ensure adequate safety measures and to promote the health and welfare of the workers employed in factories. It also prevents haphazard growth of factories through the provisions related to the approval of plans before the creation of a factory.

✓ The Shops and Establishment Act, 1954

The main objective is to provide statutory obligation and rights to employees and employers in the unorganised sector of employment, i.e., shops and establishments.

✓ The Contract Labour (Regulation and Abolition) Act, 1970

The main objective is to regulate the employment of contract labour in certain establishments and to provide for its abolition in certain circumstances and for maters connected therewith.

✓ The Mines Act, 1952

The main objective is to amend and consolidate the law relating to the regulation of labour and safety in mines.

✓ The Plantation Labour Act, 1951

The main objective is to provide for the welfare of labour and to regulate the conditions of work, in plantations.

✓ The Weekly Holidays Act, 1942

The main objective is to provide for the grant of weekly holidays to persons employed in shops, restaurants and theatres.

(iii) Laws on Industrial Relations

✓ The Industrial Dispute Act, 1947

The main objective is to provide machinery for peaceful resolution of disputes and to promote harmonious relation between employers and workers.

✓ The Trade Union Act, 1926

The main objective is to confer a legal and corporate status on registered trade unions.

✓ The Industrial Employment (Standing Orders) Act, 1946

The main objective is to have uniform standing orders providing for the matters enumerated in the schedule to the Act, that it was not intended that there should be different conditions of service for those who are employed before and those employed after the Standing Orders came into force and finally.

(iv) Laws on Social Security

✓ The Workmen's Compensation Act, 1923

The main objective is to provide compensation for workmen in cases of industrial accidental/occupational diseases in the course of employment resulting in disablement or death. Coverage for persons employed in factories, mines, plantations, the railways and others mentioned in Schedule II of the Act.

✓ The Employees State Insurance Act,1948

The main objective is to provide for health cover, medical care and cash benefits for sickness, maternity, employment injury and pensions to dependents in case of death (or) employment injury.

✓ The Employees Provident Fund Act, 1952

The main objective is to make provisions for the future of the industrial worker after he retires or for his dependents in the case of his early death.

✓ The Payment of Gratuity Act, 1972

The main objective is to maintain social security measures to provide some protection to persons employed in industrial and commercial establishment.

✓ The Maternity Benefits Act, 1961

The main objective is to regulate theemployment of women in certain establishments for certain periods before and after child birth and to provide for maternity benefits and certain other benefits.

✓ The Bonded Labour System (Abolition) Act, 1976

The main objective is to provide for the abolition of bonded labour system with a view to preventing the economic and physical exploitation of the weaker sections of the people and for matters connected therewith or incidental thereto.

✓ The Child Labour(Prohibition and Regulation) Act, 1986

The main objective is to prohibit the engagement of children in certain employments and to regulate the conditions of work or children in certain other employments.

✓ Inter-State Migrant Workmen (Regulation of Employment and Conditions of Service) Act, 1979

The main objective is to regulate the employment of inter-state migrant workmen and to provide for their conditions of service and for matters connected therewith.

✓ The Fatal Accident Act, 1855

The main objective is to provide compensation to families for loss occasioned by the death of a person caused by actionable wrong.

✓ The Beedi and Cigar Workers (Conditions of Employment) Act, 1966

The main objective is to provide for the welfare of the workers in beedi and cigar establishments and to regulate the conditions of their work and for matters connected therewith.

✓ The Employment of Children Act, 1938

The main objective is to regulate the employment of children in certain industrial employments.

(v) Environmental Laws

✓ Water (Prevention and Control of Pollution) Act, 1974

The main objective is to provide for the prevention and control of water pollution and the maintaining or restoring of wholesomeness of water, for the establishment, with a view to carrying out the purposes aforesaid, of Boards for the prevention and control of water pollution, for conferring on and assigning to such Boards powers and functions relating thereto and for matters connected therewith.

✓ Air (Prevention and Control of Pollution) Act, 1981

The main objective is to provide for the prevention, control and abatement of air pollution, for the establishment, with a view to carrying out the aforesaid purposes, of Boards, for conferring on and assigning to such Boards powers and functions relating thereto and for matters connected therewith.

✓ Environment Protection Act, 1986

The main objective is to provide for the protection and improvement of environment and for matters connected there with.

(vi) Miscellaneous Legislations

✓ The Collection of Statistics Act, 1953

The main objective is to facilitate the collection of statistics of certain kinds relating to industries, trade and commerce.

✓ The Apprentices Act, 1961

The main objective is to provide for regulation and control of training of Apprentices and for matters connected therewith.

✓ The Employment Exchange (Compulsory Notification of Vacancies) Act, 1959

The main objective is to provide for the compulsory notification of vacancies to employment exchanges.

Complementing and Supplementing Economic Growth

Entrepreneurs are the driving force behind any economy. They are risk takers, willing to roll the dice with their money or reputation on the line in support of an idea or enterprise. They are willingly assume responsibility for the success or failure of a venture and are answerable for all its facets. Economy is a vehicle where as an entrepreneur is a drier. He steers the bad and good conditions and helps the economy on sustaining its growth in good periods and preventing further slides in its bad conditions. He is essentially a visualizer and an actualiser who can visualize something and when visuallzes it he sees exactly how to make it happen. These are called as complementing and supplementing economic growth.

Social Stability and Balanced Regional Development of Industries

Entrepreneurship can be defined as the process of using private initiative to transform a business concept into a new venture or to grow and diversify an existing venture or enterprise with high growth potential. Entrepreneurs identify an innovation to seize an opportunity, mobilize money and management skills, and take calculated risks to open markets for new products, processes and services. In the activities of the entrepreneur one may recognize processes which are fundamental to social stability and change, and a focus on entrepreneurial activity can thus provide an analytical key to a dynamic study of society. Social entrepreneurship overcomes the gap between the business and the public sector as it is connected to the non profit or the third sector as well as to the concept of the social economy with emphasis on objectives to serve communities and society rather than generating a company's profit. It has been rightly said that everyone is a change maker. Social entrepreneurs are critical in this change – they have a vision, and they have a big impact. Balanced development of different parts of the country, extension of benefits of economic progress to the less developed regions and widespread diffusion of industry are among the major aims of planned development.

Role of Export Promtion and Import Substitution

Entrepreneurs in Export Promotion

Small and medium enterprises are the dynamic and vibrant sector of the Indian economy. From the socio-economic point of view, these industries promoted entrepreneurship and helps in strengthening the democratic base of a country. Every developing country needs comprehensive and integrated programmes of export developments in small scale sector. For exporting any product it requires three things:

- The development of export products
- The promotion of export market
- Setting up of Adequate Institutions

In order to export the products of small and medium enterprises, several institutions are providing export assistance to popularize the Indian products in the global market. Export business is very exacting in demand, risky in operations and rapidly changing in pattern. Following are the various institutions extending their services for the betterment and growth of export of small scale industries products:

1. Development Commissioner: The Small Industries Development Organization has been looking after the promotion and development of small scale industries in India. It has offices in all states and they are called as Small Industries Services Institutes for the development of export promotion.

2. Chief Controller of Imports and Exports: The main function of this office is to issue import license for the purchase of raw materials, machineries, tools and spares parts etc. from abroad which are not available in India. This office is headed by the Chief Controller of Imports and Exports for the execution of the import and export policies formulated by the Ministry.

3. Commodity Boards: For the production and export of various commodities, the Government of India has set up different boards in order to protect the image of different commodities in the market. There are several statutory bodies which are responsible for the production, development and marketing of their respective commodities.

4. Export Credit and Guarantee Corporation: It was set up in the year 1964, with an objective of exports risks and guaranteeing payments to the exporters as well as financing banks. It looks over the functions of export risk Insurance Corporation that had been set up in 1957. There are two types of risks covered under this scheme namely commercial risk and political risks. Commercial risk protects the insolvency of the importer, default in payment and failure to accept the documents entitling the goods where as political risk includes imposition of new import restrictions, cancellation of import license etc.

5. Export Inspection Council: It was set up by the Government of India in 1963, in order to check the quality control and pre-shipment inspection of the variety of products which are exported from India. The council was recognized by the Export (Quality Control and Inspection) Act, 1964. There are five inspection agencies which are located in different parts of the country for the purpose of checking the quality of export products.

6. Export Promotion Council: The Government of India has established Export promotion council for the promotion of Export of specific commodities or group of products. It is registered under the Companies Act as 'No profit seeking organisation'. It is providing various types of assistance in connection with the export policies, publicity and participation in exhibition and trade fares, maintaining effective liaison with industry and trade providing various information for the improvement of exports.

7. Export-Import Bank of India: It was set up in the year 1982, for extending financial assistance for the promotion of India's foreign trade. It is a statutory corporation owned by the Union Government. It coordinates the activities of institutions engaged in financing export and imports. The main activities of the bank are to increase the export of non-traditional manufactured goods, project exports and exports of technology and consultancy services etc.

8. Federation of Indian Exporters Organization: It is an apex organization which is co-ordinating and supplementing the export promotion activities of various organizations and provides integrated assistance to government recognized export houses. The various functions includes assistance towards the settlement of foreign trade disputes, acting as a forum of export promotion, sponsoring study teams and trade delegations abroad and to invite trade delegation from abroad and providing advice to the Central and State Government, local authorities in all matters relating to export trade.

9. Indian Institute of Foreign Trade: It was set up in the year 1963, by the Government of India as an apex training organization for Indian and for South and South-East Asia. It has already been successful in providing training to several executives in government as well as in industry and trade services.

10. Indian Institute of Packaging: It was set up in 1966, as a National Institute jointly by the Ministry of Commerce, Government of India and Indian Packing Industry for the purpose of maintaining the packaging standards of different Indian products. Various activities of the institute include standardization, demonstration, testing and training in the field of packaging.

11. Minerals and Metals Trading Corporation: It was established in the year 1963, in order to takeover the work of State Trading Corporation in connection with minerals and metals. It has also exporting manganese ore, Ferro-manganese, coal, Ferro-silicon and Ferro-chrome. It has set up a subsidiary unit i.e., the Mica Trading Corporation to concentrate entirely on developing the export of mica. The main objectives of MMTC are to enlarge and diversify exports of minerals, ores and concentrate other allied commodities.

12. Small Industries Service Institutes: The export promotion division of the small industries service institute renders various types of services. It is publishing a quarterly news bulletin titled 'Export News' for the benefits of small and medium enterprises. The various functions of the SISI include export consultancy services, training in export marketing, selection of units and end products, export information service including overseas trade regulations, price, renders enquiries, market potentials etc.

13. Star Trading Houses: It was established in the year 2008. The objective of the scheme is to recognize established exporters to supply Export House, Trading House, Star Trading House and Super Star Trading House with a view to building marketing infrastructure and expertise required for export promotions.

14. State Export Trading Corporation: It is a Government of India undertaking was set up in 1956. The main object of the corporation is to enlarge the scope of exports in the country and arrangements of imports at competitive prices. The corporations having four subsidiaries which are looking after the different areas such as Handicrafts and Handloom Export Corporations (1962): For export of handloom and handicrafts goods; Cashew

Corporation of India (1970): To look after the promotion, developments of cashew nuts; Project and Equipment Corporation (1971): To take over the activities of engineering and railway equipments and State chemicals and Pharmaceuticals India Limited (1976): To take over the activities of chemicals.

15. Trade Development Authority: It has been established to provide a package service in the field of export production and marketing of medium and small scale sector. The main objective of the authority is to develop the entrepreneurial export capabilities along with other assistance. It has having three divisions to discharge the above function such as information, research and analysts, merchandising division. It has also established overseas office at New York, Tokyo and Frankfurt etc.

16. Trade Fair Authority of India: It was established in the year 1977, in order to promote, organize and participate in industrial trade and other fairs and exhibitions. It has also set up different showrooms in India and abroad, undertaken promotional publicity through various communication media and developing new export items for the expansion of exports. Trade Fair Authority of India was established by merging three different units i.e., Directorate of Exhibitions and Commercial Publicity, the Indian Council of Trade Fairs and Exhibition, The Trade Fair Organisation.

EXPORT INCENTIVES

In order to promote exports and to obtain foreign exchanges, Government of India has framed several schemes. Few of the important export incentives are explained below:

(i) Duty Drawback (DBK): It is a rebate of duty chargeable on imported or excisable material used in the manufacturing of goods in and is ported. The exporter may claim drawback or refund of excise and customs duties being paid by his suppliers. The final exporter can claim the drawback on material used for the manufacture of export products. In case of re-import of goods the drawback can be claimed. Drawback is not allowed on inputs obtained without payment of customs or excise duty. There are two categories of Duty Drawbacks i.e., (i) Customs paid on imported inputs plus excise duty paid on indigenous imports; and (ii) Duty paid on packing materials.

(ii) 100% Export Oriented Units: These units are exempted from import license. They can import raw materials without payment of any customs duty provided they export their products. Since selling the entire production of units in these free trade zones outside India may not be always possible, such units may sell 25 % of their production in India. If they sell their product in India, duty equal to excise duty if the products were manufactured by another person in India or 50% of custom duty, whichever is higher becomes payable.

(iii) Deemed Export Benefits: Deemed exports means an arrangement in which the goods supplied do not leave the country and the supplier in India receives the payment for the goods. It means the goods supplied need not go out of India to treat them as 'Deemed Export'.

(iv) Duty Entitlement Passbook Scheme (DEPB): It is an export incentive scheme consisted of (a) Post-export DEPB and (b) Pre-export DEPB. The pre-export DEPB scheme was abolished w.e.f., 1.4.2000. Under the post-export DEPB, the exporter is given a duty entitlement Pass Book Scheme at a pre-determined credit on the FOB (Free on Board) value. The DEPB rates are allows import of any items except the items which are otherwise restricted for imports.

(v) Duty Exemption Scheme: It is a scheme applicable to various situations advance license, annual advance license, advance intermediate license, special imprest license etc. Advance license is granted to merchant exporter or manufacturer exporter for the import of inputs required for the manufacture of goods without payment of basic customs duty.

(vi) Exchange Earner Foreign Currency Account (EEFC A/C): It is an account maintained in foreign currency with an Authorised Dealer, i.e., a bank dealing in foreign exchange. A person resident in India is permitted to open and maintain with an authorized dealer in India a Foreign Currency Account known as Exchange Earner's Foreign Currency (EEFC) Account. Currently, EEFC accounts are permitted to be maintained in the form of non-interest bearing current accounts.

(vii) Export Promotion Capital Goods Scheme: It is a policy applicable to the Export Promotion Capital Goods (EPCG) Scheme. The scheme allows import of capital goods for pre production, production and post production at 5% Customs duty subject to an export obligation equivalent to 8 times of duty saved on capital goods imported under EPCG scheme to be fulfilled over a period of 8 years reckoned from the date of issuance of license.

(viii) Focus Market Scheme (FMS): The Scheme has been introduced on 1st April 2006. The objective of the focus market scheme is to offset the high freight cost and other disabilities to select international markets with a view to enhance our export competitiveness to these countries. The main objective of FMS is to offset high freight cost and other externalities to select international markets with a view to enhance our export competitiveness in these countries.

(ix) Focus Product Scheme (FPS): The Scheme has been introduced on 1st April 2006. It provides incentives to export of products which have high employment potential in rural and semi urban areas in order to offset the inherent infrastructure bottlenecks and other associated costs involved in marketing of such products. During the year 2010,112 new products in the focus product scheme and 5% special incentives for products such as hand tools, by-cycle, nuts and bolts, washers, sewing machines, agro products are also adversely affected due to appreciation of Indian rupee since they have virtually no import content.

(x) Marketing Development Assistance (MDA): It was introduced on 30th August, 2000. It was decided that the Small Industries Development Organisation should have a Market Development Assistance (MDA) scheme similar to the one obtaining in the Ministry of Commerce. It is a scheme aimed at encouraging exporters to access and develops overseas markets. The scheme offers funding for participation in International fairs, study tours abroad, trade delegations, publicity, etc. Direct assistance under MDA for small scale units is given for individual sales-cum-study tours, participation in fairs/exhibitions and publicity.

(xi) Served from India Scheme: It is an export promotion schemes, introduced by the Government of India to facilitate exporter of various type of services. The objective of this scheme is to accelerate growth in export of services so as to create a powerful and unique 'Served from India' brand, instantly recognized and respected world over.

(xii) Vishesh Krishi and Gram Udyog Yojana (VKGUY): It is a special Agriculture and village Industry Scheme introduced to promote employment generation in rural and semi urban areas, it has been decided to incentivise the export of Gram Udyog products i.e. village and cottage industry products by awarding a duty free scrip @ 5 per cent of free on board (FOB) value of exports under the expanded Vishesh Krishi Upaj Yojana, which has been renamed as Vishesh Krishi and Gram Udyog Yojana.

Import Substitution

Import substitution and export promotion is an alternative strategy for entrepreneurs. Both are needed for the health of any economy. While balancing the export promotion and import substitution, an economic thought has to be focused while resorting to export promotion which may leads to inflation. Export promotion should be done on the products that we have adequate in stock. We must keep our demand in view before resorting to export promotion. Import substitutions will save our hard earned foreign exchange reserve. Therefore there should be more export and less import to have a stable position in the economy.

FOREX (Foreign Exchange) Earnings, Augmenting and Meeting Local Demands

Foreign Exchange Markets in India works under the central government in India and executes wide powers to control transactions in foreign exchange. The foreign exchange market is controlled by The Foreign Exchange Management Act, 1999. Before this Act was introduced, the foreign exchange market in India was regulated by the Reserve Bank of India through the Exchange Control Department, by the FERA or Foreign Exchange Regulation Act, 1973 (Now in Foreign Exchange Management Act, 1999). Major development in Indian or world economy affects the Indian currency market. Today, India follows the Liberalised Exchange Rate Management System (LERMS), under which it is absolutely essential for corporate executives to understand how the exchange rate moves, and why.

Export Procedures and Documents

Goods are imported in India or exported from India through sea, air or land. Goods can come through post parcel or as baggage with passengers. Procedures naturally vary depending on mode of import or export. Certain documentation takes place while exporting from India. Special documents may be required depending on the type of product or destination. Certain export products may require a quality control inspection certificate from the Export Inspection Agency. Some food and pharmaceutical product may require a health or sanitary certificate for export.

Export Procedures

With the increase in competition in domestic market, stagnant market demand, low profit margins, and ever increasing input cost, it has become inevitable for manufacturers to explore new markets to increase sales and profitability, enhance production capacity Following are the preliminary steps before an export transaction begins:

1. **IEC Number:** Every individual or company exporting or importing goods require an Importer-Exporter Code Number unless specifically exempted by the Directorate General of Foreign Trade (DGFT). The IEC number is normally allotted by the regional licensing authorities.

2. **Membership-cum-registration:** Exporters are advised to become members of local Chambers of Commerce, Productivity Council or any other trade promotion organisation organized by the Ministry of Commerce or Industry.

3. **Inquiry and Offer:** It is a request from a perspective importer containing the details of goods required with details of descriptions. Inquiry may be possible either by direct contact or through various trade journals.

4. **Confirmation of Order:** After fulfilling the requisite terms and conditions, a buyer may place an order with the exporter. The exporter will have to send the confirmation of the order by sending his acceptance.

5. **Export Licence:** An export licence has to be obtained from the competent authority. Items which are banned cannot be exported and in few cases some items are controlled by means of licenses.

6. **Finance:** Sometimes pre-shipment financial assistance are provided for exporting as per the request of the exporter.

7. **Production of Goods:** After the confirmation of the order, the exporter should take necessary steps to produce the product as per the terms and conditions made in the acceptance of the offer. It is the responsibility of the exporter to ensure that the products should be delivered in time.
8. **Shipping Space:** After the confirmation of the export order, the exporter has to book the space for in the ship well in advance. Delay in contact may affect the export of requisite goods in time which may ultimately affect the foreign exchanges.
9. **Packing and Marking:** After the production, goods are properly packed and marked as per the specification provided by the customer. In case of no such specification, the packing and marking are of the standards recommended or specified. The Bureau of Indian Standards (BIS) has prescribed packing standards for certain items.
10. **Quality Control and Pre-shipment Inspection:** Before sending the products, it has to be properly inspected. In case the quality of the product is not satisfactory, it will affect the image of the exporter as well as the economy as a whole.
11. **Excise Clearance:** Before export, clearance has to be taken regarding the excise duty exemption for export products.
12. **Customs Formalities:** Without clearance from the custom authorities, goods cannot be exported to other countries. All documents related to the export business have to be submitted for inspection and clearance from customs department.
13. **Exchange Control Formalities:** As per the Reserve Bank of India notification, an exporter has to submit a declaration regarding the status of payment from s overseas buyer.
14. **Insurance:** Goods exported through ships may face some dangers as perils in the sea. The risk of such perils may be covered under an Insurance policy. General Corporation of India (GIC) is looking after the protection against sea perils through its four subsidiaries such as The New India Assurance Company Ltd., The Oriental Fire and General Insurance Company, The United India and General Insurance Company and The National Insurance Company.
15. **Shipping of goods:** After the completion of all the above formalities, now the exporter has to send the products through different means such as (i) shipping by sea, (ii) shipping by air, (iii) shipping by Post, and (iv) shipping by land.

Export Documents

There are various documents required for the export of products to foreign countries. They are:

Principal export documents	Auxiliary documents	Regulatory documents
Commercial Invoice	Proforma invoice	Gate Pass-I/Gate Pass-II
Packing list	Shipping instructions	AR4/AR4A Form
Bill of Lading	Insurance declaration	Shipping Bills/ Bill of Export
Combined Transport Document	Shipping order	Dock Challan
Certificate of Inspection/ Quality Control.	Mate Receipt	Vehicle Ticket
Insurance Certificate Certificate of Origin	Negotiation of documents	Exchange Control Declaration
Bills of Exchange		Foreign Payment Certificate
Shipment Advice		

Liberalised Exchange Rate Management System (LERMS):

LERMS introduced, from March 1992, as a dual exchange rate system in the place of a single official rate. It consisted of one official rate for select government and private transactions and the market-determined rate for the others. The working of LERMS was smooth from the beginning, contrary to the fears in some quarters that the rupee may undergo a steep depreciation. The government introduced the Liberalised Exchange Rate Management System (LERMS), and thereby ushered in a dual exchange rate regime. This system was abolished in March 1993. Since then, the external value of the Indian rupee has been determined by market forces, with the RBI intervening as and when required to provide the desired degree of stability. Trading is regulated by the Foreign Exchange Dealers Association of India (FEDAI), a self regulatory association of dealers. Since 2001, clearing and settlement functions in the foreign exchange market are largely carried out by the Clearing Corporation of India Limited (CCIL).

Decision Making Process of Entrepreneur

Decision making is the study of identifying and choosing alternatives based on the values and preferences of the decision maker. Decision making is the process of sufficiently reducing uncertainly. Several decisions have to be taken while doing business; some on the spur of the moment, some perhaps after long deliberations. Nevertheless, decisions cannot be avoided. Entrepreneurs need to have the knack to take the correct decisions. Often one cannot consult nor have the time to do so. Independent decision making is required. The essence of management is making decisions. Managers are constantly required to evaluate alternatives and make decisions regarding a wide range of matters. Just as there are different managerial styles, there are different decision making styles. Decision making involves uncertainty and risk, and decision makers have varying degrees of risk aversion. Decision making also involves qualitative and quantitative analyses, and some decision makers prefer one form of analysis over the other. Management guru **Peter F. Drucker**, has identified eight "critically important" decision making practices that successful executives follow. Each:

1. Ask "What needs to be done?"
2. Ask "What is right for the enterprise?"
3. Develop action plans
4. Take responsibility for decisions
5. Take responsibility for communicating
6. Focus on opportunities rather than problems
7. Run productive meetings
8. Think and say "we" rather than "I"

Socialisation of Entrepreneurship

Entrepreneurship is a dynamic and social process, where individuals, alone or in cooperation, identify possibilities, and do something with it by transforming ideas to practical and purposeful activity – in a social, cultural or economic context. Entrepreneurship is the character, practice and skill that combines innovativeness, readiness to take risks, sensing opportunities, heightened initiative, perceiving and mobilising potential resources, concern for standards of excellence, persistence in achieving the goal, positive orientation to problem solving and constant striving for growth and excellence.Likewise, an entrepreneurial spirit implies commitment to certain ends, adherence to self-fulfillment and also the means of realising certain ends.

The businessmen of today are concerned about social responsibilities because of the following factors:

(i) Compelling Forces: Business have been forced to consider as social obligations because of every increasing fear of public interference through the government. Various Acts in India compelling an entrepreneur to control the functioning of the business undertakings. For instance in India many Acts like Competition Act, 2002, Indian Companies Act, 1956, Indian Partnership Act, 1932 and so on are controlling the functioning of the business scenarios.

(ii) Persuasive Force: It is the duty of the business to ensure good working conditions and good standard of living for the workers, to supply with goods of acceptable quality at reasonable price which will motivate them to deal with the business.

(iii) Favourable Conditions: In large business organisation, there is a result of separation of ownership and control. The professional managers are well educated and well acquainted with the expectations of the society. They think in terms of long-range welfare and interests of the enterprise which can be achieved if they are able to satisfy the customers, shareholders, workers, society etc.

Areas of Social Responsibilities

Social responsibilities of management can be studied under two headings: (i) Internal social responsibilities, and (ii) External social responsibilities. Internal social responsibilities are concerned with assuring due process, justice, equity and morality in employee selection, training, promotion, and hiring or they may relate to such things as increasing employee productivity, or improving employee physical environment. It includes the shareholders or owners, workers, etc. External social responsibilities refer to such actions as stimulating minority entrepreneurship, improving the balance of payments, or training and hiring hardcore unemployed. It includes the consumers, suppliers, society, government etc.

Summary

Entrepreneurs and firms approaching a novel opportunity will most probably meet unique challenges. Decisions are important to carry out daily tasks as well as professional tasks. A decisive person is very successful in life. He or she is able to reach set goals. A weak decision can be a disaster. A person who vacillates while taking decisions and is not firm about them cannot be a successful businessman or woman. Making quick decisions, something entrepreneurs are often required to do, does not necessarily mean sacrificing systematic decision making. Managers can prepare themselves for making quick decisions by practicing pre-decision making. This involves keeping in mind a decision making structure, such as a series of probing questions that must be answered, as a contingency plan in the event a quick decision is needed.

Questions

SHORT ANSWER QUESTIONS

1. What do you mean by labour legislations?
2. What are Industrial Relations?
3. What do you mean by the decision making process of entrepreneur?

4. What are the various export documents?
5. What are the various export incentives in India?

LONG ANSWER QUESTIONS

1. Describe the preliminary steps followed in export business?
2. What are the different functions of personnel management? Explain in detail.
3. What are the various steps required while exporting goods to foreign countries?
4. What do you understand by the social responsibility of business? Explain the various types of factors which are linked with the social responsibility of business.

CHAPTER

WOMEN ENTREPRENEURSHIP

"Can man be free if woman be a slave? ... Well ye know...What woman is, for none of Woman Born? Can choose but drain the bitter dregs of woe, whichever from the oppressed to the oppressors flow?"

— P. B. Shelley

Chapter Overview:

At the end of this chapter, you will be able to understand:

1. Women entrepreneurship in India.
2. Traits needed for success of women entrepreneurs.
3. Women entrepreneur: profile and motivation.
4. Problems faced by women entrepreneurs.
5. Top most powerful business women in India.

INTRODUCTION

Entrepreneurship offers tremendous opportunities for women across the world by opening doors to greater self-sufficiency, self-esteem, education, and growth – not only for the women themselves, but also for their families and their employees. Women are changing the face of business ownership internationally; between one-quarter and one-third of the world's businesses are owned by women. As their numbers grow and as their businesses prosper, they will change the way the world does business.

It has become evident that if at all the development process is to be accelerated; the potential contribution by half the population cannot be ignored. In India, entrepreneurship development has been accepted as a strategy for achieving two basic objectives, i.e., promoting the spirit of entrepreneurship among the educated unemployed youths and rapid industrialization. Women have a proportionately greater presence in the informal economy and in micro enterprises; and they are less represented in formal registered SMEs.

WOMEN ENTREPRENEURSHIP – A STATE OF MIND

Women entrepreneurship is one of the key elements of growth in any economy. They initiate, organize and operate in a dynamic business environment. Women continue to play a marginal and peripheral role in the overall national context despite constituting almost half the population with a critical role in production and social processes. Government of India has defined women entrepreneurs as an enterprise owned and controlled by a woman having a minimum financial interest of 51% of the capital and giving at least 51% of employment generated in the enterprise to women. Naina Lal Kidwai, Anita Raddick and Indra Nooyi are well-known and successful woman entrepreneurs. Their successes and the success of other woman entrepreneurs have changed perceptions and brought about paradigm shifts, calling upon the women of the nation to cherish the spirit of entrepreneurship.

WOMEN ENTREPRENEUR: PROFILE AND MOTIVATION

According to **Jawahar Lal Nehru,** *"when a woman moves forward, the family moves, the village moves and the nation moves."*

An entrepreneur is a catalytic agent of change and generates employment opportunities for others. Women have innate flair for entrepreneurship. They are endured with intuition that helps them to make right choices even in a situation where experience and logic fails. They have to devote time to the family and maintain a balance between their family responsibility and business. Women entrepreneurs can play powerful role in confidence building and creating awareness in other women to promote self-reliance. A women entrepreneur is a decision maker who performs various functions to run the enterprise or to settle entrepreneurship. A women entrepreneur can retain her income and use it at her own discretion at household level. Financial independence leads to social empowerment.

There are four motivating factors which influence a woman entrepreneur.

1. **Recognition:** A woman entrepreneur is motivated by recognition in respect of admiration, regard, esteem and celebrity. It is communication tools that reinforces and rewards the most important outcomes entrepreneurs create for the business.
2. **Influence:** It is the capacity or power of a person to be a compelling force on or produce effects on the actions, behavior, opinions, etc., of others.
3. **Internal:** It is the main factor which motivates businesswomen. It is the internal factors which are very much important for the motivation. It includes creativity, respect, and happiness of other people.
4. **Profit:** It is not the true motivation which influences an entrepreneur. Welfare of the employees, payment of tax to the government, is indirectly improving the living conditions of the entrepreneur. Thus the real motivation for Apple to create and sell popular products like ipod, ipone and ipad is probably not money, but the interest.

Categories of Women Entrepreneurs in Practice in India

- **First Category**
  - Established in big cities
  - Having higher level technical and professional qualifications
  - Non-traditional Items
  - Sound financial positions
- **Second Category**
  - Both traditional and non-traditional items
  - Established in cities and towns
  - Having sufficient education
  - Undertaking women services – kindergarten, crèches, beauty parlors, health clinic etc.

- **Third Category**
  - Financially weak
  - Illiterate women
  - Involved in family business such as Agriculture, Horticulture, Animal Husbandry, Dairy, Fisheries, Agro Forestry, Handloom, Powerloom etc.

GROWTH OF WOMEN ENTREPRENEUR AND FUTURE CHALLENGES

There is a saying that, when women bring life into this world, it contributes to the society. When a women entrepreneur creates an enterprise, it generates employment opportunity which ultimately creates wealth. Hence the contributions of women entrepreneurs are a prerequisite for nation building. Growth of women entrepreneurs can be a vehicle of their socio-economic empowerment. Socio-economic empowerment is a situation when women have control over their life and resources. Women are naturally endowed with the emotions of love. This positive energy could be used in managing human resources efficiently. All the women have all the resources to manage an enterprise. Women entrepreneurship can only bring about women empowerment. Women entrepreneurship is therefore, a natural process for women and encouragement of women entrepreneurs are the only solution for women empowerment.

"Stepping stones to success.

Traits Needed for Success of Women Entrepreneurs

Women owned businesses are highly increasing in the economies of almost all countries. The hidden entrepreneurial potentials of women have gradually been changing with the growing sensitivity to the role and economic status in the society. Skill, knowledge and adaptability in business are the main reasons for women to emerge into business ventures. Women entrepreneur is a person who accepts challenging role to meet her personal needs and become economically independent. A strong desire to do something positive is an inbuilt quality of entrepreneurial women, who are capable of contributing values in both family and social life.

1. Women's entrepreneurship as an untapped source of economic growth;
2. Women have a lower participation rate in entrepreneurship than men;
3. Women choose different Industries than men do;
4. Such industries are perceived as being less important to economic growth and development;
5. Mainstream government policies and programmes do not take into account specific needs of women entrepreneurs.

Why do Women Take-up Employment?

- Push Factors
  - Death of bread winner
  - Permanent inadequacy in income of the family
  - Sudden fall in family Income
- Pull Factors
  - Need and perception of Women's Liberation, Equity etc.
  - To gain recognition, importance and social status.
  - To get economic independence
  - To utilize their free time or education
  - Women's desire to evaluate their talent

Functions and Roles Played by Women Entrepreneurs

Women have a proportionately greater presence in the informal economy and in microenterprises; and they are less represented in formal, registered SMEs.

1. Mainstream government policies and programmes do not take into account specific needs of women entrepreneurs.
2. Such industries are perceived as being less important to economic growth and development;
3. Women choose different industries than men do;
4. Women have a lower participation rate in entrepreneurship than men;
5. Women's entrepreneurship is an untapped source of economic growth;

Government Programs and Group Formation and Training for the Development of Women Entrepreneurship

Women owned businesses are highly increasing in the economies of almost all countries. The hidden entrepreneurial potentials of women have gradually been changing with the growing sensitivity to the role and economic status in the society. In order to encourage more and more women enterprises in the MSE sector, several schemes have been formulated by this Ministry and some more are in the process of being finalized, targeted only at the development of women enterprises in India. In India, many B-schools are offering programmes exclusively for women entrepreneurs. Indian Institute of Management, Ahmedabad, Indian Institute of Management, Bangalore, Indian School of Business, Hyderabad, Narsee Monjee Institute of Management Studies, Mumbai is few of them. There are some specialized training centres which provide training exclusive to the women entrepreneurs:

Association of Women Entrepreneurs of Karnataka (AWAKE):

It is the forefront of Entrepreneurship development and has earned National and International accolades for its contribution in this field of Entrepreneurship Development. The vision of the organisation is "To develop self reliance amongst women" and its mission is "Empowering women through Entrepreneurship Development to improve their economic condition". The focus of the association is on empowerment of women and youth from rural and urban areas, irrespective of their academic, social and economic background as AWAKE believes that economic empowerment of women. AWAKE has set up a special purpose vehicle 'ARISE' – a training centre for entrepreneurial excellence.

Women Entrepreneurs Association of Tamil Nadu (WEAT):

It has been established to focus on the economic empowerment of women. It is a prerequisite for overall empowerment and hence a separate association called WEAT has been created and given to the women to manage various EDP, Skill Training, Management Development Programmes etc. It conducts various training to women entrepreneurs on coir, fashion designing, garment making, sewing operator training with stipend and placement, food processing and preservation etc.

1. The Trade Related Entrepreneurship Assistance and Development (TREAD): The Trade Related Entrepreneurship Assistance and Development (TREAD) scheme for women envisages economic empowerment of women through development of their entrepreneurial skills in non-farm activities. The government's grants up to 30 per cent of the total project cost is provided to the Non-Governmental Organizations (NGOs) for promoting entrepreneurship among women. The remaining 70 per cent of the project cost is financed by the lending agency as loan for undertaking activities as envisaged in the project.

2. Mahila Coir Yojana (MCY): Mahila Coir Yojana is a woman-oriented self-employment scheme in the coir industry, which provides self-employment opportunities to the rural women artisans in regions producing coir fibre. The scheme envisages distribution of motorized ratts for spinning coir yarns to women artisans after giving training. Women spinners are trained for two months in spinning coir yarn on motorized ratt at the Coir Board's training centers.

PRODUCTIVE SKILLS AND NATIONAL PERSPECTIVE PLAN FOR WOMEN (NPPW)

Productive Skills

Women's empowerment is inextricably linked to security, economic opportunity, effective governance, and social development. It is a simple fact that no country can prosper if half its citizens are left behind. All reliable development indices show that investments in women are the single most effective poverty alleviation mechanism contributing to a society's prosperity; similarly, lack of investment in women characterizes failed states. There are two productive skills for women. They are speaking and writing. A brief description of the differences between accuracy and fluency activities are given below:

- Accuracy Activities
  - ✓ Accuracy activities are usually part of the study phase.
  - ✓ Accuracy activities are concentrated on producing correct language.
  - ✓ These activities are controlled in order to ensure accurate reproduction of language.

- Fluency Activities
  - ✓ Fluency activities are usually part of the activate phase.
  - ✓ Fluency activities are concentrated on allowing the students to experiment and be creative with language.

In order to bring effectiveness and flow of the communication, fluency has placed a major role.

National Perspective Plan for Women (NPPW)

It is a report of the core group set up by the Department of Women and Child Development, Ministry of Human Resource Development, Government of India in 1988. It was initiated to improve women's and girls access to education, women's security and the institutions that serve women, women's leadership development in both the public and private sectors, women's access to formal and informal justice mechanisms and enforce existing laws and the Constitutional guarantee of equality. It was also initiated to support and expand economic development opportunities for women and increase women's political empowerment and participation.

Developing Women as Entrepreneurs

1. Access to savings and credit.
2. Awareness and education about policy and programmes amongst women.
3. Complete family support.
4. Inculcation of personality traits like determination and strong will power.
5. Motivation of women to become economically independent and take up the challenge of starting their own business.
6. Thorough involvement of all promotional agencies in providing support in the areas of infrastructure, finance, raw materials, marketing etc.
7. Well equipped training and resource centres to meet the needs of women entrepreneurs

Prospects for Women Entrepreneurship/Emerging Opportunities

(A) Direct and Indirect Financial Support

- Different Rate Schemes
- District Industries Centres
- Mahila Udyog Needhi Scheme

- Nationalized banks
- Small Industrial Development Bank of India
- State Finance Corporations
- State Industrial Development Corporation
- State Small Industrial Development Corporations

(B) Yojna Scheme and Programmes

- DWACRA(Development of Women and Children in Rural Areas)
- Jawahar Rozgar Yojna
- Nehru Rozgar Yojna
- TRYSEM (Training of Rural Youth for Self Employment)

(C) Technological Training and Awards

- Entrepreneurship Development Institute of India (EDII)
- National Institute of Small Business Extension Training (NSIBET)
- Stree Shakti Package by SBI
- Trade Related Entrepreneurship Assistance and Development (TREAD)
- Women's University of Mumbai

(D) Federations and Associations

- Associated Country Women of the World (ACWW)
- Association of Women Entrepreneurs of Karnataka (AWEK)
- India Council of Women Entrepreneurs (ICWE)
- National Alliance of Young Entrepreneurs (NAYE)
- Self Employed Women's Association (SEWA)
- World Association of Women Entrepreneurs(WAWE)

Problems Faced by Women Entrepreneurs

1. Subordinate to men
2. Lack of suitable environment for promotion of entrepreneurship,
3. Lack of confidence to start their venture.
4. Dual role to play at workplace and at home place.

5. Not awareness of facilities provided by government
6. Competition with large scale units
7. Problems related to marketing
8. Social pressure and attitude of doubting a women's capability and restricting her freedom of movement.
9. Close scrutiny by financial institutions
10. Inadequate involvement of financial and other agencies to assist women.
11. Other problem includes religious and social taboos, conservative attitude of society, health problems, procurement of loans etc.

Suggestions for Development of Women Entrepreneurs

Following are the few suggestions for the development of women entrepreneurs:

1. Women should be considered as a specific target group for all developments.
2. Government should provide better educational facilities and schemes.
3. More Governmental schemes should be launched to motivate women entrepreneurs to engage in small scale and large-scale business ventures.
4. Adequate training programme has to be conducted for the women entrepreneur.
5. Continuous monitoring and improvement of training programmes is essential for grooming women entrepreneurs.
6. Making provision of marketing and sales assistance from government part.
7. To encourage more passive women entrepreneurs the Women training programme should be organised that taught to recognize psychological needs and express them.
8. The financial institutions should provide more working capital assistance both for small scale venture and large scale ventures.

One woman, seven roles: Indian women are playing seven roles. They are:

1. She's a Home Manager
2. She's a Finance Manager
3. She's a Relationship Manager
4. She's a Well-Being Manager
5. She's the Next-Gen Manager

6. She's a PR Manager
7. She's a Self Manager

Understanding the needs of each role, one can access the importance of women in various fields. As a home manager, she is busy with housekeeping, cooking and supervising domestic helps. She derives satisfaction from being a good wife. As a women who is a home maker, her family ones before her career. As a finance manager, she plays the lead role in all household purchases and balances the budget. She feels happy when her household budgets are managed well. As a relationship manager she develops communication link between family members. She gives top priority to the happiness within the family members as well as around the family. As a well-being manager, she provides right food to all the members in the family and provides right supplements. She sees herself as the healer and is fiercely protective about her family's health. As a next-gen manager, she is responsible for the health of the children, their growth, character and personally. As a Public Relation manager, she represents the family on social/family occasions. Her priority is to have good equation with others so that her family finds acceptance in society. Last but not least, as a self manager, she herself project as an attractive women to the world outside. Her hobbies, pastimes, health and beauty care often take a backseat for the housewife.

The 21 Leading Business Women in India

1. Akhila Srinivasan, Managing Director, Shriram Investments Ltd.
2. Chanda Kocchar, Executive Director, ICICI Bank
3. Ekta Kapoor, Creative Director, Balaji Telefilms
4. Jyoit Naik, President, Lijjat Papad
5. Kiran Mazumdar Shaw, Chairman and Managing Director, Blocon
6. Lalita D Gupte, Joint Managing Director, ICICI Bank
7. Naina Lal Kidwai, Deputy CEO, HSBC
8. Preetha Reddy, Managing Director, Apollo Hospitals
9. Priya Paul, Chairman, Apeejay Park Hotels
10. Rajshree Pathy, Chairman, Rajshree Sugars and Chemicals Ltd.
11. Ranjana Kumar, Chairman, NABARD
12. Ravina Raj Kohli, Media Personality and Ex-President, STAR News
13. Renuka Ramnath, CEO, ICICI Ventures
14. Ritu Kumar, Fashion Designer

15. Ritu Nanda, CEO, Escolife
16. Shahnaz Hussain, CEO, Shahnaz Herbals
17. Sharan Apparao, Proprietor, Apparao Galleries
18. Simone Tata, Chairman, Trent Ltd.
19. Sulajja Firodia Motwani, Joint Managing Director, Kinetic Engineering
20. Tarjani Vakil, Former Chairman and Managing Director, EXIM Bank
21. Zia Mody, Senior Partner, AZB and Partners

Women Non-Government Organisations (NGOs) in India

Few of the women Non-Government Organizations in India are playing their role in the various States:

Sl.	State	Non-Government Organizations
1.	**Bihar**	Mahila Mukti Wahini
		Seeta Gramodyog Vikas Sansthan
2.	**Chandigarh**	Nari Jagriti Manch
3.	**Chhattisgarh**	Saathi Samaj Sevi Sanstha
		Sankalp Munch
4.	**Delhi**	Mahila Haat
		Women's Action for Development
		Women's Feature Service
5.	**Goa**	Anyay Rahid Zindagi
6.	**Gujarat**	Gujarat Stree Kelvani Mandal
		Gujarat Rajya Bal Kalyan Sangh
		Mahila Punarutthan Sangh
		Mahila Samakhya Gujarat
7.	**Haryana**	Gayatri Khadi Avem Gramudyog Samiti
		Karam Bhoomi Sansthan
8.	**Himachal pradesh**	Nav Nirman Kalyan Samiti
9.	**Jammu and kashmir**	Sapna Gramen Udyog
10.	**Karnataka**	HOPE - Anti Addiction Action Group
		Jagajyothi Mahila Seva Samaj
		Jagruthi

11.	**Maharashtra**	AASRA
		Asha Niketan
		Asha Sadan
		Mahila Dakshata Samiti
		Streehitakarini
		Stree Mukti Sanghatana
		Stree Aadhar Kendra
		Shishu-Adhar-'for the Child'
		Nari Samata Manch
		Saathi
12.	**Mizoram**	Meghalaya Women's Alliance
13.	**Nagaland**	Blue Blood Clan
		Bethesda Youth Welfare Centre
		Chizami B.S. Multipurpose Society
		M Rhakho Multipurpose Society
		National Ladies Organisation Movement
14.	**Orissa**	Asha Deep
		Banabasi Seva Sansada
		Banki Anchalika Adivasi Harijan Kalyan Parishad
		Gramya Mahila Vikash Samiti
		Jeevan Rekha Parishad
		PREM-People's Right and Environment Movement
		Sakuntala Gramodyog and Social Action
		Rural Women Development Service Centre
		Sisu 'O' Mahila Kalyan Samiti
		Women Organisation for Rural Development
15.	**Pondicherry**	The Mother's Service Society
16.	**Punjab**	Mahila Samaj Kalyan Samiti
		Nishkam Sewa Ashram
17.	**Rajasthan**	Astha
		Gayatri Shiksha Sadan Sansthan
		Gharib Nawaz Mahila Avam Bal Kalyan Samiti
		Mahila Chetna Manch
		Mahila Hast Shilp Samiti

18.	**Tamil nadu**	Aasha
		Arogyam
		Asha Nivas Social Service Centre
		Jeeva Jyothi
		Stree Seva Mandir
19	**Uttar pradesh**	Laxmi Mahila Evam Bal Kalyan Sanstha
		Mahila Kalyan Evam Janam Niyantran Samiti
		Mahila Samakhya-Uttar Pradesh
		Nari Sewa Samiti
		Suraksha-Anti Dowry Demand Organisation
20.	**West Bengal**	Janasiksha Prochar Kendra
		Karma Kutir
		Sachetna
		Sahamarmi
		SAHAY
		Womens Sahayog
		Swayambhar Nari

Motivational and Empowerment Factors for Women Entrepreneurship

Following are few suggestions for development of women entrepreneurs:

1. Encourage women's participation in decision making.
2. Training in professional competence.
3. Counseling through the aid of committed NGOs.
4. Continuous monitoring.
5. Women entrepreneurship guidance cell system.
6. Better educational facilities and schemes should be extended to women .
7. Consider women as specific target group for all developmental programme.
8. Adequate training programme on management skills to be provided to women community.

Summary

In growing the venture, the entrepreneur transforms the role of acquiring resources into that of creating an intaining structures to management. Growth is a critical to entrepreneurial success. Organisational growth, however, means more than just an increase in size. It involves development and change within the organisation and changes in the way in which the organisation grows as coherent whole, organisational growth itself is best understood in a multi-faceted way. From the above study made. It can be rightly conluded that entrepreneurs are born and made. Empirical evidence shows that women contribute significantly to the running of family businesses mostly in the form of unpaid effort and skills. The value of this effort is underestimated both by the families that take it for granted and in academic studies.

Questions

SHORT ANSWER QUESTIONS

1. Explain the problem of women entrepreneurs.
2. Who is a women entrepreneur?
3. What are the various categories of women entrepreneur?
4. Why do women take-up employment?
5. What are the various functions and roles played by the women entrepreneurs?
6. What are the various women non-governmental organizations found in India?

LONG ANSWER QUESTIONS

1. Discuss the status and role of women entrepreneurs with special reference to India.
2. Explain the various problems of women entrepreneurs? How can these problems be solved?
3. Explain the functions and roles played by women entrepreneurs in India.
4. What are the various training programmes conducted by the Government for the growth of women entrepreneurship in India?
5. How can one motivate and empower the women entrepreneurs? Explain the various suggestions for the development of women entrepreneurs?

◎✧◎✧◎

UNDERSTANDING SMALL SCALE INDUSTRIES

CHAPTER

"If you are clear about what you want, the world responds with clarity."

— Loretta Staples

Chapter Overview:

At the end of this chapter, you will be able to understand:

1. Whether setting up a business is right for you?
2. Estimate whether your business will be feasible.
3. Decide how your business will operate.
4. Know where to go for assistance.
5. Know the basics of developing a business plan.
6. Know the steps to take to start your business.

INTRODUCTION

Small scale industries have developed as an integral part of the total industrial structure of a country like India. The progress of these sectors is supported by the Industrial Policy Resolutions. The Industrial Policy Resolution, 1977, has highlighted the importance of small scale industries. Growth of small scale industries is not only an economic objective but also provides certain socio economic goals of economic planning. It is helping the country by creating employment opportunities, introducing new products, diversifying the existing production line etc. It also helps the nation by promoting entrepreneurial base in rural and urban areas.

Registration of SSI Units

The main objectives of registration of a small scale industry are as follows:

1. To enumerate and maintain a roll of small industries to which the package of incentives and support are targeted.
2. To provide a certificate enabling the units to avail statutory benefits mainly in terms of protection.
3. To serve the purpose of collection of statistics.
4. To create nodal centres at the centre, state and district levels to promote small scale industry.

Registration of SSI Units (At a Glance)

1. District Industries Centre is the primary registering centre.
2. Registration is voluntary and not compulsory.
3. Two types of registration i.e. (i) Provisional (before commencement of production), (ii) Permanent (after commencement of production)
4. The Provisional Registered Certificate (RPC) is valid for 5 years and the Permanent Registered Certificate (PRC) is given in perpetuity.

Steps to set up an Industry: at a glance

Step-1: Entry Level

- Project identification
- Forms of business
- Business category
- Registration/Industrial License

Step-2: Implementation Stage

- Allotment of land
- Permission for land use
- NOC and consent under Water and Air Pollution Control Act.
- Approval for construction activity and building plan
- Sanction of water and power
- Factory and Boiler Certificate, Boiler Inspection Certificate
- Registration under State VAT Act.
- Registration under Excise

Step-3: Operational Stage

- Production
- ISI Certificate (Now as BIS)
- Quality Marking Certificate
- Code number for Exports and Imports

Small Scale Industries: Registration

Entrepreneurs will have to comply with some formalities before, during establishment and also during operational stage. Some of the application forms required to be filled up by new entrepreneurs is listed below. The requirement of forms is classified into planning, implementation and operational stage.

(A) At Planning Stage

Approcals Clearances ReauiredDepartment AUthority Responsible for Approval/Clearance

Sl.	Provisional Registration Number	District Industries Centres
1.	Application for shed or plot	State Industries Development Corporation
2.	No Objection Certificate from local authorities	Local Self-Government agencies such as Panchayat, Nagar Palika, Municipal Corporation.
3.	No Objection Certificate from Health Department	District Health Officer
4.	No Objection Certificate from Electricity Department	Electricity Department
5.	Loan Application form for Term Loan	State Finance Corporation/Nationalised Bank/ National Small Industries Corporation.
6.	Subsidy Registration Form	District Industries Centre

7.	Application for Building Plan and Estimates	Approval of Architect/Contractor
8.	Application for Bank Accounts/ Hypothecation/ Cash Credits/Working Capital Loan	Nationalised Banks
9.	Application for Air and Water Pollution – No Objection Certificate (NOC)	State Pollution Control Authorities
10.	Application for the approval of production programme for certain restricted items	District Industries Centre, Central Ministry and Small Industry Service Institutes
11.	Registration of Partnership Deed	Registrar of firms
12.	Application for Ancillary Units	Parent Companies
13.	Registration of firm	Registrar of firms
14.	Application for the Broilers and Plant lay-out of the unit	Inspector of Factories
15.	Application for the production of petroleum based products.	Director of Industries, Ministry of Petroleum
16.	Application for Excise Registration Number	Excise Department
17.	Application for Latex in rubber based products	Rubber Board
18.	No Objection Certificate from Forest Department for wood based products	State Conservator of Forests
19.	Application for essential commodity items as raw-materials	District Collector/District Civil Supply Department
20.	Application for imported raw-materials	District Industries Centre/Export-Import Boards
21.	Application for Imports.	District Industries Centre/Export-Import Boards
22.	Application for raw materials quota	District Industries Centre/Export-Import Boards

(B) At Implementation Stage

Approvals/Clearances Required	Department.Authority Responsible for Apprival/ Clearance
Application for power connection	Local Electricity Department
Application for Water	Local Authorities
Application for 'C' Form-Sales-Tax	Sales Tax Department
Application for State Sales Tax Registration	Sales Tax Department
Application for Central Sales Registration	Sales Tax Department
Application for Exemption from Sales-Tax	Sales Tax Department, District Industries Centre
Application for Exemption from Octroi Duty	Local Authorities, District Industries Centres
Centre Application for storing raw-materials	Director for Explosive

(C) At Operational Stage

Application for permanent Registration Number	District Industries Centre/Directorate of Industries
Application for Subsidy Claim	District Industries Centre
Application for Power Subsidy	Local Self Government Agencies
Application for FPO License	Food Preservation Ordinance, Food Controller
Application for Registration in case of more than 20 employees without power use/more than 10 in power oriented units.	Labour Welfare Board/Employment Exchange, Provident Fund.
Application for product marketing to the Central Government Department.	Directorate of Industries or Director General of Supply.

Clearance and Permits

Sl. Approvals/Clearances Required	Department /Authority responsible for Approvals/ Clearances
1. Incorporation of Company	Registrar of Companies
2. Registration/Industrial license/Industrial Entrepreneur Memorandum (IEM)	District Industries Centres for SSI/Secretariat for Industrial Assistance (Government of India) for large and medium industries.
3. Allotment of land	IDCO
4. Permission for land use (in case industry is located outside an industrial area)	IDCO Department of Town and Country Planning, Department of Town and Country Planning, Local authority/District Collector.
5. NOC and consent under Water and Air Pollution Control Acts	Orissa State Pollution Control Board (OSPCB).
6. Forest and Environment Clearance	Ministry of Forest and Environment, Government of India.
7. Approval of construction activity and building plan	Developmental Authority.
8. Sanction of Electricity	Distribution Companies: CESCO, NESCO SOUTHCO, WESCO, Transmission Company-GRIDCO.
9. Water Supply	Water Resources Department. .
10. Factory and Boiler clearance	Chief Inspector of Factories and Boilers.
11. Boiler Inspection Certificate	Chief Inspector of Boilers.
12. Finance	OSFC/Commercial Banks like IDBI, ICICI, SBI etc.
13. Orissa VAT Act, and Central and State Excise Act	i. Commercial Tax Department. ii. Central and State Excise Department.

14. Permanent Account Number (PAN)	Income Tax Commissioner.
15. Extraction of Minerals	State Director of Mines and Geology.
16. ISI Certificate	Regional Office of the Bureau of Indian Standards (BIS)
17. Weights and Measures	Inspector of Weights and Measures
18. Code Number for Export and Import	Regional Office of Director General of Foreign Trade.

How to Start a Small Scale Industry

The small scale industries constitutes the most vital and dynamic segment of India economy. It has emerged into a vibrant sector and expected to play a crucial role in the industrial development of the country. For the growth of the economy, small scale industries have a big role to play. It is providing considerable employment of the unskilled and skilled labourers in the country. The owner of a small scale industry visualizes the business, combines various factors of production and puts them into a going concern. In order to launch a new venture following procedure is usually followed:

1. **Decisions to be self employed:** Everybody wants to earn sufficient amount of money in order to maintain a peaceful life. There are three types of occupations which are available for every human being i.e., profession, employment and business. Certain restrictions are imposed in the profession as it requires appropriate qualifications which are prescribed by the law. Without desired qualification one cannot practice any profession. Before taking any decision to be self employed one has to ask himself few questions such as: Am I ready to become a businessman? Can I take prompt decisions independently? Do I possess self confidence and patience? Am I innovative? Decisions about self employement should be taken after satisfying the above questions.
2. **Product identification:** After taking decisions about self employement, the owner has to conduct various market survey and thorough investigations about the product. The study should be made in relation to the quality and price of other products, the level of competition in the market, demand and supply position of other products etc. Perfect study of the market will help a businessman to select the best product which can be viable in its existence.
3. **Preparation of preliminary project report:** The owner of a small scale unit will have to prepare a preliminary project report with the help of technical experts in that field. It consists of various information about the market survey, project capacity, selection of the site, plant layout, operating planning etc. It provides necessary statistical forecasting and planning to a project.

4. **Apply for registration:** Registration of a small scale industry is not compulsory but a registered unit avails several facilities from the government at a concessional rate. The registration is usually done by the Directorate of Supplies and Disposals" of the respective states. It is done free of charges. The owner of the small scale unit has to apply for registration in a prescribed form to the District Industries Officer or Assistant Director of industries. Provisional certificate is issued for one year ad the owner has to apply for permanent registration with the industry goes into production.
5. **Deciding the form of ownership:** Ownership is the right of an individual or a group of individuals to enjoy the right of possessing business assets, managing and controlling the business in the manner thinks best and ultimately bearing the gain or loss arising out of such possession or use. The selection of the suitable form of business ownership is considered at two levels i.e., while starting a new business and at a later stage when business grows and expands. The ownership can be of various types such as Sole proprietorship, Partnership, Joint Hindu Family, Cooperative and Joint Stock Company.
6. **Fixing the banks:** The books receives the deposits of money or of credit and seek profit through the extension and sale of their own credit. The bonus provids advances and loans to the owners of the small units at a low rate of interest.
7. **Power connection and water supply:** For power connection one has to contact the State Electricity Boards of the respective states on priority basis. In case of irregularity in its supply necessary alternative arrangements should be made by maintaining a standby power generator system. For water connection concerned Municipal Corporation should be contacted. Concessions are also granted to those units which are utilizing the water from irrigation projects for industrial purpose.
8. **Procurement of raw materials:** When the supply of raw materials is not locally available, one has to contact the State Directorate of Industries who ultimately recommends the same to the Joint Chief Controller of Imports and Exports. Necessary quotations are invited from the intending supplier when the government facilities are not available to a particular unit. Raw material assistance are also available from STC (State Trading Corporation), MMTC (Minerals and Metals Trading Corporation), CAPCO (Chemicals and Pharmaceuticals Corporation of India Ltd.) etc. If the materials are imported, one has to obtain an import license by applying to the Regional Licensing authorities after payment of certain prescribed fees.
9. **Location of the enterprise:** The location of a small scale industry is an important factor because unsuitable location may result in waste of efforts. The industries cannot be set up anywhere or everywhere. Majority of the small scale industries are failure

due to wrong choice of the location. Wrong selection of the location is greatly affects the production and distribution of the desired product. Selection of the site should be based on the technical, commercial and financial aspects of it.

10. **Acquiring industrial plot/shed:** For the growth of small scale industries, central as well as state governments are providing plot of land or shed depending upon the circumstances and nature of the business. The State Directorate of Industries and State Industries Development Corporations are constructing industrial sheds and developed industrial plots for allotment to small scale units. Besides the above facilities, they are also providing other benefits such as supply of electricity, establishment of banks and post office, canteen for the employees at a subsidized rate etc., for newly established business.

11. **Inviting quotations for machineries and equipment:** Before purchase of machineries and equipment for the small scale industries, the owner has to invite quotations from different suppliers. Selection of the suppliers depends upon price, quality, time of delivery, quantity of discount, terms of payment, mode of delivery and goodwill of the supplying firm. One can consult the publication of Building Machines Build India which is providing industry wise address of all machineries builders in India. Machinery are also available from NSIC (National Small Industries Corporation), SSIC (State Small Industries Corporation) on an instalment basis.

12. **Follow up sanction of loans:** There are several formalities which are to be complied with for availing the required loan amounts. An application for loan is submitted to the District Industries Officer or Assistant Director of industries in a prescribed manner. In case of industrial cooperative societies, the application form should be submitted to the Assistant Registrar, cooperative Societies. Application form should contain (i) approval schemes of loan needed (ii) details of immovable properties as a security of loan (III) an affidavit to the effect of capital investment in machinery and equipment (iv) an affidavit that property is owned by the applicant (v) quotations of at least three standard supporters in case loan is required to purchase the above.

13. **Place order for machineries and equipment:** Before placing necessary orders for the purchase of machineries and equipment one has to be certain about the reliability of the supplier. Selection is based on the following factors (i) meeting specifications and quality standards (ii) arranging the plant in time to meet production schedules (iii) sufficient amount of money to meet manufacturing requirements without causing excessive carrying expenses. Care should be taken to see that services provided by the supplier in connection with the post sale period is satisfactory.

14. **Apply for income and sales tax numbers:** The owner of a small unit has to apply for income tax and sales tax registration numbers which will be the reference numbers for submitting income tax and sales tax returns.

15. **Preparation of detailed project report:** After going through the formalities the owner has to prepare a detailed project report. It should be providing necessary information which is required for the purpose of sanction of financial assistance, while appraising of the project by the financial institutions. There are different heads under which all the information is explained. They are (i) general information (ii) project description (iii) market potential (iv) capital costs and source of finance (v) requirement of working capital (vi) economic and social variables etc. It is the final decision about the product to be manufactured and the place of industry.

16. **Appointment of personnel:** It is said that employees are the pillars of the business. For smooth functioning of the business, it is required to maintain happy relationship with the employees. This happens when they get fair wages, good working condition, stability of employment, prospects of promotion etc.

17. **Installation of machineries:** It is a technique which helps to locate different machineries in right place. The main purpose of installation of machineries in the appropriate place is to minimize the cost, maximize the use of space, maximize the output and also the productivity. It is nothing but scientific use of work area.

18. **Arrangement of finance:** Loans are available in the form of (i) assistance to technical person (ii) state participation in equity capital (iii) credit guarantee schemes and (iv) machineries on hire purchase loans, available from (a) National Small Industries Corporation (b) State small Industries Corporation (c) Small Industries Development Bank of India (d) Commercial Banks (e) Co-operative Banks (f) Regional Rural Banks etc.

19. **Conduct trial production:** After availing necessary assistance, steps should be taken to produce the product on a trial basis. The predetermined standards should be compared with the present quality, size, cost etc. The product should be inspected by the concerned officer and if it satisfies the management, indication about the final production may be given to the production department.

20. **Plan commercial production:** If the result of trial production gives positive indication then one should go for commercial production. It is nothing but a process of planning the production in advance, setting the exact route of each item, fixation of starting and finishing dates for each item etc. It is based on the principle, *"first plan your work and then work your plan".*

21. **Maintenance and management of finished stock:** Adequate attention should be given towards the maintenance and management of finished goods of a small scale industry. An effective method of stock taking helps a firm to have a control in its receipt, custody and issue of finished goods as per the demand of the product. Sufficient precautions and inspection should be observed for this purpose. There are two methods of stock taking which are usually followed in every organisation: (i) annual physical verification and (ii) perpetual inventory control. For a small firm annual physical verification method is usually appropriate.

22. **Marketing facilities:** Marketing of small industry products are becoming complex and complicated affairs. The problem of today's business is not that of production but that of sales. Due to immense competition at every step, marketing is greatly affecting the profitability of the unit. Central and State Governments are providing various marketing assistance to small scale units. Any entrepreneur can participate in this scheme either directly or through NSIC (National Small Industries Corporation). For availing marketing assistance from NSIC one has to get himself registered with NSIC.

23. **Repayment of loans:** Money borrowed should be judiciously spent so that the entrepreneur can get a steady return in order to repay the loan amount in time. It is very much essential that the loan amount should be paid in due time for betterment of the concerned unit. If any unit requires additional finance for expansion or diversification of the existing unit, then it will be available without much delay if the previous loan amount was paid in time.

24. **Avoiding sickness:** Units become sick only when it fails to generate internal surplus funds to honour its obligation towards its suppliers and creditors in time. No business unit become sick over night, rather it becomes sick over a period of time. An industrial unit becomes sick when the working conditions are so unsatisfactory that it threatens the viability of the undertaking. As far as possible practicable sickness should be avoided.

25. **Modernisation and upgradation of technology:** Modernisation can be done either by improving technology or mechanisation of production process. Government has appointed various committees to study the impact of recession on small scale units. Small Industries Development Organisation (SIDO) is also providing assistance to the small units to upgrade their technology and modernize the unit as per the suitability of the market.

26. **Exploring export promotion opportunities:** There are vast export opportunities available for small scale industries products. Central and State governments are also providing various export assistance in order to popularise the products in the global market. Exporters can obtain both pre-shipment and post-shipment advances from commercial banks at low rate of interest.

SICKNESS IN SSI: INTRODUCTION, DEFINITIONS, CAUSES, SIGNALS AND SYMPTOMS

The small scale industries play a vital role in the development of underdeveloped and developing countries. In advanced countries the normalcy of the sick unit is restored through restructuring within a short span or the unit is closed down. Developing countries cannot afford large scale unemployment of labour or of valuable productive assets on account of sickness and resultant closure of the unit. In view of this, only alternative available in developing countries is to make sincere attempts of rehabilitating the sick units. It is of utmost importance to take measures to ensure that sickness is arrested at the incipient stage itself.

Definition of 'Sick Units'

Definition of a sick unit is given by Sick Industrial Companies Act, 1985. According to the Act. "The sick industrial company is a company which has at the end of any financial year accumulated losses equal to or excluding its entire net worth and has also suffered cash losses in that financial year and in the financial year immediately preceding it." Industrial sickness especially in small-scale Industry has been always a demerit for the Indian economy, because more and more industries like – cotton, jute, sugar, and textile, small steel and engineering industries are being affected by this problem.

SICKNESS: PREVENTIVE MEASURES, CONSEQUENCES AND REMEDIAL MEASURES

Sickness and its Magnitude

An unit becomes sick when it fails to generate internal surplus funds to honour its obligations towards its suppliers and creditors in time. Sickness is a process and no unit becomes sick over night; rather it becomes sick over a period of time. This stage is called incipient stage.

There are Three Parts of the Sickness. They are:

Part-I: Detection

Part-II: Rehabilitation

Part-III: Nursing

PART-I: DETECTION

Industrial units may be regarded as sick when (i) it faces financial embarrassment and (ii) its viability is seriously threatened by adverse factors.

A: Internal Causes

(I) **Planning:** (a) Technical feasibility-Inadequate technical know-how, locational disadvantage, outdated production process; (b) Economic viability-high cost of inputs, break-even point too high, over estimation of demand, under-estimation of financial requirements, unduly large investment in fixed assets.

(II) **Implementation:** Delays in getting licenses or sanctions, inadequate mobilization of finance etc.

(III) **Production:** It consists of production management, labour management, marketing management, financial management, administrative management etc.

(a) **Production management:** Inappropriate production mix, high cost maintenance and replacement, poor quality control, poor capacity utilization etc.

(b) **Labour management:** Excessive manpower, poor labour productivity, lack of trained skilled labour or technically competent personnel, poor labour relations etc.

(c) **Marketing management:** Unscrupulous sales or purchase practices, lack of proper knowledge of the market, a limited number of customers or single or a limited number of products, poor sales realization, defective pricing policy, booking of large orders of fixed prices in an inflationary market, weak market organisations, lack of market feedback and market research, lack of knowledge of marketing techniques etc.

(d) **Financial management:** Poor financial planning, inadequate working capital, faulty costing, liberal dividend policy, general financial indiscipline, application of funds for unauthorized purposes, deficiency of funds, absence of cost consciousness, lack of effective collection machinery etc.

(e) **Administrative management:** Lack of feedback to management, lack of timely diversification, over centralization, lack of proper management information system, lack of controls, excessive expenditure on research and development, incompetent and dishonest management etc.

B: External causes

(a) Reduced lending by financial institutions.

(b) Non-availability of adequate finance at the right time.

(c) Changes in government policies with respect to excise duties, custom/export duties etc.

(d) Development of new technology.

(e) Sudden declining order from the government.

(f) Natural calamities.

(g) Adverse international developments.

(h) Chronic power shortage, transport bottlenecks etc.

PART-II: REHABILITATION (Rehabilitation of Sick Units)

The rehabilitation of sickness can be classified into three categories. They are:

(i) Sickness at birth – due to in-feasibility of the project;

(ii) Induced sickness due to incompetence of the management;

(iii) Genuine sickness – beyond the control of the promoter, inspite of the sincere efforts.

Revival of sick unit is just like fighting a battle and no army can win the battle without high courage and morale of the promoter. Several committees have been formed in order to solve the above problems of small scale sector. They are District Level Revival Committee (DLRC), District Coordination Committee (DCC), State Level Revival Committee (SLRC) and State Level Inter Institutional Committee (SLIIC) etc. But it is the high time for SFCs, banks and other government agencies for effective coordination to provide matching term loan and working capital and other concessions strictly adhering to the RBI guidelines. For rehabilitation of sick small scale units, a three tier mechanism has already been evolved by Government by forming DLC at DIC level, Sub-committee of SLRC at Directorate level and SLIIC at Government level.

PART-III: NURSING

A systematic approach in necessary to convert a sick unit into a healthy one:

(a) Analysing past performance: With business running on such a highly competitive level, it is no wonder that the process of analyzing the business results is high detrimental. These are designed to provide an economical, efficient and effective means for businesses to analyse a range of performance issues. A SWOT analysis has to be made to know the past operations for effective monitoring system and feedback.

(b) Identification of viable level of operations: The operating unit should identify the feasible levels of operations to generate the internal surplus.

(c) Determination of funds required to continue the unit at the new production level: Most importantly, the financial position of the unit, in terms of requirements of funds needed to operate at the proposed level of production, should be analyzed.

(d) Identifying key areas which contribute to the weakness of the unit and developing action plan for each weak spot.

(e) Regular periodical review to assess the progress of the unit.

FUNDAMENTALS OF MANAGEMENT FOR ENTREPRENEURS

It has become evident that, principles of management also need to receive instructions and exposure to more current issues and topics in addition to the traditional management principles. There are management experts who have given their opinion on the topic of management.

Management Experts	Abbreviation	Managerial Functions Specified
Henry Fayol	POC^3	(i) Planning and forecasting (ii) Organising (iii) Commanding (iv) Co-ordinating (v) Controlling.
Harold Koontz and	POSDC	(i) Planning (ii) Organising (iii) Staffing (iv) Directing Cyril O'Donnellv and leadership (v) Controlling.
Luther Gullick	PODSCORB	(i) Planning (ii) Organising (iii) Directing (iv) Staffing (v) Co-ordinating (vi) Reporting (vii) Budgeting.
George R. Terry	POAC	(i) Planning (ii) Organising (iii) Actuating (iv) Controlling.
Lyndall Urwick	POC^3FI	(i) Planning (ii) Organising (iii) Commanding (iv) Co-ordinating (v) Communicating (vi) Forecasting (vii) Investigating.
Ernest Dale	POSDCIR	(i) Planning (ii) Organising (iii) Staffing (iv) Direction (v) Control, (vi) Innovation (vii) Representation

BOOKKEEPING FOR SMALL AND MEDIUM ENTERPRISES:

Bookkeeping is an art and science of recording business transactions in the appropriate books of accounts in accordance with the principles of accountancy for the purpose of ascertaining the profit or loss and the financial position of the business. On the other hand, it is a system of recording all monetary dealings whether linked with goods or services in a systematic manner.

Subsidiary Books

In a small organisation, the owner himself maintains the various records of the business, but in a large organisation, it is quite difficult for recording various transactions in a limited number of books. Several books are maintained to record the business transactions. They are:

Sl.	Name	Particulars
1.	Cash Book	Records all cash transactions.
2.	Purchase Day Book	Records credit purchase of goods only.
3.	Sales Day Book	Records credit sales of goods only.
4.	Purchase Return Book	Records return of goods to suppliers.
5.	Sales Return Book	Records return of goods from customers.
6.	Bills Receivable Book	Records entries regarding bills receivables.
7.	Bills Payable Book	Records entries regarding bills payables.

Reasons for Maintaining Subsidiary Books:

There are various reasons which satisfy why subsidiary books are maintained. They are:

1. **Savings in Time:** When transactions are directly recorded in the subsidiary books it saves time as compared to the transactions recorded in journal and then posting into the ledger.
2. **Accurate:** When transactions are directly recorded in the subsidiary books it not only saves labour but also ensures accurate postings into the ledgers.
3. **Statistical Record:** Transactions recorded directly into the subsidiary books provide various statistical information to the management. It provides a quick glance on the efficiency of a particular department.

Preparation of Final Accounts

Financial information of a firm can be known through the financial statements. The main objective of the financial statement is to provide reliable information about the economic resources, change in net resources, future earning potential and to disclose other related information of the business enterprise. Financial statement builds up linkage between the firm and the users of accounting information. There are three parts:

(1)Trading Account, (2) Profit and Loss Account and (3) Balance Sheet.

Trading Account

It is prepared for a particular period. It provides the trading result of the business i.e. gross profit or gross loss. Gross profit has a direct linkage with cost of goods sold. An increase in the cost of goods sold decreases gross profit and a decrease in the cost of goods sold increases gross profit. Cost of goods sold can be calculated by the following formula.

Cost of Goods Sold = Opening stock + purchase (less purchase return) + direct expenses – closing stock

Gross Profit = Sales – cost of goods sold;

Profit and Loss Account:

It is prepared for a particular period. It provides net profit or net loss of the business. It is debited with the gross loss(if any) from the trading account with various indirect expenses such as administrative, selling, distribution etc., and credited with gross profit (if any) from the trading account, operating or indirect incomes etc. The difference between the two sides represents either net profit or net loss. When the credit side is more than the debit side it is net profit and when debit side is more than the credit side it is net loss.

Net Profit = Gross Profit + Indirect Incomes – Indirect Expenses

Balance Sheet

Balance sheet is not an account but is a statement prepared from the balances of accounts. It is a sophisticated report which serves as a valuable information to the owners and outsiders who are linked with business. Assets are the properties of the business. They are tangible objects or intangible rights owned by an enterprise. These are valuable resources owned by the business which will carry future benefits. Liabilities are the claim by outsiders on the assets of a business. In other words, it is a debt owed to someone. It follows the basic accounting equation: **Assets = Liabilities + Capital**

Working Capital: Meaning, Definitions, Factors Affecting Working Capital

Meaning of Working Capital

Every business need funds for two purposes i.e., fixed capital and working capital. Fixed capital is required for the payment towards the purchases of land, building, plant, machinery, furniture etc., whereas working capital is required for the payment towards the purchase of raw materials, payment of wages, and other expenses. Working capital is a ratio of short-term liabilities and short-term income, and it's the capital that a company needs to work with an ongoing basis. On the other hand, working capital is how much in liquid assets that an entrepreneur has on his hand. It is needed to pay for planned and unexpected expenses, meet the short-term obligations of the business, and to build the business. This is particularly true where there is a substantial time lag between making the product and receiving the money for it. It is the amount of funds which is required for the day to day management of the business. A lack of working capital makes it hard to get business loans or obtain credit. It is very important to an entrepreneur to manage its working capital carefully.

Concept of Working Capital

There are two concepts of working capital i.e. gross working capital and net working capital. Gross working capital is the amount of funds which are invested in current assets. Current assets are those assets which are converted into cash within a short period of time generally in one year. Current liabilities are those liabilities which can be payable within a short period of time generally in one year.

Current assets: Cash in hand, cash at bank, sundry debtors, bills receivables, short term investments, inventories, marketable securities, prepaid expenses, accrued incomes etc.

Current liabilities: Sundry creditors, bills payable, outstanding expenses, accrued expenses, short term advances and deposits, dividends payable, bank overdraft etc.

Kinds of Working Capital

Working capital may be classified into two categories such as:

(i) On the basis of concept, and

(ii) On the basis of time

Working capital on the basis of concept again classified into two categories such as gross working capital and net working capital. Working capital on the basis of time classified into two categories such as permanent working capital and temporary working capital.

Gross Working Capital: Total of all Current Assets

Net Working Capital: Total Current Assets – Total Current Liabilities

The accounting formula used to calculate the available working capital of a business is:

Working Capital = Current Assets - Current Liabilities

Significance of Working Capital

Working capital is required for day to day smooth running of the business just as circulation of blood is essential in the human body for maintaining life. It is sometimes said that, *"Inadequate working capital is disastrous; whereas redundant working capital is a criminal waste."* From the above statement it clearly indicates that there are three aspect of the significance of working capital. They are:

(i) Adequate working capital

(ii) Excessive or redundant working capital

(iii) Inadequate working capital

Advantages of Adequate Working Capital

Following are the various advantages of adequate working capital:

(i) Goodwill: Adequate working capital enables a business concern to pay its liabilities, whenever it becomes due which ultimately enhance goodwill of the firm.

(ii) Cash discount: Adequate working capital helps an organisation to avail cash discounts on the purchase of merchandise and raw materials. Timely payment of the cost of merchandise reduces the cost of production.

(iii) Easy loans from banks: Adequate working capital helps an organisation to avail banks loans on easy and favourable terms. A business having good credit standing and trade reputation avails loans easily.

(iv) Distribution of dividends: Adequate working capital helps a business to distribute dividends to its shareholders in right time.

(v) High morale: Adequate working capital improves the morale of the executives. It brings an environment for certainty, security and confidence which are a physiological factor for the improvement efficiency.

(vi) Sense of security and confidence: Adequate working capital can built up a sense of security, confidence and loyalty among the stakeholders.

Disadvantages of Excessive or Redundant Working Capital:

Every business requires adequate working capital for the day to day management of the business. But a question is always arises whether excess or redundant working capital is best for the business or shortage or inadequate working capital is best. Out of the above two alternatives, it can be concluded that both are bad for the business. Following are the various disadvantages of excessive or redundant working capital:

(i) Loss of goodwill: Excess of working capital brings an opportunity to invest in low rate of interest bearing securities, which ultimately affect the return on investment of the shareholders. There shareholders loose confidence in the company which ultimately reduce the good will.

(ii) Misuse of funds: Excess of working capital diverts the attention of the company to invest wisely in the most profitable investments. Due to the excess working capital it will be very much difficult to put control on the various purchases.

(iii) Inefficient management: Excessive working capital leads to the inefficiency of the business because the management is not interested to invest the funds in expanding of the business.

(iv) **Low rate of return on capital:** Excess of working capital indicates the presence of idle funds available in the business. The idle funds do not carry any interest which ultimately leads to low rate of interest on the capital employed. The low rate of return on capital ultimately affects the earnings of the shareholders in terms of reduction of dividends.

Disadvantages of Inadequate Working Capital

Following are few disadvantages of inadequate working capital:

(i) **Loss of goodwill:** A business facing inadequate working capital cannot pay its current liabilities in time. This will affect the reputation of the business and fails to avail good credit facilities.

(ii) **Losing favourable opportunities:** Inadequate working capital fails to provide favourable opportunities to invest in profitable projects. It indicates a stagnant position because of the inadequate working capital.

(iii) **Increase in business risks:** Inadequate working capital leads to increase the business risks because of the irregular payment of the business liabilities. It posess a serious threat to the survival of the business.

(iv) **Adverse effect on morale:** Inadequate working capital discourages the morale of the business executives. It brings an environment for uncertainty and insecurity which losses the confidence of the executives and ultimately loses the morale of the stakeholders.

Marginal Costing: Break-Even Point, Profit-Volume Ratio, Margin of Safety

Meaning

It is a technique of costing which is extensively used in all industries for profit planning, cost control and decision making. It is not only a method of cost ascertainment but also used for managerial decision making. Under the marginal costing, costs are classified into two categories such as fixed and variable. Fixed cost or expenses per unit very with the increase or decrease in production because it is fixed upto a certain level of product. On the other hand variable costs are very with product. Fixed costs are those expenses which are not affected by the change in the volume of output. Variable costs are directly in proportion to change in volume of production or output. The cost which increases or decreases in the same proportion in which the units produced is termed as variable cost. Direct material, direct labour, direct expenses, variable overheads are some of the examples of variable cost. Semi-variable costs contain partly fixed and partly variable and which is partly affected by fluctuations in the level of activity is known as semi-variable costs.

Application of Marginal Costing Techniques

The concept of marginal costing is an essential tool for the managerial decision making. Following are the various applications of marginal costing techniques:

- (i) Break Even Point (BEP)
- (ii) Profit/Volume Ratio (P/V)
- (iii) Margin of Safety (M/S)

(i) Break Even Point (BEP): It is otherwise known as the cost-volume-profit analysis. A break even point refers to the point of activity where the total revenues equal to the total costs. It is a point of no profit and no loss. There are two methods used to calculate the breakeven point. They are:

(a) Break Even Point (in units)

(b) Break Even Point (in amounts)

Break-even point can be calculated by using the following formula:

$$BEP = \frac{\text{Fixed Expenses}}{\text{Contribution per unit}}$$

$$\text{Or, } \frac{\text{Fixed Expenses}}{\text{Selling price per unit} - \text{Variable cost per unit}}$$

(I) Break Even Point (BEP) in units:

Illustration 1

From the following particulars given below, calculate break even point:

Fixed Expenses = Rs. 75,000, Selling price per unit= Rs. 60, Variable cost per unit = Rs. 45

Solution

Break Even Point = Fixed Expenses/Contribution per unit

= 75,000/60- 45

= 5,000 units.

(ii) Break Even Point (BEP) in values

Break even point in value can be calculated after modifying the marginal costing equation. According the equation:

Sales-Variable cost = Fixed cost + Profit

S - V= F + P

$$\frac{S-V}{S-V}=\frac{F+P}{S-V}$$ (Dividing both side by S-V)

1= F/S - V

$$1 \times S = \frac{F \times S}{S-V}$$ (Multiplying both side by S)

$$\text{Break Even Point (in Sales)} = \frac{F \times S}{S-V}$$

$$\text{Or, } \frac{\text{Fixed cost}}{\text{P/V Ratio}}$$

Try yourself

1. From the following particulars given below, calculate break even point:

   Fixed Expenses = Rs. 90,000, Selling price per unit= Rs. 65, Variable cost per unit = Rs. 35

2. From the following particulars given below, calculate break even point:
   Fixed Expenses = Rs. 1,20,000, Selling price per unit= Rs. 100, Variable cost per unit = Rs. 60.

Illustration 2

From the following particulars given below, calculate break even point:

Total variable cost: Rs. 60,000; Total Cost Rs. 90,000, Sales (15,000 units) = Rs. 90,000

Solution

Total fixed cost = Total cost – Variable cost

= Rs. 90,000 - Rs. 60,000 = Rs. 30,000

$$\text{Break Even Point} = \frac{30{,}000 \times 90{,}000}{90{,}000 - 60{,}000}$$

$$= \text{Rs. } 90{,}000$$

Try yourself

1.From the following particulars given below, calculate break even point:

Total Variable cost = Rs. 1,50,000, Total cost = Rs. 2,40,000

Sales (20,000 units) = Rs. 3,00,000. Calculate Break Even Point:

Profit/Volume Ratio

It reflects the relationship between contribution and sales of the enterprise. This ratio is presented in percentage. It is often used as a guide to profitability of business. Here, it is very important to mention that the word profit does not mean profit but contribution. It is another important formula used in marginal costing which determines the contribution from sales as a percentage of sales value. It expresses the relationship between the contribution and sales. The ratio can be shown in the form of a percentage when the calculated value is multiplied by 100. Profit/Volume ratio indicates the sound financial health of the organisation. The ratio reflects the change in profit due to the change in volume. Profit/Volume ratio can be calculated by using the following formula:

(i) Contribution/Sales i.e., C/S

(ii) $\dfrac{\text{Sales} - \text{Variable cost}}{\text{Sales}}$ i.e., $\dfrac{S-V}{S}$

(iii) $\dfrac{\text{Fixed Cost} + \text{Profit}}{\text{Sales}}$ i.e., $\dfrac{F+P}{S}$

(iv) $\dfrac{\text{Changes in Profit/Contribution}}{\text{Changes in Sales}}$

Thus if the selling price of a product is Rs., 20 and the variable cost is Rs. 12, then P/V ratio will be

$$= \frac{20-12}{20} \times 100 = 40\%$$

From the above calculation, it is clear that a sale of every Rs. 100 will bring a profit of 40% after the fixed expenses are met. Higher the P/V ratio more will be the profit and lower the P/V ratio lower will be the profit. It is the primary responsibility of the entrepreneur of any organisation to increase the P/V ratio for higher profit. The higher P/V ratio can be calculated under any one of the following alternatives:

(i) Increasing the selling price per unit.

(ii) Decreasing the variable or marginal costs.

(iii) Switching the production to more profitable products.

The P/V ratio can also be useful to calculate the break even point, value of sales to earn a desired amount of profit, variable costs, profits, fixed cost and margin of safety. Following are the various formula of calculating the P/V ratio.

(i) Break Even Point = $\frac{\text{Fixed Expenses}}{\text{P/V Ratio}}$ i.e., $\frac{F}{P/V}$

(ii) Value of sales to earn a desired amount of profit = $\frac{\text{Fixed cost + Desired profit}}{\text{P/V Ratio}}$

(iii) Variable Cost = Sales (1-P/V Ratio)

(iv) Profit = (Sales × P/V Ratio) – Fixed Cost

Illustration 3

From the following information calculate (i) P/V Ratio (ii) Fixed Cost (iii) Sales to earn a desired amount of profit of Rs. 24,000.

Sales Rs, 80,000, Variable cost 60%, Profit Rs. 8,000

Solution

Sales Rs. 80,000; Variable cost = 60% of Sales = 60% of 80,000 = Rs. 48,000

Profit/Volume Ratio: $\frac{\text{Sales} - \text{Variable Cost}}{\text{Sales}} \times 100$

$= \frac{80{,}000 - 48{,}000}{80{,}000} \times 100$

= 40%

(i) Fixed Cost = Contribution – Profit

= 32,000 - 8,000

= Rs. 24,000

(ii) Sales to earn a desired amount of profit or Rs. 24,000

Value of sales to earn a desired amount of profit = $\frac{24{,}000 + 24{,}000}{40\%}$

= Rs. 1,20,000

Illustration 4

From the following information calculate the P/V Ratio:

Years	Sales (Rs.)	Profit (Rs.)
2002	1,80,000	10,000
2003	2,00,000	35,000

Solution

Profit/Volume Ratio

$$= \frac{\text{Changes in profit/contribution}}{\text{Changes in sales}} \times 100$$

$$= \frac{35{,}000 - 25{,}000}{2{,}00{,}000 - 1{,}80{,}000} \times 100$$

$= 25\%$

Try Yourself

From the following information calculate the P/V Ratio

Years	Sales (Rs.)	Profit (Rs.)
2002	30,000	800
2003	38,000	2,000

Calculate P/V Ratio, Profit when sales are Rs. 24,000, and the sales required to earn a profit Rs. 3,800.

Margin of Safety (M/S)

Margin of safety is an important symbol of the business strength. The difference between the total sales and sales at break-even point represents the margin of safety. It is an amount of sales above the break even sales. On the other hand, sales or output beyond break even point is I is known as a margin of safety. Higher the margin of safety higher is the strengths of the business and lower margin of safety indicate dangers to the business. Following are the few alternatives which will maximize the margin of safety:

(i) Increase in the levels of production

(ii) Increase in the selling price

(iii) Reduction of the variable and fixed costs

(iv) Addition of a new product in the existing production line which is profitable one.

Margin of safety can be calculated by the use of any one alternative formula:

(i) Margin of Safety = Total Sales-Sales at Break even Point

(ii) Margin of Safety $= \dfrac{\text{Profit}}{\text{P/V Ratio}}$

(iii) Margin of Safety Ratio$= \dfrac{\text{Total Sales} - \text{Break Even Sales}}{\text{Total Sales}} \times 100$

Illustration 5

From the following particulars given below, calculate: (i) P/V ratio, (ii) Break Even Point (iii) Margin of Safety (iv) Sales required to earn a profit of Rs. 1,20,000 (v) Profit when sales are of Rs. 8,00,000, (vi) Margin of safety available to it, if the company is earning a profit of Rs. 1,40,000.

Fixed Expenses	Rs. 2,00,000
Sales	Rs. 4,00,000
Profit	Rs. 80,000

Solution

(i) **P/V ratio** $= \dfrac{\text{Contribution}}{\text{Sales}} \times 100 = \dfrac{2{,}80{,}000}{4{,}00{,}000} \times 100 = 70\%$

(ii) **Break Even Point** $= \dfrac{\text{FIxed Expenses}}{\text{P/V Ratio}} = \dfrac{2{,}00{,}000}{70\%} = \text{RS. } 2{,}85{,}714$

(iii) **Margin of Safety:** Total Sales-Sales at Break Even Point
Rs. 4,00,000 - Rs. 2,85,714 = Rs. 1,14,286

(iv) **Sales required to earn a profit of Rs. 1,20,000**

$= \dfrac{\text{Fixed Cost} + \text{Desired Profit}}{\text{P/V Ratio}}$

$= \dfrac{2{,}00{,}000 + 1{,}20{,}000}{70\%}$

= Rs. 4,57,143

(v) **Profit when sales are of Rs. 8,00,000**

Profit = (Sales × P/V Ratio) – Fixed Cost

= (Rs. 8,00,000 × 70%) – Rs. 2,00,00

= Rs. 3,60,000

(vi) **Margin of safety available to it, if the company is earning a profit of Rs.1,40,000.**

Margin of Safety= Profit/P/V Ratio= 1,40,000/70% = Rs. 2,00,000

Production Management: Production Planning and Control, Need and Phases of PPC

Meaning

Production management is an important function in all the manufacturing enterprises. Production means conversion of raw materials into finished products with the help of certain process. The main purpose of any production system is to satisfy the customers through the production of goods and services. The existence and growth of any business is depends upon the products and/or services it offers to its customers. Production function of management involves a wide range of activities from the plant location to the packing of products to be distributed by the marketing department of the enterprise. It includes (i) design of product, (ii) design of production system, (iii) production planning and control, (iv) selection of location, (v) layout of plant, (vi) selection of plant and equipment and (viii) research and development.

Production Planning and Control (PPC)

Production Planning and Control is a very important activity in any business. It is a process that comprises the performance of some critical functions of any business i.e., planning and control, which are two most basic, integral and interdependent functions. No doubt with the aid of computers and applicable software, it has made controlling every aspect of the business much easier, still the system can be made to work efficiently provided the people understand it and make it work. The planning part is always pre-operation. Control is done after execution or implementation of the planned layout and procedure.

Elements of Production Planning and Control

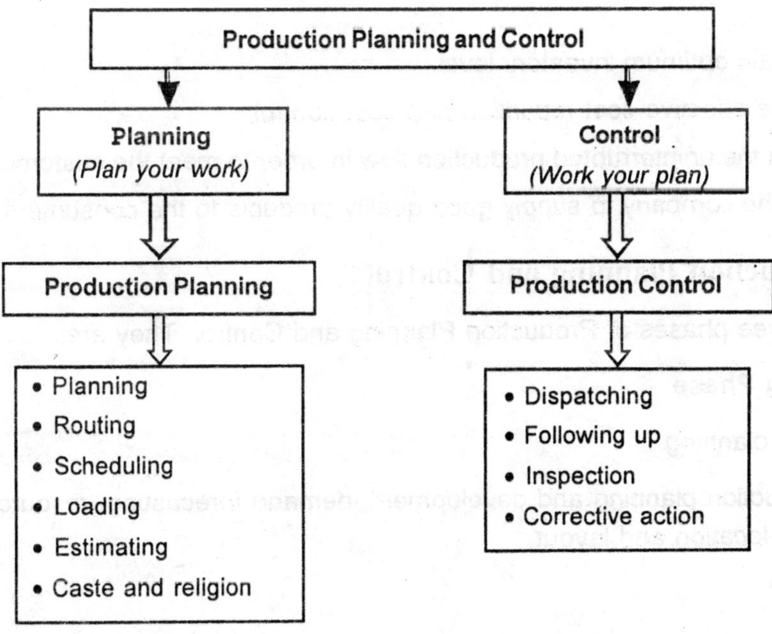

1. Production Planning: It is one of the crucial points in production planning and control. It is a process through which goods and services are created and it involves the decision relating to the work measurement, determine the work content of various operations and designing production system. It is a complex process used by manufacturing companies to optimize the efficiency of their processes. On the other hand, production planning is the projected flow of production. According to Yogi Berra, "If you do not know where you are going, you might not get there".
2. Production Control: It involves the implementation of production plan or schedules through the coordination of different activities of the organization. Production planning is the projected flow of production, while production control is the systematic approach to control the flow of projected production. Production operations are constantly evaluated, guided and directed along with plans formulated by the planning department. Production planning without production control has no meaning at all, because both are complement to each other.

Need for Production Planning and Control

Production planning and control serve as a useful tool to coordinate the various activities of the organisation. Following are the various needs of production planning and control:

1. To maintain effective and optimum utilization of firms' resources.
2. To coordinate with other departments relating uninterrupted production flow.
3. To ensure production and quality resources.
4. To organize the production facilities to achieve stated production objectives
5. To achieve the production objectives with respect to quantity and quality, time and cost.
6. To maintain optimum inventory level.
7. To ensure effective cost reduction and cost control.
8. To obtain the uninterrupted production flow in order to meet the customer's demand.
9. To help the company to supply good quality products to the consumers.

Phases of Production Planning and Control

There are three phases of Production Planning and Control. They are:

1. **Planning Phase**

   (a) Prior planning

   Production planning and development, demand forecasting, resource planning, plant location and layout.

(b) Active Planning

Process planning, capacity planning, tool planning, routing, master planning.

2. **Action Phase:** It is the execution or implementation phase:

   - Dispatching

3. **Control Phase**

(a) Progress Report:

Material control, tool control, inventory control, cost control.

(b) Corrective Action:

Expediting re-planning

MARKETING SECRETS FOR SMALL BUSINESS: 4 P'S OF MARKETING-THE MARKETING MIX

Marketing is an important segment of business activity. It is an outlet to let out the products. It is a gigantic machinery to move the goods by creating utilities of place, time and ownership. Production and marketing are the two pillars of an efficient economy. Production and consumption are the two wheels of an economy which are linked by the powerful belt of marketing. Marketing is 'Putting the right product in the right place, at the right price, at the right time'.

According to **Philip Kotler,** "Marketing is a social process by which individuals and groups obtain what they need and want through creating and exchanging products and values with others."

The marketing mix and the 4 Ps of marketing are often used as synonyms for each other. In fact, they are not necessarily the same thing. Marketing mix is a set of marketing tools designed as a simple way to focus on the main elements of marketing for a business and create a marketing strategy. It is a general phrase used to describe the different kinds of choices organizations that have to make in the whole process of bringing a product or service to market. The 4Ps, i.e., product, price, place (distribution) and promotion. It is one way, probably the best known way of defining the marketing mix, and the original 4P's came from ***E. Jerome McCarthy*** in his book *"Basic Marketing: A Managerial Approach"* in the year 1960. The 4Ps are:

- **Product (or Service):** What you are selling?
  - It includes the factors like quality, features, style, brand, packaging, warranties etc.

- **Price:** How much you are charging for your product?
  - It includes the factors like list price, discount, payment period, credit terms and also the switching cost (the cost of changing to or from a different product or service etc..
- **Place:** How people can buy your product?
  - It includes factors like distribution channels, market coverage, locations, inventory, supply chain, logistics etc.
- **Promotion:** How you tell people about your offer?
  - It includes the factors like advertisement, sales promotion, public relations etc.

The Marketing Mix: 4 Ps of Marketing

Selling vs. Marketing

	FOCUS ON	MEANS	ENDS
SELLING	Products	Aggressive selling and sales promotion	Maximize profits through sales volume.
MARKETING	Customer needs	Integrated marketing plan encompassing product, price, promotion and distribution.	Maximize profits through increased customer satisfaction

Channels of Distribution

The channels of distribution are sometimes called marketing channels. It can be defined as the collection of organizational units, institutions, or agencies within or external to the manufacturer, which perform the functions that support product marketing. It refers to systems of interdependent organisations that facilitate the movement of the physical product or service from the producer to the consumer and includes the producer, consumer and all the intermediaries involved in distribution including the internet. Channels of distribution are divided into direct and indirect forms. Under the direct channel, consumers are buying goods directly from the manufacturer and under indirect channel; they are buying goods through any one middle man. The chain of businesses or intermediaries through which goods or services passes until it reaches the end users.

It is the movement of goods and services between the point of production and the point of consumption through organizations that perform a variety of marketing activities. There are two types' products which need appropriate channel. They are:

1. **Industrial products:** The distinctive marketing features of industrial goods are there distribution for use in further production rather than for resale.
2. **Consumer products:** The distinctive marketing features of consumer goods are there distribution to the ultimate users of the product i.e., consumer.

Choice of Channels of Distribution

Following are the various factors to be considered before choosing a suitable channels of distribution:

1. **Product considerations:** It is the nature and type of the product which have an important bearing on the choice of distribution channels.
2. **Market considerations:** It is the nature and types of market which determine the choice of channels of distribution.
3. **Company considerations:** It is the nature and size of the company which determine the channels of distribution.
4. **Middlemen considerations:** It includes the nature and types of middlemen which determine the choice of channels of distribution.

Human Resource Management – Problems and Strategies

Human resources management is the process of managing the people of an organization with a humane approach. HRM can be defined as that part of management process which develops and manages the human elements of enterprise considering the resourcefulness of the organization's own people in terms of total knowledge, skills, creative abilities, talents, aptitudes and potentialities. Human Resource Management (HRM) can be defined as an organizational function which deals with issues related to people such as compensation, hiring, performance management, organization development, safety, wellness, benefits, employee motivation, communication, administration, and training. The management of human resources has now assumed as a strategic importance in the achievement of organizational growth and excellence. It is based on the golden rule, 'GIVE LOVE AND GET LOVE'.

HRM is a philosophy, while Human Resource Development (HRD) includes the activities and processes undertaken to promote the intellectual, moral, psychological, cultural, social and economic development of the individuals in an organization. It is a continuous process by which the employees are assisted in a planned way to develop capabilities.

Aspects of HRM

(i) Human Resource Planning (ii) Recruitment (iii) Selection (iv) Placement (v) Inductions (vi) Transfer and Planning (vii) Job Analysis (viii) Performance Appraisal (ix) HR Audit (x) Total Quality Management (xi) Quality of Working Environment (xii) Quality Cycle etc.

Taxation for Entrepreneurs: Income Tax, Excise Duty, Sales Tax, Vat etc.

Indian tax is regulated and administered by the Ministry of Finance under the Government of India. Taxation is the government's main source of revenue and several types of taxes are applied to different categories of the population. Taxation in India has been classified into two categories i.e., direct tax and indirect tax. Direct Tax is the tax paid to the government directly by the assessee and indirect tax is the tax levied on goods or services rather than on persons or organizations like Excise Duty, Service Tax, Securities Transaction Tax etc. In order to control the indict taxation in India; there is a series of tax laws and regulations made by the central government and state government. Since 1991 Indian taxation system has undergone tremendous reforms. The tax rates have been rationalized and tax laws have been simplified resulting in better compliance, ease of tax payment and better enforcement. The process of rationalization of tax administration is ongoing in India.

4Rs of Taxation

Indian taxation has four main purposes or effects i.e. Revenue, Redistribution, Repricing and Representation. Revenue means taxes which are raise to spend on armies, roads, schools, hospitals etc. Redistribution means transferring wealth from the richer sections of society to the poorer sections.The purpose of repricing is a process where taxes are levied to address externalities i.e. tobacco is taxed to discourage smoking. Representation indicates where ruler's tax citizens and citizens demand accountability from their rulers as the other part of this bargain.

Three tier Structure of Taxation

Union/Central Government	Income Tax (except tax on agricultural income, which the State Government can levy.), Capital Gain Tax, Customs duties, Central Excise duties, Sales Tax, Service Tax.
State Government	Sales Tax (tax on intra-State sale of goods), Stamp Duty (duty on transfer of property), State Excise (duty on manufacture of alcohol), Land Revenue (levy on land used for agricultural/non-agricultural purposes), Duty on Entertainment, Tax on Professions and Callings.
Urban/Rural Bodies	Tax on properties (buildings, etc.), Octroi (tax on entry of goods for use/consumption within areas of the Local Bodies), Tax on Markets and Tax/User Charges for utilities like water supply, drainage, etc.

Classification of Taxes

Taxation in India is classified into two categories i.e. direct and indirect.

(A) Direct Tax: Income Tax, Corporation Tax, Capital Gain Tax, Professional Tax, Agricultural Income Tax, Wealth Tax, Estate Tax, Land Revenue, Registration and Stamp Fee etc.

(B) Indirect Tax: Sales Tax, Value Added Tax, Central Sales Tax, Excise Duty, Service Tax, Fringe Benefit Tax, Banking Transaction Tax, Cenvat Credit etc.

Income Tax

According to ruling of Income Tax Act, 1961, any person whose salary from any source of income is more than the exemption limit and who qualifies as an assessee is required to pay Income Tax in accordance with the rates indicated by the Finance Act.

Learn how to calculate your Income Tax

Step I: **Gross Income:** Calculate your Annual Income. (Monthly Income X 12)

Step II: **Donations:** Calculate the total donations you have made towards various institutions in accordance to Income Tax Rules.

Step III: **Savings:** Calculate the total savings. This may include all the savings and investments mentioned in Income Tax Saving Schemes sections.

Step IV: **Taxable Income:** Follow the following rules to calculate the taxable income i.e., Step I - (Step II + Step III) = Taxable Income

Step V: **Income Tax:** When you have calculated your taxable income, refer to the income tax slabs to calculate your Income Tax accordingly.

Corporate Income Tax

Taxes which are levied on the income of companies and business corporations are known as corporation tax. Corporate income tax in India takes many forms. Primarily, this tax is aimed at domestic corporations, which in India pay a base income tax rate of 35 per cent with a 2.5 per cent surcharge. This also applies to foreign corporations that have economic bases in India e.g., Hewlett-Packard, Agro-Tech, Microsoft etc. Corporate Income Tax is applicable to all people working for a corporation.

Capital Gain Tax

The capital gains tax is another important form of Direct Tax in India. It is payable on capital gains received upon the sale of assets. It can be defined as any income generated by selling a capital investment (business stocks, paintings, houses, family business, farmhouse, etc.). Long-term Capital Gains Tax is charged if (i) capital assets are held for more than three years and, (ii) In case of shares, securities listed on a recognized stock exchanges in India, units of specified mutual funds, the period for holding is one year.

Professional Tax

It is charged on the income of professionals i.e., doctors, chartered accountants, teachers, artists, actors etc., by the state government. The professional tax rates differs from State to State. It is a State tax.

Agricultural Income Tax

Agricultural income is tax-free in India. Income earned from agricultural operations is not taxed. The reason for exemption of agriculture income from Central Taxation is that the Constitution gives exclusive power to make laws with respect to taxes on agricultural income to the State Legislature, However, while computing tax on non-agricultural income, agricultural income is also taken into consideration. This is a source of discontent in many assessments of non-agricultural income.

Wealth Tax

It is governed by the Wealth Tax Act, 1957 and is applicable for all citizens of India. It is a tax paid by the owner of the property every year till he retains the property and is depending on the market value of it. The person paying the wealth tax under the clause of the Wealth Tax Act, 1957, is known as the Assessee. The residential status of the assessee is one of the main characteristic factors for the person paying the wealth tax in India.

Estate Tax

In India, estate duty was introduced in 1953. It is a tax which is payable on the economic value of the accumulated savings and assets of a deceased person. Indian entrepreneurs are very much lucky. They can pass most of their wealth to their children without too much hindrances.

Land Revenue

Land revenue in India is a direct tax. It is received by the state governments.

Registration and Stamp Duty

Registration and Stamp Duty in India is a kind of tax that is levied on the transaction performed by means of a document or instrument as per the regulations of Indian Stamp Act, 1899. Stamp Duty is collected by the states where the transaction is carried out. On the other hand, stamp duty is paid on instruments, which are simply a document to create, transfer, limit, extend, extinguish or record a right or liability.

Sales Tax

Sales tax is an indirect tax, whose incidence is shifted by the trader to customers. It is levied on the sale of movable goods. The sales tax has been classified into two categories. They are:

- ✓ Central Sales Tax (CST): CST is 4% on manufactured goods.
- ✓ Local Sales Tax (LST): Where a sale takes place within a state, LST would be levied. Such a tax would be governed by the relevant state tax legislation. This is normally up to 15%.

Most of the Indian States have replaced Sales tax with a new Value Added Tax (VAT) from April 01, 2005.

Central Sales Tax

It is governed by the provision of Central Sales Tax Act, 1956. It is a tax levied on dealer, who carries on his business of sales and purchase of goods in the course of interstate trade or commerce. The provisions of the Central Sales Tax are (i) There should be a dealer who carries on business and (ii) he must be a registered dealer under Sales Tax Act. The Central Sales Tax is required to be paid only when the goods are traded between states. The rate of tax is 4% and it is a revenue for Central Government.

Excise Duties (Now as CENVAT)

An excise or excise tax (sometimes called an excise duty) is a type of tax charged on goods produced within the country (as opposed to customs duties, charged on goods from outside the country). The Central Government levies excise duty under the Central Excise Act, 1944 and the Central Excise Tariff Act, 1985. It is a tax on the production or sale of goods. This tax is now known as the Central Value Added Tax (CENVAT). In order to stimulate the economic growth, excise duty has been used as an instrument for fiscal policy.

Service Tax

The provisions related to Service Tax came into effect on 1st July, 1994. Service Tax in India is regulated and administered by the Central Excise Commissionerates who work directly under the Department of Revenue, Ministry of Finance, Central Board of Excise and Customs, and the Government of India. It is essentially an indirect tax where individuals are required to pay only once in a quarter. Companies can pay service tax for one month by the 25th of the following month. Although legal penalties exist for failing to pay service tax, these penalties cannot be imposed if the assessee can prove that there was due cause for failure. The service tax amount used tobe 5% when the government first launched service tax in India. In 2003, this was hiked to 8%. Usually, 10% service tax is levied on various services that are provided in the country. Creerntly, the rate of servece tax in India is 10.2% including a 2% education cess.

Value Added Tax (VAT)

It is an indirect tax and its burden is passed on to the purchaser. VAT is a multipoint tax system with provision for set off of tax paid on purchases at each point of sale. This is the tax that a manufacturer needs to pay while purchasing raw materials and a trader needs to pay while purchasing goods. Each commodity passes through different stages of production and distribution before finally it reaches the consumer. Value Added Tax (VAT) is a tax on the value addition at each stage. Under VAT system, a dealer collects tax on his sales, retains the tax paid on his purchase and pays balance to the Govt. Treasury. It is a consumption tax because it is borne ultimately by the final consumer. The tax paid by the dealer is passed on to the buyer. It is not a charge on the dealer. All business transactions carried on within a State by individuals, partnerships, companies, etc. will be covered by VAT. It will not cover small business with a turnover below a certain limit. Most of the Indian States have replaced sales tax with a new Value Added Tax (VAT) from April 01, 2005. VAT is imposed on goods only and not services and it has replaced sales tax. Other indirect taxes such as excise duty, service tax etc., are not replaced by VAT. It is implemented at the state level by State Governments. It is applied on each stage of sale with a mechanism of credit for the input VAT paid. There are four slabs of VAT:

- ✓ 0% for essential commodities.
- ✓ 1% on bullion and precious stones.
- ✓ 4% on industrial inputs and capital goods and items of mass consumption.
- ✓ All other items 12.5%.

Petroleum products, tobacco, liquor etc., attract higher VAT rates that vary from State to State.

How Value Added Tax Works

A trader registered for VAT effectively pays VAT only at one stage when he sells his goods. It has an effect on his selling price which he has paid as a part of his purchase price is charged on him by his suppliers. This is not a cost to him because he gets it back by deducting it from tax on his sales (output tax). The dealer pays VAT by deducting the tax paid on purchases (input tax) from his tax collected on sales (output tax). Hence, VAT = Output Tax-Input Tax.

For example: A dealer pays Rs.10.00 @ 10% on his purchase price of goods valued Rs.200.00. He sells the goods at Rs.250.00 and collects tax amounting to Rs.25.00 (@ 10%). He will pay Rs.5.00 (Rs.25.00- Rs.20.00) as he has already paid Rs.20.00 to his seller while purchasing those goods.

How Value Added Tax Misused

From the above discussion, it is clear that VAT encourage disclosure of complete information on business turnover. Below mentioned two examples which will clarify how VAT is being misused by the traders:

Example 1

Basic purchase of goods Rs. 20,000; 12.5% VAT on the basic purchase price i.e., Rs. 2,500 Overhead related to the goods Rs. 500, Profit margin 20 %

Particulars	Rs.
Basic purchase of goods	20,000.00
Add: 12.5% VAT	2,500.00
Value inclusive purchase price	22,500.00
Add: Overheads	500.00
Total	23,000.00
Add: 20% profit margin	4,600.00
Basic selling price	27,600.00
Add: 12.5% VAT	3,450.00
VAT inclusive selling price	31,050.00

Example 2

Basic purchase of goods Rs. 20,000; 12.5% VAT on the basic purchase price i.e., Rs. 2,500, Overhead related to the goods Rs. 500, Profit margin 20 %

Particulars	Rs.
Basic purchase of goods	20,000.00
Add: 12.5% VAT	2,500.00
Value inclusive purchase price	22,500.00
Less VAT input	2,500.00
VAT free purchase price	20,000.00
Add: Overheads	500.00
Total	20,500.00
Add: 20% profit margin	4,100.00
Basic selling price	24,600.00
Add: 12.5% VAT	3,075.00
VAT inclusive selling price	27,675.00

The VAT of 12.5% is charged on the 'Total'. Thus the VAT inclusive selling price will be 'Total' plus 'VAT'. From the above two examples, it is clear that, in example 1, the trader has overcharged his customer to the extent of Rs. 3,375.00 (31,050-27,675). Thus a trader is advised to adopt example 2 as a guideline and it overcharge the consumer. If he does, he will lose his customers.

Customs Duties

The Central Board of Excise and Customs under the Ministry of Finance manages the customs duty process in the country. Customs duty in India falls under the Customs Act, 1962 and Customs Tariff Act, 1975. Usually, the goods that are imported to the country are charged customs duty along with educational cess. The rates of basic duties vary from 0 to 30%. For industrial goods, the rate has been slashed to 15%.

Fringe Benefit Tax

These benefits are either taxed in the hands of the employees themselves or the value of such benefits is subject to a fringe benefit tax in the hands of the employer. The rationales for levying a fringe benefit tax of the personal benefit possess problems or for some reasons, it is not feasible to tax the benefits in the hands of the employees. It is proposed to levy a separate tax known as the fringe benefit tax.

Banking Transaction Tax

It was applicable to whole of India except the State of Jammu and Kashmir. It was come into force w.e.f., June 1, 2005. Tax was imposed on the cash withdrawal, encashment of term deposit, etc. From April 1, 2009, this scheme has been abolished. Taxpayers will not have to pay levy on withdrawal of cash from banks with the government withdrawing the Banking Cash Transaction Tax (BCTT). The BCTT was served a very useful purpose in enlarging the information system of the Income Tax Department since the information is also being gathered through other instruments. It was not introduced with the intention of revenue generation.

Securities Transaction Tax

Transactions in equity shares, derivatives and units of equity-oriented funds entered in a recognized stock exchange attract Securities Transaction Tax at the following rate:

- ✓ Delivery base transactions in equity shares or buyer and seller each units of an equity-oriented fund – 0.075%
- ✓ Sale of units of an equity-oriented fund to the seller mutual fund – 0.15%
- ✓ Non delivery base transactions in the above – 0.015%
- ✓ Derivatives (futures and options) seller – 0.01%
- ✓ Sales Tax Acts of various State Governments and Central Sales Act governed the application of Sales Tax/VAT.

Municipal/Local Taxes

- ✓ Octori/entry tax: Some municipal jurisdictions levy octori/entry tax on ontry of goods.
- ✓ Other State Taxes
- ✓ Stamp duty on transfer of assets
- ✓ Property/building tax levied by local bodies.
- ✓ Agriculture income tax levied by State Governments on income from plantations.
- ✓ Luxury tax levied by certain State Government on specified goods

Electronic Commerce and Small Organisations: Meaning and Evolution

In the era of liberalization superior customer service has to be the key objective of any firm to survive and grow. The components of such a business strategy would definitely include efficient sharing of sales information to understand what the consumer wants. In order to expect the business operations to lean and profitable, it requires efficient replenishment of goods and services in response to consumer's demand and efficient order management. small and medium enterprises (SME's) are critical to the economies of all countries, including developing ones. They cannot be left behind and many are already demonstrating their entrepreneurial strength by grasping opportunities offered by electronic commerce. Online marketing has only recently made it's foray, and yet it's charm, speed and time saving attributes have made it a viable option. Sitting on your chair and just a mouse click away to make a purchase, seems so simple and effortless. Internet marketing has become an energetic and economical way to buy products and services in less time, without consuming the time and energy of their customers.

Electronic commerce is a process of using electronic methods and procedures to conduct all forms of business activity to achieve organizational goals. It is a key trade promotion policy issue because of its potential to transform the way large chunks of world trade are undertaken. Electronic commerce uses different technologies and embraces a wide range of financial forms, such as electronic banking, electronic trading, electronic data interchange (EDI), electronic mail (E-mail), facsimile (Fax), electronic cataloguing, video conferencing and multimedia communications, and all forms of messaging between enterprises.

Types of Electronic Commerce Transactions

1. **Person to person:** Telephone, Fax and E-mail.
2. **Person to computer:** Mostly application based electronic forms including World Wide Web (www),
3. **Computer to computer:** EDI, smart cards and bar coded data.
4. **Computer to person:** Computer generated mail, fax and e-mail.

Computers and the internet are now widely expected to function as part of the business and social infrastructure. Transactions conducted through the internet will have enormous implications over the next few years for the international competitiveness of every country. It is a fundamental and permanent change in the way we do business. It is not only a strategic tool that reduces expenses and streamlines business procedures but also creates a competitive advantage. Global competitiveness, technological growth, opening of economy, expansion of markets and treating the whole world as a single market have necessitated the need for a continues flow of information as information works like lubricating oil to make economic system work better. For example many companies are now-a-days selling their products through amazon.com.

Benefits of Online Marketing

1. Benefits to Consumers: Convenient, Interactive and Immediate

2. Benefits to Marketers: Customer Relationship Building, Reduce Costs and Increase Efficiency, Greater Flexibility, Access to Global Markets etc.

Electronic commerce is still in its infancy, but is the fastest growing type of international, value added trade. Many consumers are hesitant to purchase items over the Internet because they do not trust that their personal information will remain private. It is rightly said by Edward da Costa, "It is difficult, and yes, it is possible." (Summing up how hard it is for SME's in developing countries to use electronic commerce successfully.)"

Small Business in International Business

The Internet presents the perfect opportunity for small businesses all over the world to meet and do business in a true international marketplace. In addition to building the perfect e-commerce website and planning the business, there are a few key tips that will help establish a good business and build a solid customer service reputation. Globalization has made international trade more essential than ever to the health of our economy. If your small business is interested in exporting or importing products or services, learn about the laws, agencies and trade organizations that can help lead to successful ventures in international commerce. In order to facilitate the international transactions. The Department of Commerce provides comprehensive information on licensing requirements for participating in international trade. They have an online application process, SNAP (Simplified Network Applications Process), which allows registered users to submit export and re-export license applications, and request commodity classifications and agricultural license exception notices through a single and secure web site. The various shipping documents are commercial invoice, bill of lading, insurance certificate, certificate of origin, certificate of inspection, dock receipts, shipper's export declaration (SED) etc.

Summary

Small-scale industry sector is a very important segment in the Indian industrial sector and would continue to play a crucial role in the Indian economy in the future. It has also been observed that many of the units in the SSI sector are today plagued with technological stagnation and their quality, efficiency and productivity have actually declined over the years. The Small Scale Industrial (SSI) sector is one of the most vital sectors of the Indian economy in terms of employment generation, the strong entrepreneurial base etc.

QUESTIONS

SHORT ANSWER QUESTIONS

1. What are the various objectives of small and medium enterprises ?
2. What are the different books maintained by an entrepreneur?
3. What are the 4Ps of marketing mix?
4. What is production planning and control?
5. What is a VAT?
6. What are the causes of sickness?

LONG ANSWER QUESTIONS

1. What are the four P's of marketing mix? Explain each of the P with suitable example.
2. What are the various electronic commerce practices found in small and medium enterprises?
3. What do you mean by marginal costing? What are the various applications of marginal costing techniques?
4. What are the various taxes imposed on the business? Explain each of them in detail.
5. What do you mean by industrial sickness? Explain the various causes and symptoms of industrial sickness in Indian small and medium enterprises.

PROJECT APPRAISAL

CHAPTER

"The seeds of every company's demise are contained in its business plan."-

— Fred Adler

Chapter Overview:

At the end of this chapter, you will be able to understand:

1. Introduction into project appraisal.
2. Meaning of Research.
3. Research process.
4. Research design.
5. Project reports.

INTRODUCTION

A project is a well defined activity, with clear cut beginning and having a desired outcome. It refers to the process of assessing in a structured way, the case for proceeding with a proposal. It is otherwise known as channelising predetermined amount of money to generate something that will assist the organisation in designing and executing its strategies.

Project appraisal is the process of examining the various dimensions of a project, be it technical, financial, social, environmental etc., and providing an assessment of the project's likelihood for success and its viability. It is the process of assessing and questioning proposals before resources are committed. It evaluates project's ability to meet its stated objectives and to provide long term economic growth in the larger framework of local and national needs.

RESEARCH: MEANING, OBJECTIVES, CHARACTERISTICS AND TYPES

Meaning of Research

Research is a voyage of discovery from the known to the unknown. It is an original contribution to the existing stock of knowledge. It is a scientific and systematic search for pertinent information on a specific topic. The Advanced Learner's Dictionary of Current English has defined research as *"a careful investigation or inquiry specially through search for new facts in any branch of knowledge."* Research is an endeavour to discover answers to intellectual and practical problems through the application of scientific method.

Objectives of Research

The objectives are:

1. To discover answers through the application of scientific procedures.
2. To construct a new procedure.
3. To explain a new phenomenon or to generate new knowledge.
4. To investigate the existing situations or problems.
5. To determine the frequency with which something occurs.
6. To test a hypothesis of a causal relationship between variables.

Characteristics of Research

1. Research involves the quest for answers to unsolved problems.
2. Research is based upon observable experience or empirical evidence.
3. Research is directed towards the solution of a problem.

4. Research by nature is a cycle.
5. Research demands accurate observation and description.
6. Research activities are characterized by carefully designed procedures.
7. Research is carefully recorded and reported.

Types of Research

1. **Descriptive research:** It is also called as statistical research. The main aim of this type of research is to describe the data and characteristics about what is being studied. This type of research is mainly done to gain a better understanding of a topic.
2. **Analytical research:** It is primarily concerned with testing hypothesis and specifying and interpreting relationships, by analyzing the facts or information already available.
3. **Applied research:** It is designed to solve practical problems of the modern world, rather than to acquire knowledge for knowledge's sake. It is carried out to find solution to a real life problem requiring an action or policy decision.
4. **Fundamental research:** It is otherwise known as basic or pure research, which is undertaken for the sake of knowledge without any intention to apply it in practice.
5. **Quantitative research:** It is all about quantifying relationships between variables. The objective of quantitative research is to develop and employ mathematical models, theories and/or hypotheses pertaining to phenomenon by the use of statistical analysis. According to **Fred Kerlinger,** 'There's no such thing as qualitative data. Everything is either 1 or 0".
6. **Qualitative research:** It is a non-quantitative type of analysis aimed at to gather an in-depth understanding of human behavior such as people's attitudes, behaviours, value systems, concerns, motivations, aspirations, culture or lifestyles of a particular phenomenon. It seeks out the 'why', not the 'how' of its topic through the analysis of unstructured information. According to **Donald Campbell,** "All research ultimately has a qualitative grounding".
7. **Conceptual research:** It is generally used by philosophers and thinkers to develop new concepts or to reinterpret existing ones. It is used in research to outline possible courses of action or to present a preferred approach to an idea or thought.
8. **Empirical research:** It is a research that derives its data by means of direct observation or experiment. It is used to answer a question or test a hypothesis a data based research.

Some Other Types of Research

1. **One-time research:** It is confined to a single time period.
2. **Longitudinal research:** It measures relationships between variables over a period of time.
3. **Diagnostic research:** It is a clinical research which aims at identifying the causes of a problem, frequency with which it occurs and the possible solutions for it.
4. **Exploratory research:** It is a type of research which provides insights into and comprehension of an issue or situation where a problem has not been clearly defined. It is the preliminary study of an unfamiliar problem, about which the researcher has little or no knowledge.
5. **Experimental research:** It is a scientific research designed to assess the effect of one particular variable on a phenomenon by keeping the other variables constant or controlled, or to test a hypothesis.
6. **Historical research:** It is a systematic collection and evaluation of data related to past occurrences in order to describe causes, effects, and trends of those events that may help to explain present events and anticipate future events. The purpose is to discover the trends in the past, in order to understand the present and to anticipate the future.

RESEARCH PROCESS: MEANING, STEPS AND CRITERIAS OF GOOD RESEARCH

Meaning of Research Process

Research is the systematic process of collecting and analyzing information to increase our understanding of the phenomenon under study. It is the function of the researcher to contribute to the understanding of the phenomenon and to communicate that understanding to others. It is a set of activities focused on the systematic collection of information using accepted methods of analysis as a basis for drawing conclusions and making recommendations.

The Research Process/Steps

There are eight steps in a research process. They are:

Steps in planning a research study:

Step-1: Formulating a research problem

Step-2: Conceptualizing a research design

Step-3: Constructing an instrument for data collection

Step-4: Selecting a sample

Step-5: Writing a research proposal

Steps in conducting a research study:

Step-6: Collecting data

Step-7: Processing data

Step-8: Writing a research report

Criteria's of Good Research

- ✓ Purpose should be clearly defined.
- ✓ Research process detailed.
- ✓ Research design should be thoroughly planned.
- ✓ High ethical standards applied.
- ✓ Limitations frankly revealed.
- ✓ Adequate analysis for decision maker's needs.
- ✓ Findings presented unambiguously.
- ✓ Conclusions justified.
- ✓ Researcher's experience reflected.

QUALITIES OF A GOOD RESEARCH

- Systematic
- Logical
- Empirical
- Replicable
- Creative
- Use of multiple methods
- Research Design

A statement of proposed identification, documentation, investigation, or other treatment of a historic property that identifies the project's goals, methods and techniques, expected results, and the relationship of the expected results to other proposed activities or treatments.

It is basically a blueprint of activities from the beginning of the research process till its completion. It includes identifying the data gathering method(s), the instruments to be used and the information will be organized and analyzed.

Resource Mapping, Environmental Analysis, SWOT Analysis

Resource Mapping

It is a method for collating and plotting information on the occurrence, distribution, access and use of resources within the economic and cultural domain of a specific community. Variations are introduced in selecting particular participant groups (e.g., gender) or in adding a further stage to generate topographic map related information through a two-stage resource mapping process.

Environmental Analysis

In fact, it would be better to call this kind of analysis as business environmental analysis through the acronym PEST analysis. PEST stands for Political, Economic, Socio-cultural and Technological. Each PEST factor plays a part in determining the overall business environment. Thus, when looking at political factors one should consider the impact of any political or legislative changes that could affect the business. If the business is operating in more than one country then it need to look at each country in turn. Political factors include laws on data protection and even environmental policy. Obviously politicians do not operate in a vacuum, and many political changes result from changes in the economy or in social and cultural moves. Although tax rates are generally decided by politicians, tax decision includes economic considerations. Technological factors include economical and environmental aspect. There is an improvement in the PEST analysis such as STEEP and PESTLE. The second E in STEEP includes ecological and environmental aspects and the L in PESTLE stands for legal or legislative. The analysis examines the impact of each of these factors (and their interplay with each other) on the business. The results can then be used to take advantage of opportunities and to make contingency plans for threats when preparing business and strategic plans.

SWOT Analysis

The SWOT analysis is an extremely useful tool for understanding decision-making for all sorts of situations in business organizations. SWOT is an acronym for Strengths, Weaknesses, Opportunities and Threats. The SWOT analysis provides a good framework for reviewing strategy, position and direction of a business proposition. SWOT analysis is very simple and useful for the analysis for business planning, strategic planning, competitor evaluation, marketing, business and product development, research reports etc. It also measures a business's market and potential according to external factors such as political, economic, social and technological. It is often helpful to complete a PEST analysis prior to a SWOT analysis. The differences between PEST and SWOT are given below:

Sl.	SWOT Analysis	PEST Analysis
1.	It measures a business unit.	It measures a market.
2.	It is a subjective assessment of data.	It is an objective assessment of data.
3.	It can be useful for all sorts of decision making.	It cannot be useful for all sorts of decision making.
4.	SWOT is not useful before PEST.	PEST is useful before SWOT.
5.	SWOT does not help to identify PEST factors.	PEST definitely helps to identify SWOT factors.
6.	It is more useful for larger business.	It can be useful for all business.

Subject of SWOT Analysis

Strengths	Weaknesses
✓ Competitive advantages ✓ Experience, knowledge, data ✓ Financial reserves, likely returns ✓ Innovative aspects? ✓ Location and geographical? ✓ Marketing-reach, distribution, awareness. ✓ Price, value, quality ✓ USP's (unique selling points)	✓ Cash-flow, start-up cash-drain ✓ Disadvantages of proposition ✓ Effects on core activities, distraction ✓ Gaps in capabilities ✓ Lack of competitive strength. ✓ Timescales, deadlines and pressures?
Opportunities	**Threats**
✓ Business and product development ✓ Market developments ✓ New markets-vertical and horizontal ✓ New USP's (unique selling points) ✓ Niche target markets ✓ Technology development and innovation ✓ Volumes, production, economies ✓ Seasonality, weather effects ✓ Sustaining internal capabilities	✓ Competitor intentions ✓ Environmental effects ✓ IT developments ✓ Legislative effects ✓ Market demand ✓ New technologies, services, ideas ✓ Political effects

Project Identification and Selection (PIS)

It is said that fixation of priorities is the first step to wisdom. Identifying and selecting the right projects is a key step to project outcomes. The development plans are prepared after thorough scrutiny and judicious selection of the most important and remunerative projects. This decision needs to be based on benefits and viability with getting this right being the most important step in the project life cycle.

Project Identification

Project identification is the first phase of the project cycle. It is undertaken to study, *"Whether we see a problem or we see an opportunity"*. Problems are undesirable situations that prevent the organization from fully achieving its purpose, goals and objectives. It helps an organization to determine whether or not resources should be dedicated to a project. There are two main activities in project identification i.e., identification of the need, prioritization and translation of need into a development schedule.

Project Selection

Identifying and selecting the right projects is a key step to project outcomes. It is a specific activity with a specific starting point and a specific ending point intended to accomplish a specific objective. The project is a notion, speculative imagining of a proposal deemed fit for a prospective undertaking. It may be defined as a proposal for investment to achieve certain objectives. It is one of the most important services which is the structured identification and selection of projects for an organization to invest in. Opportunity sensing is essential for new as well as existing entrepreneurs. Once existing entrepreneurs reach the comfort stage in their project, new business opportunities need to be identified for enterprise sustenance, growth and development. Project identification and selection has the following objectives:

1. To develop understanding of the emerging business environment for identifying business opportunities, particularly SME.
2. To generate appreciation of the scope and use of knowledge necessary for opportunity sensing so as to ensure healthy industrial growth.
3. To provide necessary skills for evaluating opportunities perceived in the newly liberalized and global environment.

Project Manager: Roles and Responsibilities

'We are ready for any unforeseen event that may or may not occur.' **Dan Quayle**

Project Manager = Task Needs + Team Needs + Individual Needs

Task Needs

The project manager should meet his task needs. Following items are coming under the task needs such as attaining team objectives, planning work, allocating resources, defining tasks, assigning responsibility, controlling and monitoring quality, scrutinizing progress, checking performance etc.

Team Needs

The project manager should meet his team needs. Following items are coming under the team needs such as appointing secondary leaders, building and upholding team spirit, setting standards and maintaining regulation, training the team, setting up systems to facilitate communication with the team, developing work methods to craft team function cohesiveness etc.

Individual Needs

The project manager should meet his individual needs. Following items are coming under the individual needs such as developing the individual, balancing team needs and task needs, balancing team needs and individual needs, performance appreciation and rewards, helping with other team member's personal problems etc.

Project Reports: How to Prepare?

Starting a new business, going into a new venture, setting up an industry requires an investment. It is essential that while preparing project report the consultant analysis the project with perfection. One has to make a thorough study of the units which are already in the same line. He should try to figure out the difficulties being faced by the units already in existence and how far same can be overcome. It is always better to learn from the mistakes of others and do not commit the same.

WHAT IS PRELIMINARY PROJECT REPORT?

In short PPR is a simple brief data-sheet which gives an insight into the following:

(i) How much money, manpower and material would be required to set up the project?

(ii) What type of machines would be required?

(iii) What are the sources of technology that would be required?

(iv) What would be the economic gains from the project?

Why Preliminary Project Report

Sometimes, it is a matter of question that when an entrepreneur could prepare the detailed project report (DPR), why a preliminary project report (PPR) is always an advisable. There are many other advantages of preparing a preliminary project report also:

(1) When an entrepreneur desires to commence a business unit, he/she has to comply with certain formalities such as provisional registration in order to set up a small-scale unit.

(2) While feeding the data in the PPR, it will help an entrepreneur in completing certain formalities in anticipation of setting up a project.

(3) The data collected by preparing a PPR forms a good take-off point for preparing a DPR when one desires to do so.

(4) It will help an entrepreneur to identify in advance the infrastructural requirements for the project and sound the concerned government agencies accordingly so that one can get necessary facilities in right time.

(5) A major contribution of PPR at the nascent stage of the entrepreneur career is that it instills confidence in entrepreneur and motivates to start the time consuming process of data collection and preparation of DPR.

PRELIMINARY PROJECT REPORT PROFORMA

1.0 GENERAL

Name of the Entrepreneur____________________

Birth date: __________ Age__________

Project____________________

Location____________________/Rented Shed__________

Types of the organisation: Proprietary/Partnership/__________

Name of the Firm:____________________

Address____________________

1.1 Educational Qualification

S.S.S. or Below	Degree/Diploma	Institute	Major Subject	Year of Passing

1.2 Technical Qualification/Training

Training	in Institute	Duration	Achievement

1.3 Work Experience (Past and Present)

Organisation	Position	Nature of Work	Duration

2.1 Production Programme

Sl. No.	Item Quantity/Year	Total	Sales	Revenue/Year	Capacity Utilisation

2.2 Machineries/Equipment

Sl. No.	Description	Nos. required	price	Total value	Name and address of the suppliers

2.3 Raw Materials

Sl. No.	Item	Total annual requirements		Source
		Quantity	Value	

2.4 Utilities

Sl. No.	Particulars	Annual Requirement	Total Annual expenses	Remarks
1	Electricity			
2	Water			
3	Coal/Oil			
4	Any Other			
5	Total			

2.5 Manpower

Sl. No.	Particulars	No.	Total Wages and Salaries (per year)	Remarks
1	Skilled			
2	Semi-skilled			
3	Unskilled			
4	Office staff			

3.0 MARKET STUDY:

4.0 COST OF THE PROJECT

4.1 Fixed Capital

Sl. No.	Item	Value (Rs.)
1	Land/Building	
2	Machinery/Equipment	
3	Furniture and Fixture	
	Total	

4.2 Working Capital

Sl. No.	Item	Duration	Quantity	Value (Rs.)
1.	Raw Materials Stock			
2.	Semi-finished Goods Stock			
3.	Finished Goods Stock			
4.	One month production expenses (Utilities + Wages + Salaries)			
5.	Total			

4.3 Total Cost of Project

Sl. No.	Particulars	Value (Rs.)
1.	Fixed Capital	
2.	Working Capital (Total of item No. 4.2)	
3.	Preliminary and pre-operative Expenses	
	Total	

Project Management: Network Techniques

Network analysis is the general name given to certain specific techniques which can be used for the planning, management and control of projects. A project is a temporary endeavour undertaken to create a "unique" product or service." It has been classified into two categories such as:

(i) **PERT: Project Evaluation Review Technique:** PERT was developed by the US Navy for the planning and control of the Polaris missile program and the emphasis was on completing the program in the shortest possible time. In addition PERT had the ability to cope with uncertain activity completion times.

(ii) **CPM: Critical Path Method:** CPM was developed by Du Pont and the emphasis was on the trade-off between the cost of the project and its overall completion time (e.g., for certain activities it may be possible to decrease their completion times by spending more money - how does this affect the overall completion time of the project?)

Why PERT/CPM?

- Controlling resource allocation
- External program review
- Internal program review
- Performance evaluation
- Planning resource requirements
- Prediction of deliverables
- Uniform wide acceptance

Summary

Project management is a carefully planned and organized effort to accomplish a specific (and usually) one-time objective, for example, construct a building or implement a major new computer system. Project management includes developing a project plan, which includes defining and confirming the project goals and objectives, identifying tasks and how goals will be achieved, quantifying the resources needed, and determining budgets and timelines for completion. It also includes managing the implementation of the project plan, along with operating regular 'controls' to ensure that there is accurate and objective information on 'performance' relative to the plan, and the mechanisms to implement recovery actions where necessary. Project management is a specialist discipline. In a well run project, there is a constant array of management issues to deal with, as well as a challenging routine of project management processes. A subset of project management that includes the processes required to ensure that the project includes all the work required, and only the work required to complete the project successfully.

QUESTIONS

SHORT ANSWER QUESTIONS

1. What do you mean by the research?
2. What are the various types of research?
3. What are the various criteria's of a good research?
4. What is resource mapping?
5. What is SWOT analysis?

LONG ANSWER QUESTIONS

1. What are the various steps in a research process? Explain each of them in detail.
2. What do you mean by the project report? Explain a sample of preliminary project report.
3. What do you mean by environment analysis? Explain the various factors of environment analysis.

CHAPTER

INSTITUTIONAL SUPPORT TO ENTREPRENEURS

"What lies behind us and what lies before us are tiny matters compared to what lies within us."

— Oliver Wendell Holmes

Chapter Overview:

At the end of this chapter, you will be able to understand:

1. The services of various Institutions to entrepreneurial business.
2. The objectives of Central Level Financial Institutions.
3. The objectives of State Level Financial Institutions.

INTRODUCTION

Industries are the backbone of any country. The progress and prosperity of any country is largely depends upon the industrial developments. An industrially advanced country creates economic self-sufficiency and increases employment opportunities. It aims at having excellent performance to get better results. It is the primary responsibilities of the Central and State Government to encourage the individuals to establish new industries. The Central Government is actively helping the state by providing various types of incentives, subsidies and other benefits.

NEED FOR INSTITUTIONAL SUPPORTS

Business growth is critical to entrepreneurial success. The potential for growth is one of the factors which distinguish the entrepreneurial venture from small business. Organisational growth, however, means more than just an increase in size. Growth is a dynamic process. It involves development and change within the organization and changes in the way in which the organization interacts with its environment. Though an organization grows as a coherent whole, organizational growth itself is best understood in a multi-faceted way. The process of liberalization and market reforms has created wide ranging opportunities for the development of small scale industries. At the same time, changing world scenario has thrown up new challenges to the very existence of the sector. The need of the hour is to suitably strengthen the sector so that it could adapt itself to the changed environment and face the challenges boldly and effectively. Following are the organisations which are providing support services to the small and medium enterprises.

1. Directorate of Industries (DIs)
2. National Small Industries Corporation(NSIC)
3. National Institute for Entrepreneurship and Small Business Development (NIESBUD)
4. National Institute for Micro, Small and Medium Enterprises (NIMSME)
5. The National Science and Technology Entrepreneurship Development Board (NSTEDB)
6. Industrial Development Bank of India (IDBI)
7. Industrial Financial Corporation of India (IFCI)
8. Small Industries Development Bank of India (SIDBI)
9. Industrial Credit and Investment Corporation of India (ICICI)
10. Industrial Reconstruction Bank of India (IRBI)
11. State Financial Corporation's (SFC)
12. State Industrial Development Corporations (SIDC)
13. Export and Import Bank (EXIM)
14. Export Credit Guarantee Corporation (ECGC)

15. Small Industries Development Organisation (SIDO)
16. State Small Industries Development Corporation (SSIDC)
17. Small Scale Industries Board (SSIB)
18. Small Industries Service Institutes (SISI)
19. Industrial Estates (IE)
20. Technical Consultancy Organisations (TCO)
21. Commercial Banks and Term Lending's in India (CB&TL)
22. District Industries Centres (DIC)
23. Directorate of Export Promotion and Marketing (DEPM)
24. Industrial Promotion and Investment Corporation of Orissa Ltd. (IPICOL)
25. Industrial Infrastructure Development Corporation of Orissa (IIDCO)
26. Orissa State Financial Corporation (OSFC)
27. Orissa Small Industries Corporation (OSIC)
28. Directorate of Technical Education and Training (DTET)
29. The Agricultural Promotion and Investment Corporation of Orissa Limited (APICOL)
30. The Orissa Film Development Corporation (OFDC)

1. Directorate of Industries (DIs)

The Directorate of Industries is an executive arm of the Industries Department and is engaged in implementation of Govt.'s policies for allround development of industries in the State by seeking coordination amongst the State level promotional corporations and other departments/agencies of the Govt. relating to industries. The Directorate of Industries is led by Development Commissioner (Industries). It is the state level office responsible for implementing the policies and programmes for industrial development in the state. These offices are the focal point at the district level to facilitate industrial development in coordination with the other departments/agencies of the Government. The plan schemes and the activities under various policies of the State-Govt. are implemented by the District Industries Centres. The powers to implement the Schemes are completely decentralization and are vested with the District Industries Centres for effective delivery mechanism at district level. Besides, the DICs are the first link of the Industry-Govt. interface for resolving various issues of industry for its all round and healthy growth. Directorate of Industries works through DIC's at the district level. The role and functions of Directorate of Industries are as follows:

Role of Directorate of Industries

- Encouraging investment in manufacturing and services sector
- Encouraging entrepreneurship
- Encouraging competitiveness in MSME sector.

Functions of Directorate of Industries

(i) To implement Industrial Policy of the Government

(ii) Suggest policy measures to the Government for effecting healthy and allround industrial development in the State in view of challenges and opportunities posed to the industry in the prevailing economic scenario.

(iii) Assist Government in formulation of various policies *viz.*, Industrial Policy, SEZ Policy, IT Policy, Package Scheme of Incentives, etc.

(iv) Implement various promotional schemes.

(v) Resolving the operational problems of industry by inter departmental coordination.

NATIONAL SMALL INDUSTRIES CORPORATION (NSIC)

National Small Industries Corporation was set up in 1955, under the Union Ministry of industries to promote and develop small scale industries in the country. It is mainly supplying indigenous and important equipment on hire purchase basis to the small scale and ancillary industries. Facilities are available to those units whose value of machinery and equipment are not exceeding 3 crores inclusive of the value of the machineries and equipment already installed. The amount of the hire purchase of machineries are directly paid to the supplier an amount will be repayable within 20 quarterly instalments. It also provides other facilities like leasing, marketing support, technological developments, encouragement to export etc. NSIC continues to remain at the forefront of industrial development throughout the country with its various programmes and projects to assist the small-scale sector in the country. Recent transitions of industrial climate and liberalization of the total economic environment within the country and international arena has witnessed the tremendous changes in the domestic as well as international markets. These sudden changes have thrown up as many opportunities as challenges to the small scale enterprises in the country.

To promote small scale sector, NSIC has launched composite Term Loan Schemes, Working Capital Finance, Raw Material Assistance, Marketing Support Programme, Tender Marketing, Technology Transfer Centres, Software Technology Parks, Exports and Special Export Programmes etc. Composite Term Loan Schemes provides entrepreneurs to acquire land and building, machinery and equipment and working capital under one roof to the tiny units. Working Capital Finance scheme aims at augmenting working capital of viable and well managed units, on selective basis in case of emergent requirements to enable them to pay-off their purchase of consumable stores, spares and production related overheads particularly electricity bills, statutory dues. Raw Material Assistance facilitates the small units on "off the shelf basis" by opening raw materials depots or godowns in different parts of the country.

NATIONAL INSTITUTE FOR ENTREPRENEURSHIP AND SMALL BUSINESS DEVELOPMENT (NIESBUD)

The National Institute for Entrepreneurship and Small Business Development (NIESBUD) was established in 1983, by the Ministry of Industry (now Ministry of Micro,Small and Medium Enterprises) Govt. of India, as an apex body for coordinating and overseeing the activities of various institutions/agencies engaged in entrepreneurship development particularly in the area of small industry and small business. The Institute which is registered as a society under Govt. of India Societies Act (XXI of 1860) started functioning from 6th July, 1983.

The policy, direction and guidance to the Institute is provided by its Governing Council whose Chairman is the Minister of SSI. The Executive Committee consisting of Secretary (Small Scale Industry and ARI) as its Chairman and Executive Director of the Institute as its Member Secretary executes the policies and decisions of the Governing Council through its whole-time Executive Director. The various functions are:

- To evolve standardised materials and processes for selection, training, support and sustenance of entrepreneurs, potential and existing.
- To help/support and affiliate institutions/organisations in carrying out training and other entrepreneurship development related activities.

Objectives

- To serve as an apex national level resource institute for accelerating the process of entrepreneurship development ensuring its impact across the country and among all strata of the society.
- To provide vital information and support to trainers, promoters and entrepreneurs by organising research and documentation relevant to entrepreneurship development.
- To train trainers, promoters and consultants in various areas of entrepreneurship development.
- To provide national/international forums for interaction and exchange of experiences helpful for policy formulation and modification at various levels.
- To offer consultancy nationally/internationally for promotion of entrepreneurship and small business development.
- To share internationally experience and expertise in entrepreneurship development.
- To share experience and expertise in entrepreneurship development across national frontiers.

NATIONAL INSTITUTE FOR MICRO, SMALL AND MEDIUM ENTERPRISES (NIMSME)

NIMSME was originally set up as Central Industrial Extension Training Institute (CIETI) in New Delhi in 1960 as a department under the Ministry of Industry and Commerce, Government of India. It was formerly known as National Institute of Small Industry Extension Training (NISIET). NIMSME (NISIET) is an organisation of the Ministry of MSMEs (Formerly Ministry of SSI), Government of India, is a premier institution and internationally reputed for promotion of MSMEs through the services like training, research, consultancy, education, extension and information. It is an autonomous arm of the Ministry of Micro Small and Medium Enterprises (MSMEs). It was decided to keep it free from the tardy and impeding administrative controls and procedures, so that the Institute can play a pivotal role in the promotion of small enterprise. The Institute was shifted to Hyderabad in 1962, and was renamed as Small Industry Extension Training (SIET) Institute. SIET, as it was fondly known for over two decades later, is managed by Governing Council, appointed by the Government of India. The Founder-Chairman of SIET is Dr P.C. Alexander, the then Development Commissioner (Small Scale Industries). NIMSME has taken gigantic strides to become the premier institution for the promotion, development and modernization of the SME sector. An autonomous arm of the Ministry of Micro, Small and Medium Enterprises (MSMEs), the Institute strives to achieve its avowed objectives through a gamut of operations ranging from training, consultancy, research and education, to extension and information services. In 1984, United Nations Development Organisations (UNDO) had recognized SIET as an institute of meritorious performance under its Centers of Excellence Scheme to extend aid. Subsequently, it was also accorded national status and SIET Institute became NISIET in the same year. To cope with the precut of globalization, the Government of India has enacted Micro, Small, Medium Enterprises Development (MSMED) Bill in the Parliament which was commenced on 2nd October, 2006. Accordingly, the institute also has emerged as an apex organisation by changing its structure as well as name as NIMSME from 11th April 2007.

THE NATIONAL SCIENCE AND TECHNOLOGY ENTREPRENEURSHIP DEVELOPMENT BOARD (NSTEDB)

It was established by Government of India in 1982, is an institutional mechanism, with a broad objective of promoting gainful self-employment amongst the Science and Technology (S&T) manpower in the country and to set-up knowledge based and innovation driven enterprises. NSTEDB functions under the aegis of Department of Science and Technology. It has representation from socio-economic and scientific Department/Ministries, premier entrepreneurship development institutions and all India Financial Institutions.

The major objectives of NSTEDB are:

- To promote knowledge based and innovation driven enterprises.
- To facilitate generation of entrepreneurship and self-employment opportunities for S&T persons.
- To facilitate the information dissemination.
- To network with various Central and State Government agencies for S&T based entrepreneurship development.
- To act as a policy advisory body to the Government agencies for S&T based entrepreneurship development.
- To generate employment through technical skill development using S&T infrastructure.

The programmes conducted by NSTEDB have created awareness among S&T persons to take up entrepreneurship as a career. The academicians and researchers have started taking a keen interest in such socially relevant roles and have engaged themselves in several programmes initiated by NSTEDB. About 100 organizations, most of which are academic institutions and voluntary agencies, were drafted in the task of entrepreneurship development and employment generation. Some of the major activities undertaken by NSTEDB are elaborated on this portal. More programmes are being evolved to suit the changing economic and market scenario. 'Science Tech Entrepreneur' magazine launched by National Science and Technology Entrepreneurship Development Board in 1995, is one of India's leading magazines on Entrepreneurship. NSTEDB, Department of Science and Technology, in its endeavour to spread information about technology-driven, knowledge-based enterprise promotion is providing the Science-Tech Entrepreneur magazine in electronic form.

Industrial Development Bank of India (IDBI)

Industrial Development Bank of India was established on July 1, 1964, as a wholly-owned subsidiary of Reserve Bank of India (RBI) under an Act of Parliament. In view of the manifold increase in its activities and diverse responsibilities, IDBI was reconstituted through legislation in 1976 enacted by Parliament and made the principal financial institution of the country. The ownership of IDBI was transferred from RBI to Government of India and various responsibilities relating to Financial Institutions and other matters connected with institutional finance previously vested with RBI were entrusted to the reconstituted IDBI. Pursuant to the amendment to IDBI Act in 1995, IDBI made its initial public offering of equity shares in July 1995, reducing Government holding to 72.14%. The amendment was also aimed at providing greater operational flexibility to IDBI. This would help IDBI in responding to the changing needs of the industrial sector in a much more prompt and decisive manner. IDBI has played a pioneering role in fulfilling its mission of promoting industrial growth in line with national plans and priorities.

The main objective of IDBI is to provide financial assistance for establishment of new projects as well as for expansion, diversification, modernisation and technology upgradation of existing industrial enterprises. IDBI is vested with the responsibility of coordinating the working of institutions engaged in financing, promoting and developing industries. IDBI has evolved an appropriate mechanism for this purpose. IDBI also undertakes wide ranging promotional activities including entrepreneurship development programmes for new entrepreneurs, provision of consultancy services for small and medium enterprises, upgradation of technology and programmes for economic upliftment of the underprivileged. IDBI's role as a catalyst to industrial development encompasses a wide spectrum of activities. It can finance all types of industrial concerns covered under the provisions of the IDBI Act. Over more than three decades of its service to Indian industry, IDBI has grown substantially in terms of size of operations and portfolio.

Products

IDBI offers a wide range of financial products. It is constantly making efforts to respond to the financial needs of the industry by expanding the scope of its existing products and services and introducing new innovative products.

Project Finance

Project finance is provided for setting up of new projects as well as for expansion, diversification, modernisation and technology upgradation of existing enterprises. IDBI provides assistance to industry in the form of term loans, both in Indian rupees and foreign currencies, underwriting/direct subscription to debt instruments/equity and also offers guarantees in respect of the term obligations of industrial concerns. IDBI operates special products for technology upgradation, energy conservation and pollution control. It also provides venture capital for the development and use of indigenous technology and adaptation of imported technology. IDBI offers to its borrowers the option of both fixed and variable interest rates which are based on IDBI's risk perception and credit worthiness of the borrowers.

Non-project finance

IDBI also provides several diversified financial products of non-project nature to meet the specific needs of existing enterprises having good performance record and sound financial position. IDBI provides asset credit in the form of line of credit for acquisition of new machinery/ equipment. It also provides credit to industrial units for financing their normal capital expenditure over a specified period. IDBI provides equipment finance in the form of Indian rupee and foreign currency loans for acquisition of specific machinery/equipment.

Corporate Loans

IDBI provides corporate loans for capital expenditure and for meeting long term working capital requirements.

Working Capital Loan

IDBI provides loan component of working capital finance to companies already assisted by it. Refinance of industrial loans medium scale projects involving capital costs ranging between Rs.3 crore and Rs.5 crore is generally financed indirectly by IDBI through refinance of industrial loans granted by state-level institutions/commercial banks.

Bills Finance

IDBI rediscounts bills of exchange and promissory notes of industrial concerns arising out of sale and purchase of indigenous machinery and capital equipment on deferred payment basis and discounted by institutions approved by it. It also directly discounts bills of exchange and promissory notes of machinery manufacturers.

Services

- **Merchant banking:** The merchant banking operations of IDBI as Category I and leading merchant banker, encompass professional advice and services to industry for issue management, loan syndication, project counseling, corporate advice, project appraisal, capital restructuring and mergers and acquisitions.
- **Debenture trusteeship:** IDBI acts as debenture trustee for holders of debentures issued by companies as also to the non-convertible debenture issues subscribed by financial institutions, banks and mutual funds on private placement basis. It also offers odd lot trustee services. It acts as security agent/mortgage trustee in respect of loans granted by domestic and foreign lenders to companies.
- **Forex services:** IDBI offers a variety of foreign exchange services namely - spot and forward purchases of currencies for letters of credit and debt servicing, placement of deposits abroad, swaps, forward rate agreements and derivative products.
- **Subsidiary for small scale sector:** IDBI had been directing considerable assistance to the small scale sector. In an effort to further intensify assistance to the small scale sector, IDBI set up a wholly-owned subsidiary, the Small Industries Development Bank of India (SIDBI), as the principal financial institution for promoting, financing and developing the industries in the small scale sector.

- **Promotional and developmental activities:** In fulfilment of its developmental role the bank continues to perform a wide range of promotional activities relating to developmental programmes for new entrepreneurs, consultancy services for small and medium enterprises and programmes designed for accredited voluntary agencies for economic upliftment of the underprivileged. These include entrepreneurship development, self-employment and wage employment in industrial sector for weaker sections of society through voluntary agencies, support to Science and Technology Entrepreneurs' Parks, Energy Conservation, Common Quality Testing Centres for small industries. With a view to making available at reasonable cost, consultancy and advisory services to entrepreneurs, particularly to new and small entrepreneurs, IDBI, in collaboration with other All-India Financial Institutions, has set up a network of Technical Consultancy Organisations (TCOs) covering the entire country. TCOs offer diversified services to small and medium enterprises in the selection, formulation and appraisal of projects, their implementation and review. Realizing that entrepreneurship development is the key to industrial development; IDBI played a prime role in setting up of the Entrepreneurship Development Institute of India for fostering entrepreneurship in the country. It has also established similar institutes in several other states. IDBI also extends financial support to various organizations in conducting studies/surveys of relevance to industrial development.
- **Institution building:** Institution building is an important facet of IDBI's activities. It has set up organizations for entrepreneurship development and technical consultancy. In view of the immense importance of capital markets in industrial development, IDBI took a lead role in setting up of several institutions for its healthy development. These are the Securities and Exchange Board of India (SEBI), National Stock Exchange of India Limited (NSEIL), and Stock Holding Corporation of India Limited (SHCIL), Credit Analysis and Research Limited (CARE), and Over The Couner Exchange of India Limited (OTCEI), Investor Services of India Limited (ISIL) and National Securities Depository Limited (NSDL).

Organization and Management

IDBI is managed by a Board of Directors headed by the Chairman and Managing Director. The Board of Directors comprises eminent industrialists, professionals, management experts and representatives of the Central Government. Day-to-day operations of IDBI are carried out under the supervision of Chairman and Managing Director assisted by Executive Directors and other executives. IDBI has a pool of competent and experienced professionals drawn from various disciplines. It has decentralized its operations and delegated authority to ensure efficient working and responsive client servicing. The Bank had commissioned Booz, Allen and Hamilton (BAH), and an international firm of management consultants, to study its role and advise on strategic repositioning so as to maintain its leadership position in the financial system. Based on their recommendations the Bank has implemented the reorganisation process at the head office and the branch offices. These changes would enable the Bank to streamline the credit delivery process and enable it to serve its customers better. An in-house Asset Liability Management (ALM) Committee has been constituted to monitor liquidity risk, interest rate risk and foreign exchange risk in a co-ordinated manner. Further, IDBI has also appointed Arthur Andersen to establish an effective ALM function. The Consultancy firm would, among other things, help develop ALM policies, establish an appropriate ALM organisation structure, identify ALM software options and assist IDBI in the pilot implementation of the ALM information process.

Industrial Finance Corporation of India (IFCI)

At the time of independence in 1947, India's capital market was relatively under-developed. Although there was significant demand for new capital, there was a dearth of providers. Merchant bankers and underwriting firms were almost non-existent. And commercial banks were not equipped to provide long-term industrial finance in any significant manner. It is against this backdrop that the government established The Industrial Finance Corporation of India (IFCI) on July 1, 1948, as the first Development Financial Institution in the country to cater to the long-term finance needs of the industrial sector. The newly-established DFI was provided access to low-cost funds through the central bank's Statutory Liquidity Ratio or SLR which in turn enabled it to provide loans and advances to corporate borrowers at concessional rates.

Liberalisation – Conversion into Company in 1993

This arrangement continued until the early 1990s when it was recognized that there was need for greater flexibility to respond to the changing financial system. It was also felt that IFCI should directly access the capital markets for its funds needs. It is with this objective that the constitution of IFCI was changed in 1993 from a statutory corporation to a company under the Indian Companies Act, 1956. Subsequently, the name of the company was also changed to "IFCI Limited" with effect from October 1999.

Focus

IFCI has fulfilled its original mandate as a DFI by providing long-term financial support to all segments of Indian Industry. It has also been chiefly instrumental in translating the Government's development priorities into reality. Until the establishment of ICICI in 1955 and IDBI in 1964, IFCI remained solely responsible for implementation of the government's industrial policy initiatives. Its contribution to the modernization of Indian industry, export promotion, import substitution, entrepreneurship development, pollution control, energy conservation and generation of both direct and indirect employment is noteworthy. Some sectors that have directly benefited from IFCI's disbursals include: "Consumer goods industry (textiles, paper, sugar); Service industries (hotels, hospitals); Basic industries (iron and steel, fertilizers, basic chemicals, cement); Capital and intermediate goods industries (electronics, synthetic fibers, synthetic plastics, miscellaneous chemicals); and Infrastructure (power generation, telecom services).

IFCI has also set up Chairs in reputed educational/management institutions and universities. A major contribution of IFCI has been in the early assistance provided by it to some of today's leading Indian entrepreneurs who may not have been able to start their enterprises or expand without the initial support from IFCI. IFCI has promoted Technical Consultancy Organizations (TCOs), primarily in less developed states to provide necessary services to the promoters of small- and medium-sized industries in collaboration with other banks and institutions. IFCI has also provided assistance to self-employed youth and women entrepreneurs under its Benevolent Reserve Fund (BRF) and the Interest Differential Fund (IDF). IFCI has founded and developed prominent institutions like: Management Development Institute (MDI) for management training and development, ICRA for credit assessment rating, Tourism Finance Corporation of India (TFCI) for promotion of the hotel and tourism industry, Institute of Labor Development (ILD) for rehabilitation and training of displaced and retrenched labor force, Rashtriya Gramin Vikas Nidhi (RGVN) for promoting, supporting and developing voluntary agencies engaged in uplifting rural and urban poor in east and northeast India. IFCI, along with other institutions, has also promoted: "Stock Holding Corporation of India Limited (SHCIL) Discount and Finance House of India Limited (DFHI) National Stock Exchange (NSE), Securities Trading Corporation of India (STCI), LIC Housing Finance Limited, GIC Grih Vitta Limited, and Bio-tech Consortium Limited (BCL).

Small Industries Development Bank of India (SIDBI)

The SIDBI was established on April 02, 1990, under an Act of Parliament, the Small Industries Development Bank of India Act 1989, as a wholly-owned subsidiary of Industrial Development Bank of India, the premier development bank in the country. It was delinked from IDBI w.e.f., March 27, 2000. SIDBI is headed by the Chairman and Managing Director. The mission of SIDBI is to empower the Micro, Small and Medium Enterprises (MSME) sector with a view to contributing to the process of economic growth, employment generation and balanced regional development. The main objectives of SIDBI are (i) to serve as the principal financial institution for promotion, financing and development of industry in the small scale sector, (ii) to co-ordinate the functions of the institutions engaged in promoting, financing or developing industry in the small scale sector. Since its establishment SIDBI has been facilitating and steadily enhancing the flow of financial and developmental assistance to the small scale sector. It provides promotional, developmental and support services to SSI sector in collaboration with voluntary organisations and multilateral/international agencies. SIDBI has identified five broad thrust areas of assistance. They are :

- **Technology up-gradation and transfer:** In order to develop the technology up-gradation, SIDBI has identified two thrust areas, i.e., cluster approach for technology up-gradation and collaboration and MoUs (Memorandum of Understandings) with multilateral/International agencies for technological improvement and transfer. The technology up-gradation and modernisation efforts of the bank are aimed at identifying the needs of the industry in terms of process technology, environment management, quality management, common facilities centre etc. and at initiating efforts to address these needs. The bank identifies and implementing agency for each clusters which in turn examines the specific transfer and provides escort services. The bank has also entered into a MoU with Small Industries Development Organisation (SIDO) which *inter-alia*, provides for joint initiatives of technology up-gradation in six more clusters. In order to improve and transfer technology, the bank has made MoU with Asian and Pacific Centre for Transfer of Technology (APACTT) which is a regional institution of the United Nations under the aegis of Economic and Social Commission for Asia and the Pacific (ESCAP). A MoU was signed in 1994, with Small Industries Development Organisation (SIDO), envisaging up-gradation of technology in the SSI sector ad development of SSIs as ancillaries to defense and large establishments, while the facilities of SIDO through its various outfits in the form of Small Industries Service Institutes (SISIs). A MoU was also signed between SIDBI and Council of Scientific and Industrial Research (CSIR) which is the largest industrial R&D organisation in India engaged in promotion and development of indigenous technologies and utilization of indigenous resources with a network of 40 labs and has developed over 2300 process/technologies of which around 2000 have been licensed to over 6,000 licensees.
- **Marketing including exports:** Despite the availability of adequate credit for various project requirements, it is difficult especially for SSI units to source credit for intangible activities like marketing, brand promotion, advertising, participation in trade fairs and executing sample export orders for overseas market entry.The increasing competitiveness in the Indian markets and opening up of export opportunities have made quality a factor of paramount importance. Total Quality Management (TQM) and ISO-9000 certification have been gaining recognition as effective systems for building up and maintaining quality systems in organisations. Recognising the need greater awareness on these concepts, the bank has undertaken a major campaign to organize participative workshop all over the country. Associations like FICCI (Federation of Indian Chambers and Commerc and Industry) Quality Forum, ASSOCHAM and CII and specialist agencies like TQM Consultants (P) Ltd., and National Productivity Council (NPC).

- **Rural industrialization:** The bank firmly believes that development of viable and self-sustaining micro-enterprises in rural unemployment, urban migration, under-utilization of know-how and latent rural resources, in turn, reducing the imbalances in regional development. The Bank has adopted a comprehensive approach in formulating specific programmers aimed at promotion of informal income generating activities and micro and tiny enterprises in the rural areas with a special emphasis on backward areas and women.
- **Management development:** The Bank is concerned with the need for management development and performance improvement of SSI units. In line with such objectives, SIDBI has initiated the Small Industries Management Assistantce Programme (SIMAP) launched with the objective of developing a cadre of industrial managers specifically trained to assist small scale entrepreneurs in their multiple responsibilities and at the same time, opening up new avenues of productive employment for young graduates who are otherwise not professionally qualified.
- **Environment management and pollution control:** Pollution and environmental degradation caused by industrial sources pose a serious threat to the sustainability of economic development of the country. The small scale sector which accounts for a significant portion of the total industrial production in the country is found wanting an adopting pollution control measures. The reasons for this are manifold – technological obsolescence, inadequate understanding of the manufacturing process and lack of awareness of technologies which can prevent pollution, physical and financial constraints of the units, to name a few, are acting as impediments to ringing out pollution-free operations by the small units. For assisting SSI units in complying with pollution control norms, the bank has adopted a two pronged approach of not only encouraging implementation of corrective measures by the existing units, but also ensuring adoption of preventive practices by the new units.

SIDBI has been adopting a proactive role not just to imbibe technological optimism among SSIs but also to set in motion the multi-dimensional process of modernisation, which includes credit, marketing, infrastructure, services, management, skill development etc. However, SIDBI being a relatively new institution, needs funds support on soft terms to foster the growth of SSIs and to meet their aspirations. SIDBI is the principal financial institution for the promotion financing and development of industries in the small scale sector and to co-ordinate the functions of the institutions engaged in similar activities. It is otherwise known as an apex institution to strengthen the existing financial agencies and to reach the cottage, village, tiny and small scale industries which are spread throughout the country. Various activities of SIDBI are:

(i) Refinance Assistance.

(ii) Bill Rediscounting Schemes.

(iii) Scheme for Equity support (Seed Capital Scheme and National Equity Fund Scheme).

(iv) Direct Assistance to NSIC and SSIDC (National Small Industries Corporation, State Small Industrial Development Corporation).

(v) Schemes of Direct Assistance (Equipment Finance Scheme, Venture Capital Fund Scheme, Project Finance Scheme).

(vi) Mahila Udyami Nidhi.

(vii) Single Window Assistance Scheme.

Industrial Credit and Investment Corporation of India (ICICI)

The Industrial Credit and Investment Corporation of India Limited (ICICI) incorporated at the initiative of the World Bank, the Government of India and representatives of Indian industry, with the objective of creating a development financial institution for providing medium-term and long-term project financing to Indian businesses. The Industrial Credit and Investment Corporation of India or ICICI was established on 5th January, 1955, to assist industrial units in the private sector. It was sponsored by the World Bank. The primary object of ICICI is to assist industrial units in the private-sector. The ICICI is managed by a board of 11 directors out of whom 7 directors are elected by Indian shareholders, 2 by British shareholders, 1 by American shareholders and the remaining 1 is nominated by Government of India, It has a full-time chairman and a general manager. The ICICI is empowered to accept foreign currency loans. Loan provided by the World Bank is dominating feature. Besides World Bank loan, the ICICI is also obtaining loans from IDBI, IBRD, AID and KFW of the Federal Republic of Germany, America, Britain and also from Government of India. The main objects of ICICI are as follows:

- To assist in the creation, expansion and modernization at industrial units in the private sector.
- To encourage the inflow and participation of foreign capital in the private sector industrial units.
- To expand the investment market in India.

Functions: The main functions of ICICI are as follows:

- To sponsor and underwrite new issues.
- To provide medium and long-term loans to industrial units in the private sector.
- To guarantee loans taken from other private sources.
- To furnish managerial, technical and administrative advice to industrial units by the private sector.

- To make funds available for reinvestment.
- To advance loans in foreign currency towards the cost of imported capital equipments.
- To extend guarantee for deferred payments.
- To purchase the shares and debentures of new companies

Industrial Reconstruction Bank of India (IRBI)

The Industrial Reconstruction Bank of India (IRBI) came into being on 20th March 1985, by converting the erstwhile Industrial Reconstruction Corporation of India. It provides assistance for reconstructions and rehabilitation of the sick industrial units by granting those loans and advances, underwriting shares and debentures etc.

State Financial Corporation's (SFC)

State Financial Corporation was established in the year 1951, to provide financial assistance to the industries located in the various states. There are 18 SFCs in India. The main object of SFCs is to grants loan and advances to industrial concerns repayable within a period of not exceeding 20 years. In every states of India respective SFCs are introducing several schemes of liberalized finance in order to attract talented entrepreneurs. Various schemes of SFCs are technical entrepreneur schemes, soft loan scheme, schemes for self employment of educated employed persons, composite loan schemes etc.

State Industrial Development Corporations (SIDC)

The State Industrial Development Corporations (SIDCs) were under the Companies Act, 1956, as wholly owned undertakings of the governments with the specific objectives of promoting and developing and large industries in their respective states/union territories. SIDC extends financial assistance in the form of rupee loans, underwriting subscriptions to shares/debentures, guarantees, letters of credit on behalf of its borrowers. SIDCs undertake of promotional activities including preparation of feasibility reports, conducting industrial potential, surveys entrepreneurship training and development programmes and developing industrial areas/ estates. Some SIDCs also offer a package of developmental services that include technical guidance, assistance in plant location and co-ordination with other agencies. With a view to providing infrastructural facilities for the establishment of industrial units, SIDCs are involved in the setting up of industrial growth centres. To keep pace with the hanging economic environment, SIDCs have initiated various measures to expand the scope of their activities and have entered into various fee-based activities. Of the various SIDCs in the country, those in Andaman and Nicobar, Arunachal Pradesh, Daman and Diu and Dadra and Nagar Haveli, Goa, Manipur, Meglalaya, Mizoram, Nagaland, Tripura, Pondicherry and Sikkim also act as

SFCs to provide assistance to small and medium enterprises and act as promotional agencies for this sector. State Industrial Development Corporation operate at slightly higher level than SFCs though these institutions are also primarily working as development banks promoting industrial projects in small and medium scale.

Export and Import Bank (EXIM)

It was set up on 1st January, 1982, for extending financial assistance for the promotion of India's foreign trade. It is a statutory corporation owned by the Union Government. It coordinates the activities of institutions engaged in financing export and imports. The main activities of the bank are to increase the export of non-traditional manufactured goods, projects exports and exports of technology and consultancy services. It is providing two types of assistance i.e. funded and non-funded. Funded assistance includes direct finance to exports, technology ad consultancy services, overseas investment, financing, pre-shipment credit, export bill rediscounting and refinancing of export credit. Non-funded assistance includes guarantee towards advances and performance guarantee towards retention and raising finance abroad. Its functions include:

- Extending loans and advances to banks and financial institutions notified by the Central Government for the purpose of export and import.
- Financing Indian joint venture abroad.
- Providing technical, administrative and financial assistance to parties in connection with exports and imports.
- Dealing with foreign exchange.
- Undertaking International Merchant Banking Services.
- Conducting research, survey, techno-economic study for the promotion of International Trade.
- Collecting, compiling and disseminating market and credit information in connection with International Trade.

Export Credit Guarantee Corporation (ECGC)

Export Credit Guarantee Corporation of India Limited was set up in the year 1964, with an objective of exports risks and guaranteeing payments to the exporters as well as financing banks. It looks over the functions of Export Risk Insurance Corporation that had been set up in 1957, by the Government of India to strengthen the export promotion drive by covering the risk of exporting on credit. Two types of risks are covered under this scheme. They are commercial risk and political risks; Commercial risk protects the insolvency of the importer, default in payment and failure to accept the documents entitling the goods. On the other hand political risk includes imposition of new import restrictions, cancellation of import license, cost of additional handling and transporting due to interruption of voyage, loss of any other factors which are not covered by commercial insurers. Being essentially an export promotion organization, it functions under the administrative control of the Ministry of Commerce and Industry, Department of Commerce, and Government of India. It is managed by a Board of Directors comprising representatives of the Government, Reserve Bank of India, banking and insurance and exporting community. Export Credit Guarantee Corporation of India provides export credit insurance to the exporters of India. The organization comes under the power of Ministry of Commerce, Government of India. It got incorporated in 1983. The various services of ECGC in India are:

- To protect the exporters against the loss in export, the corporation provides variety of credit risk insurance.
- For the benefit of exporters in dealing with banks and financial institutions, the ECGC provide guarantees to those institutions.
- In the form of equity or loan the corporation also provides help to Indian companies to make joint ventures overseas.

Special Schemes of ECGC includes transfer guarantee, overseas investment guarantee and exchange fluctuations, risk covers etc.

What does ECGC do?

- Provides a range of credit risk insurance covers to exporters against loss in export of goods and services.
- Offers guarantees to banks and financial institutions to enable exporters to obtain better facilities from them.
- Provides Overseas Investment Insurance to Indian companies investing in joint ventures abroad in the form of equity or loan

Export Credit Guarantee Corporation is required for the smooth functioning of all aspects relate to exports of goods. Payments for exports are prone to risks even in good times and in the present political and economically changing scenario the risk is even higher in regards to the payments. Factors like a coup, an outbreak of a war or civil war, problems in balance of payment and such other risks can happen at anytime. Besides all these, commercial risks of a foreign buyer becoming bankrupt are enhanced due to the prevailing political and economic uncertainties. To tackle all these and various other issues related to exports, it is very important to have an organization like Export Credit Guarantee Corporation to safeguard the interest of the exporter.

Small Industries Development Organisation (SIDO)

The Small Industries Development Organisation is an apex body and nodal agency established by the Government of India in the year 1954, for formulating, coordinating and monitoring the policies and programme for the promotion and development of small scale industries. Development Commissioner is the head of the SIDO and supported by various other advisers. It provides comprehensive range of common facilities and services including consultancy in techno-economic managerial training, testing, marketing assistance etc. It also provides various types of consultancy and services through its network of 30 small industries service institutes, 30 branch SISI, 41 extension centres, 4 Regional Testing Centres, 7 Field Testing Station, 3 Central Footwear Training Centres, 1 Product and Process Development Centres etc. It also providing training facilities to the unemployed graduates, engineer entrepreneurs, diploma holders etc. The above training facilities are usually provided by National Institute for Small Industries Extension and Training, Entrepreneurship Development Instituteof India, Electronic Service and Training Centres etc. The functions of SIDO are classified into three categories such as functions relating to co-ordination, industrial development and extension. SIDO has been renamed as Micro, Small and Medium Enterprises Development Organisation.

State Small Industries Development Corporation (SSIDC)

State Small Industries Development Corporations (SSIDC) was set up in various states as private limited bodies in order to undertake number of commercial activities. The concerned State/Union Territories are responsible for the needs and development of small, tiny and village industries in their jurisdiction. The activities of the corporation includes: procure and distribute scarce raw materials, supply of machineries on hire purchase basis, construction of industrial estates or sheds, providing assistance in export marketing, extending financial, technical and managerial assistance.

Small Scale Industries Board (SSIB)

Small Scale Industries Boards is an apex advisory body established in the year 1954, in order to provide various advices to the Government for the development of small scale industries. It is operated by the help of a chairman who is the industry minister of Government of India. The board comprises of 50 members including State industry minister. It consists of other members such as secretaries If various departments, public sector undertakings, financial institutions etc., who are contributing their integrated services for the growth and development of small scale industries.

District Industries Centres (DIC)

The Industrial Policy Resolution of 1977, which was announced by the government of India on 23rd December 1977, highlighted to make every district head quarters as the focal point for the development of small and cottage industries. The State Government has established the DIC at the district level in order to provide all sorts of facilities to the industries at one place. The DICs were planned to deal with all services and support assistance required by small and cottage industries. District Industries Centres was started on 1st May 1978, to provide integrated administrative services at the district level under a single roof. Every DIC is headed by a General Manager, supported by seven functional managers or assistant managers and other support staffs. The post of a general manager is substituted by project manager if a district is having two numbers of DICs. Each functional manager will be specialist in his area and would deal with one of the following subject like economic investigation, raw materials, small scale, marketing, research, extension and training, credit and cottage industries. DIC has been declared as the Nodal Agency for the district for implementation of Prime Minister's Rozgar Yojna (PMRY) which is new as PMEGP. It undertakes continuous potential survey of the area to identify the types of feasible venture in industries, business and service sectors in each block, urban body for the benefit of the entrepreneurs. It is acting as the path finder to beneficiary in setting and running the business. Beneficiaries are required to keep in touch with the general manager or project manager to become a successful entrepreneur. In the modern era DICs are the torch bearer of educated unemployed youth in their attempt to become a successful entrepreneur. DIC provides various types of assistance which includes; identification of a suitable scheme, preparation of feasibility report, arrangement for supply of machineries and equipment, providing of raw materials, credit facilities, and inputs for marketing and extension services, quality control and research etc.

Functions of DIC

(i) Having successfully implementing the project and repaid block capital amount in full, if the entrepreneur wants to expand the existing venture or diversify the line of activity to achieve higher goal the DIC will help in formulation of viable scheme and recommend to banks for finance.

(ii) To allot Govt. land/shed in Industrial Estates.

(iii) To appraise loan applications for financial assistance to the entrepreneurs with financing institutions.

(iv) To arrange EDP training.

(v) To arrange exhibition, fair and publicity and visit of industrialists to trade fairs and different Industrial Estates of other States.

(vi) To arrange marketing outlets through liaisioning with Government or procurement agency.

(vii) To arrange training course for development of entrepreneurs through licensing with different organization or promotional agencies.

(viii) To assess the requirements of various raw materials and recommend to government for allotment for production purposes.

(ix) To assist revival of sick SSI Units.

(x) To extend benefits to the Micro, Small and Medium Enterprises such as capital investment subsidy, sales-tax/value added tax (VAT) exemption, electricity duty exemption etc.

(xi) To grant Entrepreneurs Memorandum-I and Entrepreneurs Memorandum-II for Micro, Small and Medium Enterprises.

(xii) To grant Preliminary Registration Certificate (PRC) and Permanent Registration Certificate (PMT) to the entrepreneurs.

(xiii) To identify projects to prepare project report to provide guidance to prospective entrepreneurs and enrich them with all sorts of information for setting up of Micro, Small and Medium Enterprises.

(xiv) To identify prospective entrepreneurs to take up viable projects.

(xv) To identify viable projects and make demand survey on the available resources of the district and plan for promotion of viable industries in the area.

(xvi) To liaison with IDCO for allotment of land and built-up shed with other infrastructure facilities in favour of Micro, Small and Medium Enterprises.

(xvii) To liaison with medium/large enterprises to ascertain their annual requirement of purchase and details of by-products, waste products as to identify and set-up ancillary and downstream enterprises.

(xviii) To maintain up to date data on SSI Sector.

(xix) To monitor the health of existing SSI units and the progress of those in the pipe line.

(xx) To monitor the implementation of the Prime Minister's Rozgar Yojana. (Now as PMEGP)

(xxi) To prepare viable and feasible project reports.

(xxii) To provide necessary marketing assistance.

(xxiii) To recommend different incentives as per the industrial policy of the State Govt.

(xxiv) To recommend financial proposals to Orissa State Financial Corporation/Financial Institutions/Banks etc.

(xxv) To recommend for power connection.

(xxvi) To solve the problems of the industrial units at the district level.

(xxvii) To strengthen the guidance cell to solve the problems of the entrepreneurs.

(xxviii) To update the library in different DICs by procuring different handbooks relating to industries.

Small Industries Service Institutes (SISI)

Small Industries Services Institutes was set up in order to provide consultancy and training to small entrepreneurs.The new name of SISI is MSME-DI (Micro,Small and Medium Enterprises Development Orgnisation. The activities are coordinated by the Industrial Management Training Division of DCSSIs office with the help of 30 Small Industries Service Institutes and 30 Branch Small Industries Service Institutes. The various programme includes; selection of units and end products, conducting entrepreneurship development programme, providing technical support services, providing export information services which includes overseas trade regulations, price, tenders , enquiries etc. The export promotion division of the small Industries Service Institute renders various types of services. It is publishing a quarterly news bulletin titled *'Export News'* for the benefits of small scale industries. The various functions of the SISIs include:

- Export consultancy services.
- Training in export marketing.
- Selection of units and end products.
- Export information service including overseas trade regulations price, tenders, enquiries, market potentials etc.

Industrial Estates (IE)

Industrial estates are today perceived as an integral part of development strategies of many countries worldwide. The environmental impacts from a concentration of large number of industries in a small area or an unplanned Industrial Estate, can pose a serious threat to both local and global sustainable development initiatives. The formation of ecologically balanced industrial systems can result in numerous environmental and economic benefits. Feedback examines the relevance of industrial symbiosis and carrying capacity concepts and proposes an integrated approach towards Industrial Estate planning in India.

Technical Consultancy Organisations (TCO)

Technical Consultancy Organisations (TCOs) provide a complete set of consultancy services to small and medium enterprises, individual entrepreneurs, Government departments and agencies, various state level institutions, commercial banks and other various institutions. Over the years they have diversified their services to include:

- Project conceptualization and other related services. Guidance regarding the selection of projects:
  - ✓ Preparation of feasibility studies and detailed project reports.
  - ✓ Capital structuring
  - ✓ Project appraisals and risk analysis
  - ✓ Project management design
- Credit Syndication:
  - ✓ Preparation of application for assistance from financial institutions/Banks, offer documents and information memorandum.
  - ✓ Syndication of domestic and foreign loans and post sanction follow up.
- Documentation of project reports:
  - ✓ Assistance in preparing various project specific agreements including credit documents.
- Restructuring of Projects:
  - ✓ Turnaround strategy design including rehabilitation.
  - ✓ Mergers and Acquisitions, Assistance in BIFR approvals, Assistance in striping/ sale of units/management tie-up.
  - ✓ Purchase, sale and transfer of Assets.
  - ✓ Separation, liquidation, disposal of non-strategic ventures
- Management Consultancy and Corporate Planning.
- Valuation of Assets.
- Stock Audits
- Assessment of Working Capital
- Project Monitoring Consultancy
- Securitisation Services
- Secretarial Assistance
- Training
- Entrepreneurship Development Programmes

Commercial Banks and Term Lending's in India

SBI and its subsidiary banks and other nationalized banks provide liberal term loans and working capital to small scale entrepreneurs and these loans are advanced for purchase of machine and material and to the technical entrepreneurs to encourage self employment. Specialized institute like, Central Institute of Tool Design, Hyderabad, Central Tool Room, Ludhiana and Kolkata, Central Institute of Hand Tool, Jalandhar, Institute for Design of Electrical Measuring Instruments (IDEMI) Mumbai, Integrated Trading Centre, Nilokhedi, National institute of Small Industry Extension, Hyderabad and National Institute for Entrepreneurship and Small Business Development. They conduct special courses, programmers, workshops, training programmers for the benefits of small scale industries.

State Government Organisations and Corporations involved in the promotion of Industries in Orissa:

Directorate of Export Promotion and Marketing (DEPM): Directorate of Export Promotion and Marketing has been set up to promote export of goods from the State of Orissa and to provide marketing assistance to SSI units of the State. It disseminates market intelligence and overseas tender/trade enquiries among the existing and potential exporters/entrepreneurs of Orissa for their active participation. It renders guidance in export processing, pricing of export items and on availability of different incentives for exports, granted by Government of India. It endeavours to establish infrastructure including establishment of Export promotion Industrial Park etc. This Directorate registers SSI Units and concludes rate contract for purchases by Government departments and undertakings.

Industrial Promotion and Investment Corporation of Orissa Limited (IPICOL): It was established with the principal objective of promoting large and medium scale industries in the State of Orissa. IPICOL through the Industrial Co-ordination Bureau provides assistance and guidance to entrepreneurs in project identification, project finance, preparation of project report, getting registration and license, obtaining clearance from various authorities and statutory bodies and removal of operational constraints for medium and large scale units. It promotes industries in joint sector by way of equity participation. It provides financial and managerial support for revival of sick units. The Foreign Investment Division of IPICOL is the single contact point for the NRIs and the foreign investors desirous of making investment in industrial projects.

Industrial Infrastructure Development Corporation of Orissa (IIDCO): It is the Nodal Agency for providing industrial infrastructure needs to the entrepreneurs intending to establish industrial ventures in Orissa. The various services rendered by IIDCO are:

- Establishment of industrial areas, industrial estates, functional estates, growth centres etc.
- Allotment of developed plots and built up sheds to entrepreneurs on long term leasehold basis.
- Allotment of commercial shops.
- Creation, improvement and maintenance of infrastructural facilities.
- For the projects in large and medium sectors which cannot be set up within the existing Estates, IIDCO helps them in identifying and acquiring private for the industry.

Industrial growth centres of about 1000 acres each are being established at Duburi, Chhatrapur and Jharsuguda. Three mini growth centres are also being established at Khurda, Rayagada and Paradeep under the Integrated Infrastructure Development Scheme of Government of India.100 acres of land will be developed for each Growth Centres. Export Promotion Industrial Park, of about 205 acres of land with necessary infrastructure is being set up at Bhubaneswar under the Ministry of Commerce, Government of India. An Industrial park is being set up at Paradeep as a joint venture with M/s Bang Pekong, Thailand with state of the art facilities. A Software Complex is being set up at Bhubaneswar for development of Electronic Projects with about 2,00,000 sqft, area to accommodate different soft ware companies. A Petro Chemical Complex at Paradeep over 3000 acres is being developed close to the proposed refineries of Indian Oil Corporation and Nippon Denro.

Orissa State Financial Corporation (OSFC): It was established in 1956, under the State Financial Corporations Act, 1951, with the main object of providing loan assistance to the tiny, small and medium scale industrial concerns. OSFC has a decentralized system of working with 6 Regional Offices and 23 Branch Offices throughout the state to cater to the needs of the entrepreneurs. OSFC provides loan assistance for the construction of factory building, purchase of plant and machinery, to meet electrification and installation expenses, for renovation ad modernisation of existing units. The corporation also provides working capital assistance under single window scheme and short term working capital schemes. It extends term loan up to a maximum of Rs.150.00 lakhs for acquiring fixed assets, for setting up industries and also provides working capital assistance under single window scheme. Priority is given to small and tiny sector industrial units in backward areas. The corporation provides term loan upto Rs. 150.00 lakhs to small and medium scale industries. Term loans are also provided to hotels, nursing homes and clinics, transport operators, quality control equipment, a pollution control equipment, for modernisation, diversification and rehabilitation of existing industries. It also gives assistance to women entrepreneurs under "Mahila Udyam Nigam" scheme. It provides assistance under National Equity Fund for project cost upto Rs.10.00 lakhs and extends assistance under factoring services.

Orissa Small Industries Corporation (OSIC): The Orissa Small Industries Corporation plays a vital role for promotion of small scale industries in the State. It provides marketing assistance and raw material assistance. It deals with quality raw materials like iron and steel, aluminium, wax, rubber, plastics, coal, bitumen etc. OSIC also imports scare raw materials to meet the requirements of small scale industries. The OSIC has been granted the status of a recognised export house by the Government of India. It extends finance for the purchase of raw material credit scheme and also factors the bills of SSI units. It also obtains bulk orders for projects and products and offloads the same to the competent local SSI units.

Directorate of Technical Education and Training (DTET): Directorate of Technical Education and Training looks after the planning, implementation and monitoring of technical education at degree, diploma and craftsman training level. The State of Orissa is one of the very few States in the country where the technical education is under the direct administrative control of the Department of Industries. For rapid industrialisation, the role of technical education need not be ever emphasized. The Industrial Policy 1996, has stressed the need for development of technical education and also encouraging participation of the private sector in the area so that the existing and upcoming industries do not face shortage of adequately skilled manpower.

The Agricultural Promotion and Investment Corporation of Orissa Limited (APICOL)

It is the promotional organisation for providing assistance to agricultural enterprises and agricultural investors to begin, process, expand or modernise their enterprise. It helps promotion of agro-based industries in the State.

The Orissa Film Development Corporation (OFDC)

Orissa Film Development Corporation is the nodal agency for growth, and development of film industries in the State. Various concessions, incentives are being extended to the exhibitors and film producers according to the industrial policy of the state through the corporation. In collaboration with the National Film Development Corporation, this State Government undertaking gives financial assistance to cinema houses for production of films, and creation of infrastructure in the state for production of films. The Corporation helps new entrepreneurs of cinema houses by way of refund of entertainment of tax as per the Industrial policy of the State Government. It also provides subsidy to producers of Oriya feature films.

SUMMARY

The financial institutions in India are playing a major role in the economic development of the country. The financial institutions in India are divided into two categories such as regulatory institutions and intermediaries. There are various agencies constituted at National level, which provides financial assistance to the small and medium scale industries in setting up various industrial projects. These institutions are also providing financial assistance for the modernisation, expansion and diversification programmes of existing units.

Businesses, for instance, depend on financial institutions for money. When they can not get it, unemployment rises, mortgage and other credit defaults increase, people and businesses stop spending money, which reduces income for other people and businesses, and reduces tax revenue for governments, which causes them to cut spending, which causes more unemployment, and so on. Financial institutions are the businesses and organizations involved in the collection and distribution of money. They develop the methods and procedures that allow them to collect money from depositors and lend it out to borrowers. They develop the financial securities and provide the financial markets where lenders, borrowers, investors, speculators, and hedgers can exchange money for future payments in the form of interest, for ownership interests, such as stocks, for the payment of future contingent claims, such as with options and derivatives, and for sharing risk, such as the pooling of insurance premiums for financial protection. This pooled money is then given as loans or as an investment to businesses and other organizations to finance specific projects or to provide financing for other needs.

QUESTIONS

SHORT ANSWER QUESTIONS

1. What are the various objectives of the National Science and Technology Entrepreneurship Development Board (NSTEDB)?
2. What are the functions of National Institute for Micro, Small and Medium Enterprises (NIMSME).
3. What are the functions of Directorate of Industries?
4. What is OSIC? Explain the functions of OSIC in the state of Orissa?
5. Write short notes:
   (a) APICOL
   (b) OFDC
   (c) DTET

LONG ANSWER QUESTIONS

1. What are the major financial Institutions assisting the small industries? Explain the role played by them.
2. Explain the objectives and functions of National Institute for Entrepreneurship and Small Business Development (NIESBUD).
3. Explain the role and functions of District Industries Centre in the entrepreneurship development.
4. What are the various state government organisations and corporations involved in the promotion of industries in Orissa.
5. Explain the function and role played by Technical Consultancy Organisations (TCOs).
6. Write short notes:

   (a) Industrial Estates

   (b) State Financial Corporation

   (c) Export Credit Guarantee Corporation

(Case studies are compiled from published sources and are intended to be used as a basis for class discussion only.)

CASE STUDY-1

AMUL-The Taste of India

The Amul Dairy Cooperatives had been around since 1946, in India It is one of the world's largest milk producing countries. It enjoys brand equity because of the contribution made by Dr. Verghese Kurien (born on Nov 26, 1921 at Kojhikode, Kerala) is known as the 'Father of the White Revolution in India' and also the 'Milkman of India'. He was not only a visionary, an administrator, an engineer, but also the one who transformed India into one of the world's largest milk producing countries.

Amul (Anand Milk Union Limited) registered on December 14, 1946, is a dairy cooperative movement in India. It is a brand name managed by an apex cooperative organisation. Originally marketed by the Kaira District Co-operative Milk Producers' Union Limited (KDCMPUL), Anand. Shri Tribhuvandas Patel was the Chairman of KDCMPUL, to set up a processing plant. This marked the birth of AMUL. Dr. Verghese Kurien was posted as a dairy engineer at the Government creamery, Anand in May 1949. The Kaira District Co-operative Milk Producers' Union (KDCMPUL) was taken over by the Gujarat Cooperative Milk Marketing Federation Limited (GCMMF) in 1973. It is based in Anand town of Gujarat which is known as the natural home to enterprising spirit.

Dr. Verghese Kurien was the Chairman of the Gujarat Co-operative Milk Marketing Federation Limited (GCMMF), an apex cooperative organisation that manages the Amul food brand. He is credited with architecting Operation Flood-the largest dairy development programme in the world. The brand name Amul sourced from the Sanskrit word "Amoolya" means priceless. Amul inspired "Operation Flood" and heralded the "White Revolution in India". Today, Amul collects, processes and distributes over a million litres of milk and milk products per day, during the peak, on behalf of more than a thousand village cooperatives owned by a half million farmer members. India's first Prime Minister Jawahar Lal Nehru visited Anand to inaugurate AMUL factory and he embraced Dr. Kurien for his groundbreaking work.

The White Revolution

In 1965, the then Prime Minister of India, Shri Lal Bahadur Shastri, created the National Dairy Development Board (NDDB) to replicate the program on a nationwide basis citing Kurien's "extraordinary and dynamic leadership" upon naming him chairman. Kurien also set up GCMMF

(Gujarat Cooperative Milk Marketing Federation) in 1973 to sell the products produced by the dairies. Today GCMMF sells AMUL brand products not only in India but also overseas. The White Revolution heralded by Amul under the leadership of Dr. Verghese Kurien boosted India's milk production.

Amul is the largest co-operative movement in India. It is the market leader in butter, whole milk, cheese, ice cream, dairy whitener, condensed milk, saturated fats and long life milk. Various brands of Amul are Amul Butter, Amul Milk Powder, Amul Ghee, Amulspray, Amul Cheese, Amul Chocolates, Amul Shrikhand, Amul Ice cream, Nutramul, Amul Milk and Amulya. These have made Amul a leading food brand in India. It follows a unique business model, which aims at providing 'value for money' products to its customers, while protecting the interests of the milk-producing farmers who are its suppliers as well as its owners. Amul has remained the undisputed market leader since its inception by offering quality products at competitive prices.

Ranking

It has ranked Amul as the 73rd Best Brand in its ranking of Top 1000 brands of Asia-Pacific based on a consumer survey conducted in Australia, China, India, Japan, Korea, Hong Kong, Malaysia, Singapore, Taiwan and Thailand. Amul's rank has jumped from 83rd in 2009 to 73rd during the year 2010. AMUL has positioned itself as "Taste of India " and have ensured that their communication is in line with their positioning strategy. Amul has been ranked among the largest dairy businesses in the world by International Farm Comparison Network (IFCN). The IFCN analyses global dairy trends and guides the stakeholders in the dairy sector in over 80 countries. Amul has been ranked at No. 21 in the world based on the milk production during the year 2007.

Amul has been ranked as No. 1 dairy brand, ahead of leading food and dairy brands of the Asia Pacific region like Kraft, Dutch Lady, Dumex, Walls, Anchor, Magnolia and Everyday. Out of the top 1000 brands, Amul is positioned as 73rd compared to the other Indian Brands such as Kingfisher (140), ICICI Bank (182), State Bank of India (226) and Tata (256) to name a few. The turnover of Amul during the year 2008-2009, is Rs. 67.11 billion as compared to the year 2007-2008, as Rs. 52.55 billion.

Strategy

Amul follows an umbrella branding strategy. Amul is the common brand for most product categories produced by various unions: liquid milk, milk powders, butter, ghee, cheese, cocoa products, sweets, ice-cream and condensed milk. Amul's sub-brands include variants such as Amulspray, Amulspree, Amulya and Nutramul. The edible oil products are grouped around

Dhara and Lokdhara, mineral water is sold under the Jal Dhara brand, while fruit drinks bear the Safal name. By insisting on an umbrella brand, GCMMF not only skillfully avoided inter-union conflicts but also created an opportunity for the union members to cooperate in developing products.

Strengths of Amul

- ✓ **Quality:** Amul has a brand name because of its quality. No brand survives long if its quality does not equal or exceed what buyer expects. As a food product, the brand must always represent the highest hygienic, bacteriological and organoleptic standards, it must taste good and it must be good.
- ✓ **Value for Money:** Amul has maintained a level, i.e., value for money. If a customer buys an Amul product, she gets what she pays for and more. Amul has resisted the common practice of raising prices, charging what the market would bear.
- ✓ **Availability:** Availability of a brand is very much essential to sustain in the market. Amul has created a positive brand image by supplying to the market where customer wants it.
- ✓ **Future of Amul:** AMUL's future plans include introduction of a web-based business-to-business ordering system for dealers/stockist and e-transaction capability at the level of the village cooperative.

QUESTIONS

1. What are the various factors required to launch a brand?
2. What are the various qualities that are posed with Dr. Verghese Kurien to establish Amul-the taste of India?
3. What are the various strategies to be followed in order to sustain a brand in the market?

(Case studies are compiled from published sources and are intended to be used as a basis for class discussion only.)

CASE STUDY-2

NIRMA-Rags to Riches

Dr. Karsanbhai Khodidas Patel (popularly known as Karsanbhai Patel) is the man behind the hugely successful brand, Nirma. When Karsanbhai Patel, the founder of the brand, started selling his detergent powder, he decided to call it Nirma, derived from the name of his daughter Nirupama. The picture of a little girl twirling around in her white frock with the familiar jingle *'Washing Powder Nirma'* comes to our mind. The jingle, which was first aired on radio in 1975, was broadcast on television in 1982. It is one of the longest running jingles and the spot has seen very few changes since the time it was first aired. The white dancing girl, featured in Nirma's television advertising, is perhaps the most enduring image of the brand. Purnima is the advertising agency that has been handling brand Nirma's creative and media mandate for the last 40 years and has been consistently focusing on the value-for-money angle. It's simple and catchy jingle-*'Dudh si safedi Nirma se aye, rangeen kapda bhi khil khil jaye'* has continued to echo in the drawing rooms of middle-class Indian homes through the decades. While the jingle stresses on the product, it also salutes the savvy and budget-conscious Indian housewife.

Nirma is one of the most recognizable Indian brands is a classic example of the success of Indian entrepreneurship in the face of stiff competition. Nirma took on the might of giant multinationals and wrote a new chapter in the Indian corporate history. Dr. Karsanbhai Patel, son of a small-time farmer and a qualified Science Graduate, is the founder of Nirma. In the year 1969, Dr. Patel was working as junior chemist in Government Laboratory. In the night Karsanbhai used to make detergent in the 100 Sq. ft., back yard of his home, using bare hands and bucket. After making the detergent, Karsanbhai used to pack it in polythene bag and sold it door-to-door. He priced the detergent at Rs. 3 per kg, when the available cheapest brand in the market was Rs. 13 per kg. It was really an innovative, quality product with indigenous process, packaging and low-profiled marketing, which changed the habit of Indian housewives' for washing their clothes.

In 1960s and 1970s, the domestic detergent market had only premium segment, with very few players and was dominated by MNCs. In a short span of time, with indigenous process, packaging and low-profiled marketing, Nirma created an entirely new market segment in domestic marketplace and quickly emerged as dominant market player. Nirma rewrote the marking rules and its success story became one of the widely discussed case studies in the B-schools across the world.

In a short span, Nirma created an entirely new market segment in domestic marketplace, which is, eventually the largest consumer pocket. In the 1980s Nirma catapulted Surf, which was a well-established detergent product by Hindustan Lever Limited (Now as Hindustan Unilever Limited), and occupied the top slot in the detergent products segment-a slot it has made its own. In 1990, Nirma entered the toilet soap market and today it is the second largest toilet soap brand in India. Today, Nirma has one of the largest volume sales with a single brand name in the world. His is a legendary rags to riches journey during which he shattered established business theories and rewrote new ones. He offered a quality detergent powder, using indigenous technology, at a third of the prevailing price, without compromising on the product. After establishing its leadership in economy-priced detergents, Nirma foray into the premium brand segment, in cakes and detergents are equally successful. It built up 30% market share in the premium detergent segment and achieved a greater than 20% share in the premium soaps market.

Some of the Institutional Bodies Run by Nirma are

- ✓ Nirma Institute of Technology
- ✓ Nirma Institute of Management
- ✓ Nirma Institute of Pharmaceutical Sciences
- ✓ Nirma Institute of Diploma Engineering
- ✓ Nirma Labs

Nirma's social development areas are

- ✓ Nirma Memorial Trust and Nirma Foundation
- ✓ Chanasma Ruppur Gram Vikas Trust

Some of Nirma's products are:

(i) **Consumer Products-** Soaps (Nirma Bath Soap, Nirma Beauty Soap, Nirma Lime Fresh Soap, Nima Rose, Nima Sandal), Detergent (Nirma Washing Powder, Nirma Detergent Cake, Super Nirma Washing Powder, Super Nirma Detergent Cake, Nirma Popular Detergent Powder, Nirma Popular Detergent Cake), Edible Salt (Nirma Shudh), Soaps, Scouring Products (Nirma Clean Dish Wash Bar, Nima Bartan Bar).

(ii) **Industrial Products-** LAB (Linear Alkyl Benzene), Soda Ash, Pure salt, AOS (Alfa Olefin Sulfonate), Sulfuric Acid, SSP (Single Super Phosphate), Sodium Silicate Glycerin, Vacuum Evaporated Iodized Salt,

Strengths of Nirma

1. **Value for money:** Nirma is synonymous with value for money, committed to offer better quality products and services to the consumers.
2. **Services:** Nirma is a customer-focused company committed to consistently offer better quality products and services that maximise value to the customer.

This customer-centric philosophy has been well emphasized at Nirma through:

- ✓ Continuously exploring and developing new products and processes.
- ✓ Laying emphasis on cost effectiveness.
- ✓ Maintaining effective Quality Management System.
- ✓ Complying with safety, environment and social obligations.
- ✓ Imparting training to all involved on a continuous basis.
- ✓ Teamwork and active participation all around.
- ✓ Demonstrating belongingness and exemplary behaviour towards organisation, its goals and objectives.

Future of Nirma

Nirma's vision visualises itself as a vibrant, pro-active and widely admired, ethical corporate citizen. Nirma believes, that exemplary achievements on the business points are not enough in the making of a good corporate citizen. In fulfillment of this role as a responsible part of the society and environment in which one operates, Nirma has undertaken a host of activities in the educational and social development areas. India is a one of the largest consumer economy, with burgeoning middle class pie. In such a widespread, diverse marketplace, Nirma aptly concentrated all its efforts towards creating and building a strong consumer preference towards its 'value-for-money' products. It was way back in '60s and '70s, where the domestic detergent market had only premium segment, with very few players and was dominated by MNCs.

Questions

1. What are the various factors required to launch a brand?
2. How Dr. Karsanbhai Patel was success by competing in the market?
3. What are the various strategies to be followed in order to sustain a brand in the market?

Small and Medium Enterprises at a Glance

Types of Enterprises

	Investment ceiling for Plant, Machinery/Equipment	
	Manufacturing Enterprises	Small Scale Service & Business Enterprises
Micro	Upto Rs. 25 Lakh	Upto Rs. 10 Lakh
Small	More than Rs. 25 Lakh upto Rs 5 Crore	More than Rs. 10 Lakh upto Rs 2 Crore
Medium	More than Rs.5 Crore upto Rs 10 Crore	More than Rs.2 Crore upto Rs 5 Crore
Large	Above Rs 10 Crore	Above Rs 5 Crore

What are The New Names of The Following Organisations?

Sl.No.	FORMERLY	NOW
1.	Ministry of Industry	Ministry of Micro, Small and Medium Enterprises
2.	NISIET (National Institute of Small Industry Extension Training, Hyderabad.)	NIMSME (National Institute for Micro, Small and Medium Enterprises, Hyderabad.)
3.	SISI (Small Industries Service Institute.)	MSME-DI Micro, Small and Medium Enterprises (Devolopment Institute.)
4.	SIDO Small Industry Development Organisation.	MSME-DO Micro, Small and Medium Enterprises Development Organization.

Prime Minister Employment Generation Programme (PMEGP):

Prime Minister's Employment Generation Programme (PMEGP) is a credit linked subsidy programme administered by the Ministry of Micro, Small and Medium Enterprises (MoMSME), Government of India. Khadi & Village Industries Commission (KVIC), a statutory organisation under the administration of Ministry of MSME is the nodal agency at national level for implementation of the scheme. At state level the scheme is implemented through Khadi & Village Industries Commission (KVIC), Khadi & Village Industries Board (KVIB) and District Industries centers. It has been introduced by merging the two schemes, namely, Prime Minister's Rojgar Yojana (PMRY) and Rural Employment Generation Programme (REGP).

The Margin Money (Govt. Subsidy) admissible under PMEGP is as follows:

Categories of beneficiaries under PMEGP	Rate of (Margin Money) Subsidy (of project cost)	
Area (location of project/unit)	Urban	Rural
General Category	15%	25%
Special (including SC/ST/OBC/Minorities/Women, Ex-servicemen, Physically handicapped, NER, Hill and Border areas etc.	25%	35%

SME Rating Agency of India Limited (SMERA)

SME Rating Agency of India Limited (SMERA) is the country's first rating agency that focuses primarily on the Indian SME segment. SMERA's primary objective is to provide ratings that are comprehensive, transparent and reliable. This would facilitate greater and easier flow of credit from the banking sector to SMEs. It is a joint initiative by SIDBI, Dun & Bradstreet Information Services India Private Limited (D&B) and several leading banks in the country.

What is SME Rating?

- ✓ SMERA Rating is an independent third-party comprehensive assessment of the overall condition of the SME, conducted by SME Rating Agency of India Limited.
- ✓ It takes into account the financial condition and several qualitative factors that have bearing on credit worthiness of the SME.
- ✓ SMERA Rating consists of 2 parts, a Composite Appraisal/Condition indicator and a size indicator.
- ✓ SMERA Rating categories SMEs based on size, so as to enable fair evaluation of each SME amongst its peers.
- ✓ An SME unit having SMERA Rating would enhance its market standing amongst trading partners and prospective customers.
- ✓ SMERA Ratings take into account industry dynamics by factoring in a system through which an SME could compare its strengths and weaknesses with those of other companies in the same line of business. This is done through statistically derived industry benchmarks for various ratios.

Rating Indicator

		Financial Strength		
		High	Moderate	Low
Performance Capability	Highest	SE1A	SE1B	SE1C
	High	SE2A	SE2B	SE2C
	Moderate	SE3A	SE3B	SE3C

	Weak	SE4A	SE4B	SE4C
	Poor	SE5A	SE5B	SE5C

Rating Scale: Applicants can avail of two types of ratings under SMERA.

A. For SME Units not eligible for rating fee subsidy:

Category	Fees	Service Tax 10.3%	Total
Turnover	Rs.	Rs.	Rs.
< 50 Lacs	30,000	3,090	33,090
50 to 200 Lacs	36,000	3,708	39,708
> 200 Lacs	48,000	4,944	52,944

B.NSIC SMERA Rating Fee for SSI Units eligible for subsidy

Category	Fees	Service Tax 10.3%	Total
Turnover	Rs.	Rs.	Rs.
< 50 Lacs	7,500	773	8,273
50 to 200 Lacs	9,000	927	9,927
> 200 Lacs	12,000	1,236	13,236

(Source: www.smera.in)

BIBLIOGRAPHY

1. Entrepreneurship Development Institute of India, Ahmedabad, "*A Handbook for new entrepreneurs.*"
2. Bright, P.S., "*Bright's How to be an Entrepreneur*", M/s Bright Careers Institute, Delhi.
3. Saleem, Shaikh "*Business Environment*, M/s Pearson Education, New Delhi.
4. Desai, Vasant, "*Dynamics of Entrepreneurial Development and Management-principles, projects, policies and programmes*". M/s Himalaya Publishing House, Mumbai.
5. Khanka, S.S., "*Entrepreneurial Development*", M/s S. Chand & Co. Ltd., New Delhi.
6. Sahay, A. and Sharma, V., "*Entrepreneurship and New Venture Creation*", M/s Excel Books, New Delhi.
7. Charantimath, Poornima M., "*Entrepreneurship Development and Small Business Enterprises.*" M/s Pearson Education, New Delhi.
8. Gupta, C.B. and Srinivasan, N.P., "*Entrepreneurship Development in India*", M/s Sultan Chand and Sons, New Delhi.
9. Badi, R.V. and Badi, N.V., "*Entrepreneurship*", M/s Vrinda Publications (P) Ltd., Delhi.
10. Aswathappa, K., "*Essentials of Business Environment*", M/s Himalaya Publishing House, Mumbai.
11. Saibaba, Rudra, "*Fundamentals of Entrepreneurship*", M/s Kalyani Publishers, New Delhi.
12. Kaplan, Jack M., "*Patterns of Entrepreneurship*", M/s Wiley India (P) Ltd., New Delhi.
13. Rao, P.C.Kesava, "*Project Management and Control*", M/s Sultan Chand and Sons, New Delhi.
14. Desai,Vasant, "*Small Scale Industries and Entrepreneurship*", M/s Himalaya Publishing House, Mumbai.
15. Wickham, Philip, "*Strategic Entrepreneurship*", M/s Pitman Publishing.